Romeo and Juliet

ARDEN EARLY MODERN DRAMA GUIDES

Series Editors:

Andrew Hiscock
University of Wales, Bangor, UK and Lisa Hopkins,
Sheffield Hallam University, UK

Arden Early Modern Drama Guides offer practical and accessible introductions to the critical and performative contexts of key Elizabethan and Jacobean plays. Each guide introduces the text's critical and performance history, but also provides students with an invaluable insight into the landscape of current scholarly research, through a keynote essay on the state of the art and newly commissioned essays of fresh research from different critical perspectives.

A Midsummer Night's Dream edited by Regina Buccola

Doctor Faustus edited by Sarah Munson Deats

King Lear edited by Andrew Hiscock and Lisa Hopkins

1 Henry IV edited by Stephen Longstaffe

'Tis Pity She's a Whore edited by Lisa Hopkins

Women Beware Women edited by Andrew Hiscock

Volpone edited by Matthew Steggle

The Duchess of Malfi edited by Christina Luckyj

The Alchemist edited by Erin Julian and Helen Ostovich

The Jew of Malta edited by Robert A Logan

Macbeth edited by John Drakakis and Dale Townshend

Richard III edited by Annaliese Connolly

Twelfth Night edited by Alison Findlay and Liz Oakley-Brown

The Tempest edited by Alden T. Vaughan and Virginia Mason Vaughan

Further titles in preparation

Romeo and Juliet

A Critical Reader

Julia Reinhard Lupton

Bloomsbury Arden Shakespeare
An imprint of Bloomsbury Publishing Plc
B L O O M S B U R Y
LONDON • OXFORD • NEW YORK • NEW DELHI • SYDNEY

Bloomsbury Arden Shakespeare
An imprint of Bloomsbury Publishing Plc

Imprint previously known as Arden Shakespeare

50 Bedford Square
London
WC1B 3DP
UK

1385 Broadway
New York
NY 10018
USA

www.bloomsbury.com

BLOOMSBURY, THE ARDEN SHAKESPEARE and the Diana logo are trademarks of Bloomsbury Publishing Plc

First published 2016

British Library Cataloguing-in-Publication Data
A catalogue record for this book is available from the British Library.

ISBN: HB: 978-1-4742-1636-4
PB: 978-1-4725-8926-2
ePDF: 978-1-4742-1637-1
ePub: 978-1-4742-1638-8

Library of Congress Cataloging-in-Publication Data
A catalog record for this book is available from the Library of Congress.

Typeset by Fakenham Prepress Solutions, Fakenham, Norfolk NR21 8NN
Printed and bound in India

CONTENTS

ILLUSTRATIONS

SERIES INTRODUCTION

The drama of Shakespeare and his contemporaries has remained at the very heart of English curricula internationally and the pedagogic needs surrounding this body of literature have grown increasingly complex as more sophisticated resources become available to scholars, tutors and students. This series aims to offer a clear picture of the critical and performative contexts of a range of chosen texts. In addition, each volume furnishes readers with invaluable insights into the landscape of current scholarly research as well as including new pieces of research by leading critics.

This series is designed to respond to the clearly identified needs of scholars, tutors and students for volumes which will bridge the gap between accounts of previous critical developments and performance history and an acquaintance with new research initiatives related to the chosen plays. Thus, our ambition is to offer innovative and challenging guides that will provide practical, accessible and thought-provoking analyses of early modern drama. Each volume is organized according to a progressive reading strategy involving introductory discussion, critical review and cutting-edge scholarly debate. It has been an enormous pleasure to work with so many dedicated scholars of early modern drama and we are sure that this series will encourage you to read 400-year-old play texts with fresh eyes.

Andrew Hiscock and Lisa Hopkins

ACKNOWLEDGEMENTS

Our collective work on this volume was facilitated by a two-day meeting in Irvine, California in June 2014, funded by the W/Shakespeare Multi-Campus Working Group through the University of California Humanities Research Institute. Activities included attending a rehearsal of *Romeo and Juliet* for UCI's New Swan Shakespeare Festival; our thanks to artistic director Eli Simon for accommodating our group. Julian Jiménez Heffernan advised on Spanish versions of the story. Kirk Davis generously provided his copy-editing expertise to this enterprise; his energy and abounding good will are much appreciated.

NOTES ON CONTRIBUTORS

Shaul Bassi is Associate Professor of English and Postcolonial Literature at Ca' Foscari University of Venice. His research, teaching and publications are divided between Shakespeare, postcolonial studies, and Jewish studies. His recent publications include *Shakespeare in Venice: Exploring the City with Shylock and Othello* with Alberto Toso Fei (Elzeviro 2007), a critical edition of *Othello*, translated by Alessandro Serpieri (Marsilio 2009), *Visions of Venice in Shakespeare* with Laura Tosi (Ashgate 2011), *Experiences of Freedom in Postcolonial Literatures and Cultures* with Annalisa Oboe (Routledge 2011), and *Shakespeare's Italy and Italy's Shakespeare: Place, 'Race', and Politics* (Palgrave Macmillan 2016).

Joseph Campana is Alan Dugald McKillop Chair and Associate Professor of English at Rice University. He is a poet and arts critic as well as a scholar of Renaissance literature. He is the author of *The Pain of Reformation: Spenser, Vulnerability, and the Ethics of Masculinity* (Fordham UP 2012), and two collections of poetry, *The Book of Faces* (Graywolf 2005) and *Natural Selections* (University of Iowa Press 2012), which received the Iowa Poetry Prize. He reviews the arts for a variety of publications and is currently at work on *The Child's Two Bodies*, a study of children and sovereignty, and *Dancing Will: Shakespearean Choreographies*.

Christopher Dearner is a Ph.D. candidate in English at the University of California, Irvine, where he is writing a dissertation on affordances and the topography of intention in early modern drama.

Rebeca Helfer is Associate Professor of English at the University of California, Irvine. Rebeca is the author of *Spenser's Ruins and the Art of Recollection* (University of Toronto Press 2012). She is currently working on a book about the art of memory and poetics, tentatively titled 'The Art of Memory and the Art of Literature in Early Modern England'.

Naomi Conn Liebler is Professor of English and University Distinguished Scholar at Montclair State University. She is the author of *Shakespeare's Festive Tragedy: The Ritual Foundations of Genre* (Routledge 1995); co-editor of *Tragedy: A Theory Reader* (Longman 1998), and editor of *The Female Tragic Hero in English Renaissance Drama* (Palgrave 2002) and of *Early Modern Prose Fiction: The Cultural Politics of Reading* (Routledge 2007). A former Trustee of the Shakespeare Association of America, she has published over 40 articles and book chapters on Shakespeare and other Renaissance and modern dramatists. Her current research focuses on Shakespeare's representations of old age in the plays and poems.

Julia Reinhard Lupton is Professor of English and Comparative Literature at the University of California, Irvine and the author or co-author of four books on Shakespeare, including *Thinking with Shakespeare: Essays on Politics and Life* (University of Chicago Press 2011) and *Citizen-Saints: Shakespeare and Political Theology* (University of Chicago Press 2005). She is the co-editor with Graham Hammill of *Political Theology and Early Modernity* (University of Chicago Press 2012). She is a Trustee of the Shakespeare Association of America and a former ACLS and Guggenheim Fellow.

M. Barbara Mello teaches early modern literature at California State University, Long Beach. In 2012, she earned her Ph.D.

at the University of Southern California in Early Modern English Literature and Culture. Currently, she is working on a manuscript entitled *From the Hellmouth to the Witch's Cauldron: Cooking and Feeding Evil on the Early Modern Stage*, a study of the intersection of theatre, religion, gender and the culinary arts.

Ian Munro is Associate Professor of Drama at the University of California, Irvine. He is the author of *The Figure of the Crowd in Early Modern London: The City and Its Double* (Palgrave Macmillan 2005) and the editor of *A Woman's Answer is Never to Seek: Early Modern Jestbooks, 1526–1635* (Ashgate 2007). He is currently working on a book about Shakespeare and wit.

Robert N. Watson is the Neikirk Distinguished Professor of English at UCLA. His books include *Shakespeare and the Hazards of Ambition* (Harvard University Press 1985), *Ben Jonson's Parodic Strategy* (Harvard University Press 1987), *The Rest is Silence: Death as Annihilation in the English Renaissance* (University of California Press, 1994), *Throne of Blood* (Palgrave Macmillan 2014), several editions of Jonson's plays, and *Back to Nature: The Green and the Real in the Late Renaissance* (University of Pennsylvania Press 2008), which was named both the year's best book on early modern English literature and the year's best book of ecocriticism. His poetry has appeared in *The New Yorker* and other journals. He has received Guggenheim, NEH and ACLS fellowships, and various awards for innovative teaching and public service.

William N. West is Associate Professor of English, Classics, and Comparative Literary Studies at Northwestern University and co-editor of *Renaissance Drama*. He is the author of *Theatres and Encyclopedias in Early Modern Europe* (Cambridge University Press 2002) and co-editor of Robert Weimann's *Author's Pen and Actor's Voice: Writing and Playing in*

Shakespeare's Theatre (Cambridge University Press 2000) and *Rematerializing Shakespeare: Authority and Representation on the Early Modern English Stage* (Palgrave Macmillan 2005). He is completing a book to be called *Understanding and Confusion in the Elizabethan Theaters*, on the experiences associated with early modern playing and playgoing.

TIMELINE

Christopher Dearner

1320: Completion of Dante's *Divine Comedy*, which mentions the Montecchi and the Cappelletti.

1476: Publication of Masuccio Salernitano's *Novellino*, which contains a novella with plot similarities to *Romeo and Juliet*.

1524: Luigi Da Porto's 'Hystoria novellamente ritrovata di due nobili amanti' sets the action of earlier *Romeo and Juliet*-like stories in Verona and introduces the names Romeo and Giulietta.

1554: Publication of Matteo Bandello's 'La sfortunata morte di dui infelicissimi amanti', which expands on the plot of Da Porto's 'Hystoria'.

1559: Pierre Boaistuau translates Bandello's novella into French under the title 'Histoire troisième de deux Amants' in his collection *Histoires tragiques*, which is the principal source for Arthur Brooke's and William Painter's English versions.

1562: Brooke publishes 'The Tragicall Historye of Romeus and Juliet', which was likely used by Shakespeare in the construction of *Romeo and Juliet*.

1567: Painter publishes *The Palace of Pleasure*, an English rendering of the Romeo and Juliet story that was also probably known to Shakespeare.

1596–7?: *Romeo and Juliet* is likely performed for the first time between 22 July 1596 and 14 April 1597.

1597: Publication of *An Excellent Conceited Tragedie of Romeo and Juliet*, the first or 'bad' quarto of the play (Q1), probably based on memorial reports by actors.

1599: Publication of *The Most Excellent and Lamentable Tragedie, of Romeo and Juliet,* the second or 'good' quarto (Q2) on which all subsequent editions are largely based.

1603: Likely date for the earliest performance of Lope de Vega's *Los Castelvines y Monteses*, a Spanish rendering of the Romeo and Juliet story.

1609: Publication of third quarto of *Romeo and Juliet* (printed from Q2).

1622–3?: Publication of fourth quarto of *Romeo and Juliet* (printed from Q3, with reference to Q1).

1623: Publication of first folio edition ('First Folio') of Shakespeare's plays, under the title *Mr. William Shakespeares Comedies, Histories, & Tragedies*. The text of *Romeo and Juliet* in the First Folio is derived from Q3 and refers to Q4. The Prologue has been cut.

1662: Samuel Pepys attends (and disparages) a production of *Romeo and Juliet*.

1679: Thomas Otway's *The History and Fall of Caius Marius*, which incorporates elements from *Romeo and Juliet*, is first performed, with Elizabeth Barry and Thomas Betterton in the leading roles.

1691: Gerard Langbaine's *An Account of the English Dramatick Poets* refers to *Romeo and Juliet* as 'amongst the best of our author's works'.

1744: Theophilus Cibber stages version of *Romeo and Juliet* with himself cast as Romeo and his daughter cast as Juliet, the first staged version of *Romeo and Juliet* since Otway's *Caius Marius* displaced it on the stage.

1750: David Garrick stages his own version of *Romeo and Juliet* in reaction to Cibber's version, which the former hated. Garrick's version, which removed Rosaline from the play and gave Romeo and Juliet a final scene together before their deaths, was dominant on the stage until the middle of the nineteenth century and persisted as an acting script until the beginning of the twentieth.

1765: Samuel Johnson publishes his *Preface to Shakespeare*, including commentary on *Romeo and Juliet*.

1785: Earliest recorded performance of *Romeo and Juliet* in Italy under the name *Tragedia Veronese*. Staged in Venice and based on Ducis's French version.

1803: John Philip Kemble produces a slightly altered version of Garrick's script.

1807: Two separate 'family-friendly' versions of *Romeo and Juliet* are published, one in Thomas and Harriet Bowdler's *Family Shakespeare* and one in Charles and Mary Lamb's *Tales from Shakespeare*.

1810 Coleridge begins his 'Lectures on Shakespeare', which would run until the following year. His lecture on *Romeo and Juliet* is primarily concerned with Mercutio and the Nurse.

1811: Vincenzo Galleotti's adaptation of *Romeo og Giulietta* performed by the Danish Ballet, which is generally seen as the earliest balletic production.

1817: William Hazlitt publishes *Characters of Shakespear's Plays*, which spends more time on the protagonists than Coleridge's lectures had done.

1817: Lord Byron visits Verona and the supposed tomb of Juliet.

1823: Francesco Hayez paints *Romeo and Juliet's Last Kiss*.

1830: Vincenzo's *I Capuleti e I Montecchi* produced; like many other nineteenth-century Italian adaptations, it focuses more on Italian sources than on Shakespeare's play.

1832: *Characteristics of Women: Moral, Poetical, and Historical* published by Anna Jameson. Her work is the first systematic analysis of Shakespeare's heroines by a woman.

1839: Hector Berlioz produces an operatic version of *Romeo and Juliet* strongly influenced by Garrick's stage version. Indeed, he would go on to marry Henriette Smithson, who played Juliet in an 1827 Paris production of Garrick's play.

1845: Charlotte Cushman appears in a London production of *Romeo and Juliet*, which would replace Garrick's as the standard stage version. Charlotte appeared as Romeo and her sister Susan played Juliet. This version returns Rosaline to the story and excises the added final dialogue between Romeo and Juliet.

1871: H. H. Furness publishes his variorum edition of *Romeo and Juliet*.

1900: Edward Dowden edits *Romeo and Juliet* for Arden Shakespeare.

1904: Publication of A. C. Bradley's *Shakespearean Tragedy*, which notably does not include a chapter on *Romeo and Juliet*.

1912: Lawrence Trimble's film *Indian Romeo and Juliet* released, which tells the Romeo and Juliet story amidst a war between the Mohicans and Hurons.

1916: Theda Bara's silent version of *Romeo and Juliet* released.

1924: Agnes Mure Mackenzie's pioneering feminist work *The Women in Shakespeare's Plays* published.

1930: Ettore Solimani begins to collect letters left at Juliet's supposed tomb, where he is employed as a keeper; this work will later become the Juliet Club.

1935: Sergei Prokofiev composes his groundbreaking balletic adaptation *Ромео и Джульетта* (*Romeo and Juliet*).

1935: John Gielgud's production of *Romeo and Juliet* starring Laurence Olivier premières at the New Theatre in London.

1935: Irving Thalberg sends a troupe to Verona to research libraries and photograph several locations for Cukor's filmic adaptation.

1936: Release of George Cukor's *Romeo and Juliet* through MGM, which would become the standard film version until Zeffirelli's 1968 adaptation. Cukor's version was ultimately not shot in Italy for political reasons and featured a set design based on Hayez's *Last Kiss*.

1940: Première of Sergei Prokofiev and Leonid Lavrovsky's balletic adaptation of *Romeo and Juliet*.

1946: W. H. Auden's lectures on Shakespeare delivered at the New School for Social Research, which included a treatment of *Romeo and Juliet*. The lectures would not be published until 2000.

1947: Peter Brook produces a *Romeo and Juliet* for the Royal Shakespeare Company that cuts the final reconciliation scene.

1957: *Narrative and Dramatic Sources of Shakespeare*, Geoffrey Bullough's monumental work on Shakespeare's sources, published.

1957: Broadway production *West Side Story*, the result of a collaboration between Arthur Laurents, Leonard Bernstein, Stephen Sondheim and Jerome Robbins, which is set in New York City's upper west side during the mid-1950s.

1960: Franco Zeffirelli's *Romeo and Juliet* production at the Old Vic with Judi Dench and John Stride as Juliet and Romeo. Zeffirelli's version focuses on the generational conflict.

1965: Kenneth MacMillan's *Romeo and Juliet* produced by the Royal Ballet, which deployed Prokofiev's score and remains one of the most-seen balletic adaptations of the play.

1968: Franco Zeffirelli's filmic adaptation of *Romeo and Juliet* released, which replaced Cukor's version as the standard filmic adaptation. It remains, with Luhrmann's updated version, one of the iconic film versions to this day.

1972: Statue of Juliet placed in courtyard of Verona City Museum; the right breast of the statue has since been worn shiny by repeated contact, as touching it is reported to bring luck.

1973: Terry Hands' RSC production of *Romeo and Juliet*, which foregrounds homoerotic aspects of the relationship between Romeo and Mercutio, and features the latter dismembering a female doll.

1976: Carmelo Bene's postmodern production of *Romeo and Juliet*, which features multiple gender switches of characters. Interpolates Shakespeare with Da Porto's text and Bellini's music.

1979: BBC releases widely taught video version of *Romeo and Juliet* (including a young Alan Rickman as Tybalt).

1980: Publication of *The Woman's Part: Feminist Criticism of Shakespeare*, edited by Carolyn Lenz, Gayle Greene and Carol Neely with an essay on *Romeo and Juliet* by Coppélia Kahn, 'Coming of Age in Verona'.

1980: Publication of the second Arden edition of *Romeo and Juliet*, edited by Brian Gibbons; a revised version appears in 1996.

1981: Marjorie Garber's 'Women's Rites' published in the volume *Coming of Age in Shakespeare*.

1986: Michael Bogdanov's famous production for the Royal Shakespeare Company. Commonly called 'The Alfa Romeo *Romeo and Juliet*', Bogdanov's version is set in a materialistic, wealthy Verona.

1986: Northrop Frye's *Northrop Frye on Shakespeare* published. Frye's treatment of *Romeo and Juliet* focuses on the oxymora present in the play.

1986: Jacques Derrida's 'Aphorism Countertime' published, which analyses names and the act of naming in the balcony scene of *Romeo and Juliet*.

1987: Julia Kristeva's '*Romeo and Juliet*: Love-hatred in the Couple' published, which presents a post-Lacanian reading of the play.

1989: Robert Lepage's *Romeo and Juliet in Saskatchewan* staged in Saskatoon. Lepage's version features Anglophone Montagues and Francophone Capulets.

1992: Intercultural adaptation of *Romeo and Juliet* staged by Grupo Galpão in Rio de Janeiro that incorporated elements of street theatre, *commedia dell'arte* and acrobatics.

1994: Bilingual adaptation of *Romeo and Juliet* with a Palestinian Romeo and Israeli Juliet directed by Fouad Awad and Eran Bene'el. The production was a joint effort of the Khan and El-Qasaba Theatres.

1994: Dympna C. Callaghan publishes 'The Ideology of Romantic Love: The Case of Romeo and Juliet'.

1996: Baz Luhrmann's filmic modernization *Romeo + Juliet* released. Shot in Mexico City and set in 'Verona Beach', the movie retains the original dialogue but reimagines the families as competing mafia empires.

2000: Clare Stopford's version of *Romeo and Juliet*, set in contemporary Cape Town, is performed at the Maynardville Open Air Theatre.

2003: Bilingual version of *Romeo and Juliet* produced in Taiwan, staged in both Taiwanese and Mandarin.

2005: *Kino and Teresa* performed at the Autry National Center. This version of the Romeo and Juliet story, produced by Native Voices and written by James Lujan and directed by Kenneth Martines, was set in seventeenth-century Santa Fe, during conflicts between the Pueblo Indians and Spanish settlers.

2005: Bruno Barreto's *O Casamento de Romeu e Julieta* performed, a version set among feuding Paulistano soccer clubs.

2005: Ari Sandel's film *West Bank Story* released, a version of the *Romeo and Juliet* story set in competing falafel stands.

2005: Edward Clug's ballet *Radio and Juliet* first performed. This version features the music of Radiohead, incorporates two film sequences and pairs a single Juliet with six interchangeable Romeos.

2006: Nancy Meckler's RSC production of *Romeo and Juliet* sets the Shakespearean play within a frame tale involving two warring Sicilian clans participating in an annual ritual.

2008: *In Fair Palestine* produced by Ramallah high-school students and subsequently screened worldwide.

2008: Marjorie Garber's *Shakespeare and Modern Culture* published.

2009: Alexa C. Y. Huang's *Chinese Shakespeares* published.

2010: Rupert Goold's RSC production of *Romeo and Juliet* replaces Received Pronunciation with a variety of regional accents.

2010: Eve Annenberg's film *Romeo and Juliet in Yiddish* depicts wayward Chasidic youth attempting to translate *Romeo and Juliet*.

2010: The Nature Theatre of Oklahoma produces a version of *Romeo and Juliet* based on remembered fragments of the play.

2011: Alexei Ratmansky produces a celebrated version of *Romeo and Juliet* for the National Ballet of Canada that continues the tradition of the story as imagined in Prokofiev's score.

2012: *Romeo and Juliet in China*, a collaboration between the National Theatre Company of Korea and the National Theatre Company of China, premières. It is set during the Cultural Revolution.

2012: Paul Kottman's 'Defying the Stars: Tragic Love as the Struggle for Freedom in Romeo and Juliet' published in *Shakespeare Quarterly*. Kottman's essay argues for the philosophical seriousness of the play.

2012: Publication of the third Arden edition of *Romeo and Juliet*, edited by René Weis.

2012: Monadhil Daood's *Romeo and Juliet in Baghdad* premières as part of the International Shakespeare Festival. Daood's version incorporates a Shiite Romeo and Sunni Juliet and ends with Paris blowing himself and the two lovers up in a church.

2013: Bijan Sheibani's production at The Shed (a venue of the National Theatre in London) casts the Montagues as diasporic Africans and the Capulets as south Asian.

2013: Mats Ek's ballet, *Juliet and Romeo*, performed by the Royal Swedish Ballet. The production uses multiple mobile walls to dramatize Juliet's perspective.

2014: Verona commissions a replica Juliet statue to replace the original, worn down by years of contact.

2015: *The Hollywood Reporter* states that Sony Pictures is going to make *Verona*, a new film adaptation of *Romeo and Juliet*.

Introduction

Julia Reinhard Lupton

Cut him out in little stars

(3.2.22)

In her 'Gallop apace' soliloquy (3.2.1–31), Juliet begs the night to come more quickly so that she can receive her lover in the secrecy of her bedroom. Throughout the passage, Juliet invokes a teeming, velvet darkness, a 'black mantle' (15) gleaming with its own forms of illumination. She imagines darkness providing a cover for modesty: 'Hood my unmanned blood, bating in my cheeks' (14).[1] Juliet draws the image from falconry, the aristocratic art of training wild hawks as hunting birds by blindfolding them. Although her emphasis falls on hiding herself from view, the blood rising in her cheeks also casts its own special light, her face suddenly aglow with the shock of its own desire and her whole being ready to perceive the world anew through arousal's intensification and crossing of the senses.[2] 'Lovers', she declares, 'can see to do their amorous rites / By their own beauties' (8–9); touching each other, the partners' skin and body parts become instruments of sense, serving as virtual light sources in the night-curtained bed.

At the centre of 'Gallop apace' is one of the play's most beautiful and also most disturbing images of the light resident in erotic darkness:

Give me my Romeo, and when I shall die
Take him and cut him out in little stars,
And he will make the face of heaven so fine
That all the world will be in love with night

(3.2.21–4)

'To die' is both to undergo orgasm and to pass from this life. Juliet imagines seeing stars against the bright dark of her eyelids when she closes them in ecstasy, and she wants to convert that optic effect into a cosmic spectacle for the whole world to enjoy. She also already anticipates the death of both lovers and is beginning to plan their aesthetic afterlife. In myths of stellification, borrowed from Ovid's *Metamorphoses*, mortals are transformed into stars or constellations, but at the expense of their bodily integrity. Imagining her lover's glowing body as a sheer radiant material, Juliet plans a work of repair and commemoration that also requires cutting and dispersal. The speech itself cuts from the terror of Act 3, Scene 1, whose bloody action has just yielded the corpses of Mercutio and Tybalt. The violence of the preceding scene enters the urgent erotics of Juliet's soliloquy through the divine scissor work that stellification requires. The speech is itself cut off by the arrival of the Nurse, who bears the rope ladder that will enable the lovers' union, but also brings the news of the brawl in the square: 'Enter NURSE wringing her hands, with the ladder of cords in her lap.'[3]

The great Victorian critic Walter Pater (1839–94) identified Juliet's 'Gallop apace' speech as an epithalamium or classical wedding song, usually chanted by a bridegroom eager for the night to come. Pater saw the speech as part of the play's exquisite dramatization of verse forms, beginning with the sonnet through which the lovers compose their first encounter in Act 1; cresting in the epithalamium here in Act 3; and fading into the *aubade*, or morning song, in Act 3, Scene 5's lark and nightingale duet.[4] Spreading its silken wings of imagery just past the mid-point of the drama, 'Gallop apace' manifests many key issues and factors for the play's interpretation and performance, from Juliet's tender–terrible mix of erotic forwardness, maiden modesty and poetic mastery; to the drama's affinity with musical performance and lyric form; to its oxymoronic alternation between scenes of radically different mood;[5] to Shakespeare's capture of sensory forms of knowledge through poetic images; to the play's mythic origins and extraordinary diffusion across many media and world stages. For it is the later theatrical, literary, educational and entertainment industries that have indeed cut Romeo and Juliet out in little stars: fashioned them into the souvenirs and icons, celebrities and landmarks, porn avatars and teen idols, in what has become a global brand for young love.[6]

The story of Romeo and Juliet has always been an international one. Early references to the 'Montecchi e Cappelletti' appear in Dante's *Purgatorio*, locating the feud if not the lovers' story itself in the lived history of late medieval Verona. The story of the lovers was rendered into Italian prose by Masuccio Salernitano (1476), Luigi Da Porto (1524) and Matteo Bandello (1554), translated into French by Pierre Boaistuau in 1559, and then rendered into English by Arthur Brooke (1562) and William Painter (1567). Shakespeare, who likely wrote the play in the latter half of 1596,[7] relied most immediately on Brooke's poem, which had been reprinted in 1582 and 1587, but was aware of Painter's prose novella and the participation of the Romeo and Juliet story in what Shaul Bassi calls 'a larger cultural system and network of influences'.[8] That system was Italian in origin but European in scope; in addition to the French translation, there was also a Spanish play by the great playwright Lope de Vega, *Los Castelvines y Monteses,* which appeared in the decade after Shakespeare's play.[9] The internationalism of the play's origins continues to colour its afterlife, with major versions in Italian and French opera that combine Shakespearean and European sources and motifs. Globally the play has inspired an abundance of adaptations, which often employ the story of the feud to explore ethnic, religious and caste tensions and use Shakespeare's semi-ethnographic engagement of dance, festival and holiday to draw local performance traditions into the frame of Western drama.[10] The relative autonomy of many adaptations from Shakespeare's text and the return of earlier European sources in later Continental retellings bear witness to the tenacity, resilience and reach of the Romeo and Juliet phenomenon, which swirls around its definitive Shakespearean articulation but continues to gather energy from multiple sources, later media and global variations.[11] (See essays in this volume by Shaul Bassi, Ian Munro and Joseph Campana.)

What makes *Romeo and Juliet* so enduring? It is a popular school text because of its straightforward yet resonant and emotionally engaging plot, centring on two characters who are deeply attractive in their extreme youth, verbal precocity and capacity for commitment. The play brilliantly uses the spatial affordances of the theatre, incorporating gallery, inner stage and back stage as well as the centre and edges of the plateau in a sequence of dynamic actions that juxtapose the ensemble work of street fights, games of hide-and-seek and group dancing with intimate domestic exchanges and erotic duets. The simple arc of the story gains precision against the amplitude of its world: what William N. West calls in this volume the 'inexplicable, unpredictable variety of immanence, all the things that are here in all the ways they are'. The play's attention to urban space, domestic space and the space of the stage is scaffolded on mythic archetypes of heavenly ascent, infernal descent and erotic quest.[12] Unlike many other plays by Shakespeare, there is no double plot and very little disguising. The language is by and large appealing and accessible, alternating between moments of intense lyric beauty and inventiveness, and passages of naturalistic clarity, along with banter and brawling. The play's sparkling beauties float atop incessant ripples of everyday unhappiness: Lady Capulet's marital disappointments and maternal inhibition, the Nurse's family losses, Mercutio's jilting by Romeo, Capulet's domineering yet fragile fatherhood. These same features also make *Romeo and Juliet* highly performable: the play moves quickly in a tautly urban space, with no novelistic 'double time' as in *Othello* or great shifts in setting as in the romances. The focus on the two lovers is supplemented by a representative cast of secondary characters who fill out the play's generational and civic world with parents, peers, mentors, magistrates and servants, endowing everyone in the audience with someone to think with. (In this volume, see William N. West's account of the play's seeding with multiple worlds.)

This is a play not of good and evil, but of error and accident, which stem from multiple sources and thus communicate the contingencies of human life. In Ruth Nevo's estimation, 'it is less "tragic" because the vision of evil in it is less deep, less complex, less comprehensive ... Here all is at a lower pitch; nearer to the commonplace and ordinary.'[13] As Naomi Conn Liebler suggests in this volume, 'Barely hidden in the rhapsodic language is a sense that the play magnified for close scrutiny everything that a contemporary sensibility needed in order to understand the complexity of non-tragic life.'[14] Although we admire the lovers for their courage and fidelity, we also recognize the precipitousness of their actions and their, often stunning, lack of judgement. Tybalt is brash and arrogant, while Mercutio, charming and verbally gifted, becomes needlessly pugnacious at exactly the wrong moment. Lady Capulet lacks the confidence and intimacy to speak frankly with her daughter about matters of the heart and refuses to take her daughter's side against her husband later in the play. Capulet adores Juliet and enjoys managing the finer details of home entertainment, but retreats into the most abrupt authoritarianism when the household is shaken by the death of Tybalt, an event whose full import he cannot understand. Paris courts Capulet more than Juliet, recalling Lysander's rejoinder to his rival Demetrius in *A Midsummer Night's Dream*: 'You have her father's love, Demetrius: / Let me have Hermia's; do you marry him.' (1.1.93–4)[15] Benvolio, an early version of Horatio, aspires to embody his name, meaning 'good will', yet he fails to keep the peace, perhaps because he too, as Mercutio implies, harbours a history of quarrelling (3.1.15–29).

If Romeo and Juliet as well as Mercutio and Tybalt demonstrate the lack of judgement that characterizes youth, the Friar and the Nurse join the Capulets and Montagues in dispelling any promise that years bring wisdom. Privy to the 'shrift' or confessions of the young lovers, the Friar agrees to support their secret marriage in the hopes of healing a body politic poisoned by vendetta, but he over-judges his ability to engineer a solution to a situation that swiftly spins out of his control. The Friar enters the play gathering herbs and meditating on their capacities to poison as well as heal: 'Within the infant rind of this weak flower / Poison hath residence and medicine power' (2.3.19–20).[16] Yet doctoring social relationships turns out to be riskier than treating physical bodies or individual souls. His carefully dispensed sleeping potion, designed to liberate the lovers into a better future, dramatizes the limits of technocratic solutions to the inherent unpredictability of human action.

The Nurse is both more comic than the Friar and ultimately darker than he. Borrowed from the bawdy procuresses of Roman comedy, she gleefully assists her young charge in the elopement. Even when Tybalt lies dead and Romeo has been exiled, the Nurse provides the rope ladder that allows the marriage to be consummated. When the union with Paris seems inevitable, however, the Nurse abruptly withdraws her support of the secret marriage: 'Romeo's a dishclout' to Paris, she says with disingenuous bravado, leaving Juliet to her own devices (3.5.220). Spoken like a true bawd, the Nurse retreats into a self-interested pragmatism shaped by her own status as a paid subordinate. The inherent contradiction of her position – she has been hired to love another woman's child in place of her own dead daughter Susan – unexpectedly links the tragic action of the play to the division of labour among social groups and the ambivalences that these class relations cause. The Friar manifests the dangers of spiritual *superiority*, while the Nurse reveals the dangers bred by social *inferiority*. Although one would be going too far to suggest that Shakespeare implies through this double critique of 'above-ism' and 'below-ism' a vision of more democratic forms of civic life, the play is certainly interested in the role that entrenched institutions and inherited hierarchies play in deforming moral outlooks and constraining possibilities for action.

The extraordinary exchange shared by the Nurse, Juliet and Lady Capulet in Act 1, Scene 3 is a dramaturgical and existential exploration of the constrictions visited by class and gender norms on all three women. The scene plays the intimacy of the Nurse and Juliet against the distance between Juliet and her mother. Juliet may sit on the Nurse's lap or press against her bosom, poses frequently featured in performance shots. Meanwhile, Lady Capulet strives for closeness when she sends the Nurse away, but loses confidence and calls the Nurse back. During the ensuing conversation, Lady Capulet can exude alienation, impatience or regret by moving either downstage (and thus soliciting identification with the audience) or upstage (doubling her distance). Whereas *Hamlet* splits the father into two figures, Hyperion and the satyr, *Romeo and Juliet* divides the maternal function between the chatty, overindulgent Nurse and the inhibited and disaffected mother. The full emotional range of the scene, reflecting the extraordinary largesse of the play as a whole, depends on the shifting organization and on-going comparison of intimacies, from the warmth of bodies that touch to the palpable coolness of persons that drift.

Juliet and Romeo

But what of the lovers? Of the two, Juliet is the more distinctive and self-aware. In the balcony scene, Juliet imagines Romeo as a young falcon in training, kept on a leash like a pet.[17] The image indicates Juliet's dawning appreciation of her capacity to manage this brand-new relationship, despite her extreme youth and highly sheltered childhood, though the image also presents a fantasy of mastery (boyfriends are *not* like pull toys or baby animals) that breeds disaster. Later in the play, it is Juliet, not Romeo, who declares that the evening nightingale, not the morning lark, sings outside their window on the dawn of Romeo's departure to Mantua, but then sends him away. If she expresses more sexual urgency than Romeo, she is also more articulate about the risks they are courting. Although Romeo recounts his sense of foreboding to his peers before he goes to the fateful party, Juliet exercises moral judgement (rather than mere presentiment) when she declares on her balcony, 'Although I joy in thee, / I have no joy of this contract tonight; / It is too rash, too unadvised, too sudden' (2.2.116–18). In these brilliant and beautiful scenes, Juliet expresses her emergent erotic curiosity in images appropriate to her youth and upbringing, while also strikingly modern in their forwardness, sense of freedom and dawning attention to moral complexity, justly attracting much commentary in the history of criticism (see Liebler, 'The Critical Backstory').

As Ian Munro demonstrates in this volume, later performances respond to Juliet's erotic initiative by either dampening her growing awareness of her own capacity for action (producing a more docile Juliet) or by heightening the sense of youthful confrontation with the constraints of tradition, and thus intensifying what is most compelling and disturbing in the play. Julia Kristeva takes these transgressive elements to a new level of fantasmatic intensity that involves gender role-play and even sex change: 'Each acting out both sexes in turn they thus create a foursome that feeds on itself through repeated aggression and merging, castration and gratification, resurrection and death' (cited Liebler, 'The Critical Backstory'). Robert Watson and Stephen Dickey, also intuiting the play's hidden scenarios of sexual violence, focus on the aggression implicit in a range of allusions associating Romeo with mythic rapists, in order to grant Juliet a different kind of autonomy, that of 'find[ing] her own way into the uncertain meaning of her own uncertain story, and pay[ing] for her final triumph over such categories with her life'.[18]

In Act 3, Juliet finds herself progressively without support. Her mother abandons her with the same harshness as her father, and perhaps the same self-interest as the Nurse: 'Talk not to me, for I'll not speak a word, / Do as thou wilt, for I have done with thee' (3.5.203–4). Armed with the potion provided by the overzealous Friar, Juliet considers calling the Nurse and her mother back, but, realizing that they have both forsaken her, she describes her situation, 'My dismal scene I needs must act alone' (4.3.19). In calling up first the corpse and then the ghost of Tybalt along with the bones of her forefathers, she is both picturing the absolute loneliness of the grave and populating her room with familiar images in order to gather some kind of audience to witness her act. Juliet exercises courage in taking the sleeping potion in full knowledge of a range of real and imaginary risks, but the private nature of her act limits the scope of a virtue that more properly belongs to public speech and action. Cordelia is courageous when she decides not to play the love test in *King Lear*; in *All's Well That Ends Well,* Helena is courageous in practising medicine at court and then choosing Bertram as her spouse; Hermia in *A Midsummer Night's Dream* and Imogen in *Cymbeline* are courageous when they defend their marriage choices to their fathers in front of others. Juliet helps initiate this line of verbally adventurous, sexually confident and authority-testing heroines, but she chooses to practise a more secretive form of bravery whose immediate consequence is not to expand her capacities for action by setting her loose in the wider world (Cordelia to France, Helena to Italy, Hermia to the forest, Imogen to Wales, Marina to the sea and the city), but instead to induce the most rigid passivity: a sleep like death that delivers her inert body to a suffocating tomb. Her suicide can be staged as either a radical act of self-determination or as a sorry submission to the absolutistic tropes of eternal love that her story has come to emblematize. My own evaluation of Juliet honours her courage most certainly, but I also measure that courage against the more public virtues practised by other heroines in Shakespearean drama.

Romeo seems rasher and less intelligent than Juliet, and his fidelity has a more compromised cast to it. Tzachi Zamir argues that in the figure of Romeo, Shakespeare diagnoses love as 'a motion of *withdrawal* from wisdom' in which the lover plays down 'certain possibilities of thought' and silences 'both internal and external skeptical voices'; according to Zamir, Romeo's is an assumed rather than a natural stupidity.[19] Indeed, Romeo is in many ways a master of withdrawal; he is absent from the first street fight because he prefers 'the covert of the wood' (1.1.123) and the 'artificial night' of his bedroom (1.1.138) to the camaraderie of his friends, and his decision to 'be a candleholder and look on' (1.4.38), rather than join the dancing, is the inactive action that allows him to admire Juliet from a distance. In the game of hide and seek outside the Capulet orchard, Benvolio notes that Romeo 'hath hid himself among these trees / To be consorted with the humorous night' (2.1.30–1). Consorting with the humorous night means becoming one with its thick and languorous atmosphere. 'Humorous' evokes not dry wit, but damp melancholy; whereas Juliet arrives aglow with life story, Romeo is a man of shadows, a muted observer who becomes an actor almost by accident. Although his reticence can make him seem a lesser character than Juliet, it also gives Romeo his own depth and complexity, a quality captured in William Hazlitt's famous characterization of Romeo as Hamlet in love.[20]

And Romeo is always in love: the *amor* that roams in his name is his vocation and his symptom, his solution and his problem. He enters the play smitten with Rosaline, an embarrassment excised by some adapters of the text. With infatuation comes bad poetry, in the form of love clichés occasionally enlivened by new thought ('O heavy lightness, serious vanity, / Misshapen chaos of well-seeming forms' [1.1.176–7]). Since Rosaline 'hath Dian's wit' (1.1.207) – she is a distant moon goddess who refuses to return his love – Romeo's affectionate outpourings are comically one-sided.

When he meets Juliet, they speak by composing a sonnet together, mutuality replacing monologue in a meeting that is both artful and spontaneous, as many critics have noted (see Helfer, 'The State of the Art'). Under Juliet's influence and in response to the delights and resistances of her own separate being, Romeo's wits sharpen, his mood lightens and his poetry soars. In the words of Paul Kottman, 'Romeo is forced to halt his rhapsody and to recognize Juliet as a free agent ... it is her own free actions, her freedom, that Romeo must apprehend if he is to recognize her.[21] In *As You Like It* and *Twelfth Night*, Shakespeare will elaborate this fundamental scenario by making his besotted men relinquish the self-indulgent rewards of unilateral love-making for the deeper challenges and higher pleasures of dialogue with women who broker their own distinctive settlements with Renaissance norms of beauty and behaviour. This too, takes courage.

Yet despite the new forms of freedom that Romeo acknowledges and exercises in response to the luminous reality of Juliet, he nonetheless allows himself to be drawn into combat with Tybalt, a choice that he sees as reasserting his manhood after being 'made ... effeminate' by Juliet's beauty (3.1.116). The play dramatizes the costs of such manhood: at the grave, Romeo slaughters Paris, a deed sometimes cut from productions because of its sheer gratuity, but included by Shakespeare to show the on-going consequences of the duelling in Act 3, where Romeo realizes that, 'This day's black fate on moe days doth depend, / This but begins the woe others must end' (3.1.121–2). (Hamlet's character is darkened by a similar rashness: both suffer from a certain trigger-happiness.) In the Capulet monument, Romeo correctly sees in Juliet's sleeping body signs of life, but he fails to deduce from them her true condition, downing the poison just moments before she wakes up. In this scene and throughout the drama, Romeo proves himself capable of real verbal wit and poetic invention, but not possessed of very good judgement. The hero of acknowledgement (Kottman) is also the poet of disavowal (Zamir). The truth and power of the play lies in our admiration of the lovers' achieved mutuality and the forms of individuation brought about by their recognition of each other, coupled with our sense of the terrible loss and wilful stupidity represented by their deaths.

Horrified by the part he has played in Mercutio's mortal wounding, Romeo protests, 'I thought all for the best' (3.1.106). This poignant line reveals, not only Romeo's good intentions, his own *benvolio*, but also his realization that his comprehension of the situation in which he finds himself is limited and provisional. This moment of recognition also grasps the quality of the tragic in this play. The difference between what the characters intend and what their actions cause opens the semantic and affective range of tragic irony. Unlike *Hamlet*, *Lear*, *Macbeth* or *Othello*, everyone in this play is, in Romeo's words, seeking 'the best' – for themselves and their lovers, for their children and their charges, or for the city – but they find their good intentions rebounding on themselves and their neighbours, thanks to a mix of fateful decisions and unpredictable mishap.

I say 'fateful' but not 'fated' decisions: though the play toys with the idea of 'star-crossed lovers' whose destiny is preordained by higher powers or generic conventions, Shakespeare's dramatic interest lies in the consequences of human action within a realm of contingency that includes plague, poor postal service and infant mortality. The mix of chance and choice makes *Romeo and Juliet* a 'romantic' and not a 'classical' tragedy: romantic not only because it involves the death of two lovers rather than the fall of princes, but because its story incorporates elements of fortune or randomness more closely associated with the great Greek and medieval romances than with the tighter plot mechanisms and stricter causality of classical tragedy. When Romeo compares himself to a pilot navigating uncharted waters (2.2.82–4), he evokes a whole romance tradition of wandering and misadventure that begins with Odysseus and stretches to include Hero and Leander, Cupid and Psyche, and Jack and Rose in the film *Titanic*. Yet the drama is more tightly organized than some critics have allowed. Although chance prevents the successful completion of the Friar's plan, Laurence's machinations are themselves a response to the immediate consequences of Romeo's actions. Having unintentionally exposed Mercutio to harm, Romeo must choose between two evils: remaining true to Juliet by not avenging his friend against her kinsman, but losing face in the masculine world of honour; or avenging a death to which he in part contributed, but risking his standing in the city as well as the possibility of reconciling with the Capulet family at some amenable moment in the future. In the words of Ruth Nevo, the scene marks 'a finely turned *peripetia* [tragic reversal] in which the protagonist is responsible for his actions, though he is not accountable for the circumstances in which he must act, and in which these actions recoil ironically upon his own head'.[22] In a landmark essay on the play, Paul Kottman attests to the primacy of ethical freedom in *Romeo and Juliet*, an affirmation of the play's seriousness shared and extended in this volume in essays by Watson and West.[23]

Genre and beyond

It is a commonplace in criticism to note that *Romeo and Juliet* begins as a comedy, with young lovers who meet through masking, find their love blocked by warring parents and orchard walls and, assisted by go-betweens, find solutions to the impasses they encounter through inventive ploys, such as the rope ladder supplied by the Nurse or the cover of confession provided by the Friar. The obstacles to their union, which are external and eminently surmountable in Acts 1 and 2, take on a very different cast in Act 3, when Romeo's murder of Tybalt revives in the present time of the play the 'ancient quarrel' (1.1.102) 'bred of an airy word' (1.1.87) that appears to have already been waning, as we see in Capulet's toleration of the masked Romeo at the party. (See Watson on Capulet in this volume.) In comedy, constraints remain largely external and admit to solution. In tragedy, constraints stem from the actions of the hero himself, whose deeds reorganize the social world, creating impasses that rope ladders can't surmount. Neither strictly external nor fully internal, tragic constraints concern the hero's conflicted relationships with others, conflicts wrought by his own actions. Romance introduces another kind of constraint, namely the element of chance and accident, which can yield both comic and tragic consequences and resolutions. The intercepted invitation in Act 1 leads to the meeting of Romeo and Juliet, while the missed letters of Act 4 derail the Friar's plan to reunite them; in both cases, letters are instruments of communication whose success is not guaranteed. *Romeo and Juliet*, then, is a romantic tragedy built out of comic materials, whose impulses continue to shape the dénouement. Thus, the double death in the tomb, for all of its wanton wastage, also resonates as a marriage that issues in the kinds of social conciliation and rebirth associated with festive plays like *A Midsummer Night's Dream*.

However, to say that the play is built out of several genres is not to say that it is mixed in form, like the tragicomedies and romances of later Shakespeare. What is most striking about the play's architecture is its successful binding of tragic, comic and romance tendencies into an existential and aesthetic unity that is dramatic first, and genre-bound second. Thus Watson writes that the lovers' reconciliation of Eros and Thanatos has also 'merged conventionally opposed genres'.[24] The play garners laughter up to the end, though the quality of that laughter changes as the play moves from the antics of rival gangs, illiterate servants and jocular buddy talk to the spectre of a friar stumbling on tombstones, a lover armed with crowbar and poison rather than flowers or lyre and a grieving husband unwilling to trust the evidence of his eyes. Although I am too conscious of the facts of literary history to accept wholesale Kottman's stronger claim that 'generic categories are useless when it comes to Shakespeare', his iconoclastic argument discloses something important about the continuous if variegated space of action in *Romeo and Juliet*.[25] The Nurse is asked to procure the ladder *before* the violent events in the square and she brings it to the expectant Juliet *after* the tragic turn has already occurred. Deployed in full knowledge of Tybalt's death, Romeo's exile and the new constraints those facts represent, the rope ladder charts a soft highway between the comic and tragic movements of the play, allowing a comic action (the consummation of a marriage and the circumvention of parental wishes) to unfold within a tragic space hemmed in by more intractable realities. The turn or *peripeteia* from comedy to tragedy is native to both tragedy and comedy themselves, which share the structural features of reversal, recognition and dramatic irony. The crowbar that Romeo brings to the Capulet monument also belongs simultaneously to tragedy and comedy. Used in Antipholus of Ephesus' forced entry into his own house in *The Comedy of Errors*, the crowbar links Romeo to grave robbers and day labourers, threatening to demote him from tragic hero to comic villain/*villein* (peasant). (A crowbar also figures in that most Shakespearean of comic operas, Mozart's *The Marriage of Figaro*.) Romeo's crowbar serves to pivot the scene from the exterior of the tomb to the interior, and between more realistic and more mythic settings, affiliating Romeo with Orpheus seeking Eurydice in the underworld. The rope ladder is a connecting device; the crowbar is a tool for prying and leveraging. Both props facilitate movement among modes and moods, and both point us back to the social relationships, technical knowledges and environmental interactions that sustain the theatre. Both props also lift the play beyond genre, towards the more existential zone that Shakespeare will visit in *King Lear* and *Macbeth*.

According to Kottman, the lovers die neither for the city, nor for naught, nor even for each other, but for themselves: *Romeo and Juliet* is 'the story of two individuals who *actively claim* their separate individuality, their own freedom, in the only way that they can – through one another'.[26] In this volume, Watson argues that the play converts 'life-denying antitheses into more generous and generative syntheses that express the real intricacy of human experience'.[27] Hugh Grady, not unlike Kottman and Watson, recovers the play's 'utopian spirit', its cultivation of 'a space in which love and desire persist even when they are represented as defeated by larger forces'.[28] That utopian space is actively conjured and represented in Romeo's glimpse of Juliet in the tomb as he drags Paris's corpse into the monument:

> I'll bury thee in a triumphant grave.
> A grave – O, no, a lantern, slaughtered youth,
> For here lies Juliet, and her beauty makes
> This vault a feasting presence full of light.
>
> (5.3.83–6)

In architectural parlance, 'lantern' refers to the windowed structure erected above a dome to let light into the room below. A lantern is also a portable lighting appliance, often carried on stage to indicate night-time. Whereas earlier Romeo had imagined the tomb as a flesh-eating monster, here the same space becomes the scene of a fabulous feast, recreating the party in which Romeo had first seen Juliet teaching the torches to burn bright. The lantern of the grave is the last theatrical space built out of and around the meeting of the lovers: what illuminates the grave is the lovers' own co-presence in it. Its glowing bounds recall the sonnet room that Romeo and Juliet built together through poetic form and the press of palms and lips, and it also re-gathers the curtained bed that Juliet imagines will be lit by their shared 'beauties'. Finding life in death, this piece of imaginary scenography is also Romeo's counterpoint to Juliet's fantasy of stellification. In Hugh Grady's terms, both Romeo's feasting presence and Juliet's star-spangled banner enclose 'the play's elemental themes [love and death] in self-conscious patternings that fashion a symbolic triumph of desire over death in an idealized aesthetic sphere'.[29]

Yet what also shines in the funeral monument is dramatic irony, the cool light of reason and the warm light of romance tempering each other. After all, Juliet glows because – she is not dead. Romeo's final blazon – 'Beauty's ensign yet / Is crimson in thy lips and in thy cheeks, / And death's pale flag is not advanced there' (5.3.94–6) is horrible because it is true. If the image of the grave as feasting presence returns us to the dazzling hospitality of Act 1, it also illuminates a zone marked by contingency, error, bad timing and misprision. The challenge for readers, audiences and theatre-makers is to grasp the quality of triumph that irradiates the death scene without attributing to the lovers more wisdom than they possess. It is this challenge, rather than literary mixture or hybridity as artistic ends in themselves, that is ultimately at stake in the play's merging of comic and tragic materials.

Tightly constructed, well paced and populated by complex and lively characters whose good will exposes them to misfortune in a manner that affiliates them intimately and immediately with the lived worlds of readers and spectators, this play has enjoyed a rich and varied reception in theatres and classrooms for many centuries. It has not, however, been a critical favourite, either largely ignored by readers like Hegel and Bradley as somehow less than serious, or exposed as ideological symptom by the play's most trenchantly sceptical readers, including Jonathan Goldberg and Dympna Callaghan.[30] The play found champions, however, in Coleridge, Hazlitt, Pater and Frye, while the rich modal and geographical range of theatrical responses to *Romeo and Juliet* has inspired innovative reception studies by Marjorie Garber, Richard Burt and Mark Burnett. Meanwhile, whether they respect the play or not, historicists always find plenty to ponder in Verona's teeming cityscape, from burial practices, street fighting and calendar reform to dream theory and ancient physics.[31] Beyond historicism, reception and critique, *Romeo and Juliet* has attracted philosophical attention from readers whose ranks include René Girard, Jacques Derrida, Julia Kristeva, Paul Kottman and Tzachi Zamir. This volume is dedicated to the exploration of *Romeo and Juliet* in its romantic obfuscations and kitsch variations, as well as its ideational intensities and emotional truths, and it seeks to sound those depths and shallows in both readerly and theatrical experience.

1

The Critical Backstory[1]

Naomi Conn Liebler

In *New Readings vs. Old Plays* (1979), Richard L. Levin offers this challenge to serious critical readers of Shakespearean drama:

> If ours is an Age of Criticism, as we have frequently been told, then it can also be called the Age of the Reading, since that is the dominant form in which most of our criticism is taught and practiced [*sic*] ... Indeed the identification of literary criticism – or more precisely, literary interpretation – with the reading has become so well established that it is usually assumed without question, and as a result we can easily forget that this is a relatively recent phenomenon. The great critics of the past may have occasionally used the word, but they have not left us anything that we would recognize as a reading in the modern sense.[2]

Levin identifies a watershed moment in Shakespearean criticism, correctly observing that the concept of 'readings' or 'approaches,' and the 'ism' labels (e.g. Marxism, feminism, 'old' and 'new' historicisms) that frame them would have been unrecognizable to critics of earlier generations. The battles themselves, however, are not new. In the eighteenth century, Samuel Johnson pointed to similar kinds of 'debates' that began to show up as soon as competing editions began to 'correct' the First Folio, the first collection of Shakespeare's plays, compiled in 1623, seven years after he died, by two of his fellow actors, John Heminge and Henry Condell. The eighteenth century argued over issues of diction and decorum and a neoclassical obsession with Aristotelian unities, whereas the twentieth focused on interpretation and thematic 'readings'. Much like Levin, Johnson thought such debates were unproductive and pointless, as he writes in the *Preface to Shakespeare* (1765):

> It is no pleasure to me, in revising my volumes, to observe how much paper is wasted in confutation. Whoever considers the revolutions of learning, and the various questions of greater or less importance, upon which wit and reason have exercised their powers, must lament the unsuccessfulness of enquiry, and the slow advances of truth, when he reflects, that a great part of the labour of every writer is only the destruction of those that went before him. The first care of the builder of a new system, is to demolish the fabricks [*sic*] which are standing. The chief desire of him that comments an authour [*sic*], is to shew how much other commentators have corrupted and obscured him. The opinions prevalent in one age, as truths above the reach of controversy, are confuted and rejected in another, and rise again to reception in remoter times. Thus the human mind is kept in motion without progress.[3]

For Johnson, disabling the views of one's predecessors seemed a waste of time and intellect, and it happened consistently enough to provoke this satirical overview. As these lines remind us, literary criticism has a history; it is subject to fashions in thinking and, like the literature it studies, reflects the biases and values of the decades that produce it. Even critical neglect can seem a kind of commentary: in the twentieth century several important critics were *not* moved to write about this play: A. C. Bradley, Stanley Cavell, Jan Kott, T. S. Eliot, Kenneth Burke, Bertolt Brecht, and we are left to wonder why. Others offered only brief comparative references – 'as in *Romeo & Juliet*' – a paragraph or a sentence suggesting that simply naming the play is enough to trigger recognition of a shared experience, but no sustained discussion. More recent critics, on the other hand, have minded the gaps and filled them, attending carefully to the play's semantic and performative complexity, producing the variety of contesting 'readings' that Levin observed.

It is therefore worth noting that one popular approach to the play, built and sustained across four centuries, rests upon language as both its medium and its message – on the consequences of words spoken and unspoken, messages undelivered and misread, and on the question of whether the name of a thing or a person makes any real difference at all. A common ground emerges that links these critical responses. Despite differences in assessments of the play as inspiring or morally disturbing, romantic or banal, appropriate or inappropriate for younger readers and audiences, taken together, this critical discourse illuminates one trend in responses to the play: long before (and again after) the post-Freudian era in literary criticism began to analyse dramatic texts and performances under the persistent light of character analysis, critics have shared a fascination with paradox and oxymora that extends across an arc of four centuries.

From the beginning

The earliest critical notice of *Romeo and Juliet* must have been Francis Meres's 1598 observation of 'true-harted Julietta' who 'did die upon the corps of her dearest Romeo',[4] which Katherine Duncan-Jones notes was 'likely to recall an especially memorable stage tableau',[5] since the stage direction did not appear in print until the twentieth century. After that first-run notice, critical assessments emerging early in the Restoration were not much bothered about the play's content: if it was by Shakespeare, it was likely acceptable, except for Samuel Pepys's famous condemnation in a *Diary* entry for 1 March 1662. Pepys had gone to see it 'the first time it was ever acted [after the Restoration reopened the theatres]; but it is a play of itself the worst that ever I heard in my life, and the worst acted that ever I saw these people do, and I am resolved to go no more to see the first time of acting, for they were all of them out more or less',[6] though he does not mention why he thought so. In contrast, in *An Account of the English Dramatick Poets* (1691), the first comprehensive attempt at literary biography and criticism in English, Gerard Langbaine accounted *Romeo and Juliet* 'amongst the best of our author's works',[7] similarly without stating a reason.

By the mid-eighteenth century, *Romeo and Juliet* became the subject of 'proprietary' concerns in several senses of the term. Actors, editors and critical audiences alike took what they considered 'ownership' of the play, correcting and emending each other's corrections and emendations, and the Shakespeare Re-write industry was launched. In 1750, Arthur Murphy, playwright, barrister, and biographer of the famous actor David Garrick, described a twelve-night 'theatre war' when Garrick played Romeo to George Anne Bellamy's Juliet at Drury Lane, after Spranger Barry and Susannah Cibber, Garrick's original actors, decamped to mount their own production at Covent Garden. Murphy was equally horrified by both productions' attempts to pass off aging actresses as teenage Juliets, while also altering the plays to dilute or delete any language that might spark a passion or even refer to one. His aim in the essay is 'chiefly to consider whether SHAKESPEARE has been improved by the alterations lately made in this play', referring to Garrick's often-quoted intention to 'clear the Original as much as possible from the Jingle and Quibble' that (he said) had impeded a number of stage revivals, and to clear Romeo of the taint of fickleness seen in his sudden shift of affection from Rosaline to Juliet.[8] Neither production, Murphy wrote, was 'fitted for the characters as drawn by the poet'.[9]

> They all seem to want what no actor can truly feign, no spectator can thoroughly be deceived in; I mean that degree of puberty, which is but just to be distinguished from childhood ... Who therefore can help laughing to see a mother of children endeavouring to impose herself upon us for a raw girl just in her teens, and to hear her whining in this strain:
>
> Give me my ROMEO, night, and when he dies,
> Take him and cut him into little stars, &C. ...
>
> Or a great huge tall creature about six foot high, and big in proportion, wishing
>
> O that I were a glove upon that hand
> That I might touch that cheek ...
>
> with a thousand other instances of a like nature.[10]

Garrick regretted Shakespeare's neglect of the Bandello original in favour of either the French or English translations, excusing it on grounds that Shakespeare simply had not read Bandello. In fact, a preference for the Italian model seems to have overtaken a number of commentators around this time. Editor Brian Vickers includes an anonymous 'Account of the Novel and Play of *Romeo and Juliet*' from 1764 that enumerates the differences between Shakespeare's version and Bandello's, and prefers unequivocally the Italian ending:

> In Bandello, while the dying husband is holding, as he supposes, the lifeless body of his wife in his arms, and shedding the last tears for her death, she awakes, opens her eyes, gazes on him, and entreats him to carry her out of the

> monument. Romeo is for some moments lost in a transport of surprise and joy, but, reflecting that he is poisoned, and must shortly die, and leave her, his agonies return with double force, and the mutual distress of the lovers, as they discover their situation, is in the highest degree tender and affecting.

Like Garrick, the author here too opines: 'the best apology for Shakespeare having omitted' Bandello's incidents 'is that he never saw them'.[11]

Taken together, these eighteenth-century comments suggest two striking critical data: (1) there were numbers of attendees at both Covent Garden and Drury Lane who were learned enough to have read Bandello or Boaistuau,[12] though Brooke's English poem does not seem to have caught their attention; (2) these emenders and adaptors and their audiences assumed an ownership of Shakespeare entitling them to alter the text of the play to suit (what they perceived to be) current aesthetic appetites. Rather than ignore a Shakespeare who did not give them what they wanted, they preferred to bend the Shakespearean text to coterie tastes. Shakespeare was literally appropriated as 'our author'.

The romantic turn / child-protective services and reversals

By the turn of the nineteenth century, some English sensibilities required other kinds of surgical alterations. Although, arguably, no collective group in English cultural history loved Shakespeare more than the Romantics did, among them only Coleridge and Hazlitt left sustained discussions. Coleridge's magisterial essay was one of the *Lectures on Shakespeare* delivered in 1810–11, but not written down until 1818.

That was also the year of the second edition of Thomas and Harriet Bowdler's *Family Shakespeare*,[13] whose first version, under Harriet's name, came out in a small volume (12°) in

1807, the same year as Charles and Mary Lamb's family-friendly, cleaned-up *Tales from Shakespeare*. Romanticism's ownership of Shakespearean drama was tempered from the start by a prissy caution about the hazards of exposing 'young' readers to the passions signalled in these plays. The newspaper advertisement for the Bowdler edition of 1818 assured readers that: 'My great objects in this undertaking are to remove from the writings of Shakespeare, some defects which diminish their value; and, at the same time, to present to the Public an edition of his Plays, which the parent, the guardian, and instructor of youth, may place without fear in the hands of the pupil, and from which the pupil may derive instruction as well as pleasure; may improve his moral principles while he refines his taste, and without incurring the danger of being hurt with any indelicacy of expression.' The edition itself promised via its subtitle that '*Nothing Is Added to the Original Text: But Those Words And Expressions Are Omitted Which Cannot With Propriety Be Read Aloud In a Family*.' Among the defects and indelicacies expunged or altered were, predictably, Mercutio's line, 'the bawdy hand of the dial is now upon the prick of noon' (2.4.108–9), which became 'the hand of the dial is now upon the point of noon.' Samson's line in the opening scene about thrusting women to the wall (1.1.15) and Romeo's 'nor ope her lap to saint-seducing gold' (1.1.212) were removed altogether, which may in the long run have done less violence to the play than the Lambs' alterations, which summarized some twenty plays, seldom quoting from any of them.

Lamb knew Coleridge from their school days at Christ's Hospital in London; we can speculate – even imagine – a debate running from their youth through their professional lives about the moral aptness of the play one of them goes on to praise and the other to redact. Coleridge was primarily interested in the Nurse (and Mercutio), the two main characters whose lines were (literally) 'Bowdlerized'. He has to remind himself, about two-thirds of the way through one of the lectures, that he is supposed to talk about the protagonists:

> It remains for me to speak of the hero and heroine, of Romeo and Juliet themselves; and I shall do so with unaffected diffidence, not merely on account of the delicacy, but of the great importance of the subject. I feel that it is impossible to defend Shakespeare from the most cruel of all charges – that he is an immoral writer – without entering fully into his mode of pourtraying [*sic*] female characters, and of displaying the passion of love. It seems to me, that he has done both with greater perfection than any other writer of the known world. ('Seventh Lecture', 68–9)

Though clearly aware of the charges of 'immorality' made against Shakespeare, Coleridge declines to name names; his good friend William Hazlitt, however, has no such scruples. Commenting on Juliet's wedding-night speech – 'Gallop apace, you fiery-footed steeds' – Hazlitt is explicit, quoting this speech in full, out-rhapsodizing Coleridge, and explaining that:

> We the rather insert this passage here, inasmuch as we have no doubt it has been expunged from the Family Shakespear. Such critics do not perceive that the feelings of the heart sanctify, without disguising, the impulses of nature. Without refinement themselves, they confound modesty with hypocrisy ... It has nothing forward, nothing coy, nothing affected or coquettish about it; – it is a pure effusion of nature. It is as frank as it is modest, for it has no thought that it wishes to conceal. It reposes in conscious innocence on the strength of its affections. Its delicacy does not consist in coldness and reserve, but in combining warmth of imagination and tenderness of heart with the most voluptuous sensibility. Love is a gentle flame that rarefies and expands her whole being.[14]

Hazlitt is equally eloquent about Romeo:

> Romeo is Hamlet in love. There is the same rich exuberance of passion and sentiment in the one, that there is of thought

> and sentiment in the other. Both are absent and self-involved, both live out of themselves in a world of imagination. Hamlet is abstracted from everything; Romeo is abstracted from everything but his love, and lost in it ... He is himself only in his Juliet; she is his only reality, his heart's true home and idol. The rest of the world is to him a passing dream.[15]

Coleridge has less to say about the protagonists. But long before the end of the seventh lecture, he arrives at what he really wants to talk about – Mercutio and the Nurse:

> Mercutio is a man possessing all of the elements of a poet: the whole world was, as it were, subject to his law of association ... By his loss it was contrived that the whole catastrophe of the tragedy should be brought about: it endears him to Romeo, and gives to the death of Mercutio an importance which it could not otherwise have acquired ... Had not Mercutio been rendered so amiable and so interesting, we could not have felt so strongly the necessity for Romeo's interference, connecting it immediately, and passionately, with the future of the lover and his mistress.[16]

This last sentence compacts Coleridge's great appeal as a critic, and probably the reason people attended his lectures (as they did) in great enough numbers to move them from pub room to assembly room. For him, the characters on the stage embody and elicit credible human emotions, responses and engagements. He doesn't judge them: he roots for the side that wins his affection, and explains why we should as well.

Coleridge applies the same appeal to recognizable experience. Working against what he calls the 'traditional view' that Shakespeare's characterization reflects careful real-life observation, he argues that *that* much observation would have been impossible:

> Now, I appeal confidently to my hearers whether the closest observation of the manners of one or two old nurses

> would have enabled Shakespeare to draw this character of admirable generalization? Surely not. Let any man conjure up in his mind all the qualities and peculiarities that can possibly belong to a nurse, and he will find them in Shakespeare's picture of the old woman: nothing is omitted. This effect is not produced by mere observation. The great prerogative of genius ... is now to swell itself to the dignity of a god, and now to subdue and keep dormant some part of that lofty nature, and to descend even to the lowest character – to become everything, in fact, but the vicious.
>
> Thus, in the Nurse you have all the garrulity of old-age, and all its fondness; for the affection of old-age is one of the greatest consolations of humanity. I have often thought what a melancholy world this would be without children, and what an inhuman world without the aged.[17]

She is in this something like the sonnets' 'dark lady' or 'young man' – a distillation of qualities and characteristics that add up to a generic 'nurse', and require no specific or actual model. For Coleridge, it does not matter whether she talks too much, or has trouble keeping up with Mercutio's teasing, or settles for vicarious maternity in the Capulet household with a philosophical shrug about her late husband and daughter. He likes the way she thinks visually, like the Romantic poet himself. She recalls in clear chunks of imagery the toddler Juliet's tantrum over weaning, her response to the Nurse's husband's joke about falling backward, the earthquake that shook the dovehouse wall and her identification with the Nurse's dead child Susan (1.3.17–49). Coleridge loves this long-winded speech for its indispensable content: 'More is here brought into one portrait than could have been ascertained by one man's mere observation, and without the introduction of a single incongruous point.'[18]

He comes to rest on the 'natural' diction of the characters, focusing on Romeo's discovery speech in Act 1:

> Here's much to do with hate, but more with love.
> Why then, O brawling love, O loving hate,
> O anything of nothing first create,
> O heavy lightness, serious vanity,
> Misshapen chaos of well-seeming forms,
> Feather of lead, bright smoke, cold fire, sick health,
> Still-waking sleep that is not what it is.
>
> (1.1.173–9)

The play's oxymora turn out to be the single element – of both plot and diction – that captured equally the attention of critics from the Romantics to the end of the twentieth century. Coleridge helpfully explains why they matter so much to him:

> I can understand and allow for an effort of the mind, when it would describe what it cannot satisfy itself with the description of, to reconcile opposition and qualify contradictions, leaving a middle state of mind more strictly appropriate to the imagination than any other, when it is, as it were, hovering between images. As soon as it is fixed on one image, it becomes understanding; but while it is unfixed and wavering between them, attaching itself permanently to none, it is imagination ... the result being what the poet wishes to impress, namely, the substitution of a sublime feeling of the unimaginable for a mere image.[19]

We can hear an almost exact echo of Theseus' well-known invocation of the poet's pen shaping, locating and naming the work of imagination as it 'bodies forth / The forms of things unknown' (*MND* 5.1.14–15). The semantic paradoxes and contradictions function as a verbal equivalent to the situational and active contradictions performed in the play from beginning to end, and Coleridge's fine poetic sensibilities to language and character-in-language invite his (and Shakespeare's) readers to 'hear' action in the dramatic poetry.

Other Romantics shared Coleridge's and Hazlitt's enthusiasm for the emotional intensities of the play. In 1826,

Henry Mercer Graves, a minor playwright, poet and 'political commentator', sought the patronage of George Canning, statesman and briefly Prime Minister, by dedicating to him (but perhaps too late; Canning died the following year) his *Essay on the Genius of Shakespeare*, where he notes that 'The character of Romeo is that of the most perfectly drawn lover I ever read … in pathos, feeling, and overwhelming depth of passion.'[20] Juliet is 'all love, all gentleness, all woman. Love is her life and being. She lives in Romeo.'[21] Graves compares Juliet with Ophelia, and Romeo with Hamlet, and finds in each case that the earlier iteration surpasses the later in any respect he cares to notice.

In the next generation, Edward Dowden's *Shakspere: A Critical Study of His Mind and Art* (1875)[22] seems to have been the only sustained discussion of the play in the Victorian era; except for this, *Romeo and Juliet* once again slipped into neglect, its occlusion nowhere more obvious than in its omission from Bradley's *Shakespearean Tragedy* (1904).[23] Dowden also links *Romeo and Juliet* with *Hamlet,* arguing that *Romeo and Juliet* is Shakespeare's first tragedy and *Hamlet* his second (effacing altogether *Titus Andronicus* and *Julius Caesar*). He finds the earlier play 'steeped in passion', the later 'steeped in meditation'; Romeo is 'the man of the South' while Hamlet is 'the Teuton, the man of the North'.[24] These binaries stand as a common characterological thread setting a continuum from Romantic to Victorian to Edwardian that carries forward well into the mid-twentieth century. Characters are for these later poets and critics 'all *something*' contrasted with others who are 'all *something else*'. Dowden too loves this play's collection of oxymora, which he calls 'the sought-out phrases, the curious antitheses, of the amorous dialect of the period'.[25] In these antitheses he finds the core of the genre: 'Shakspere was aware that every strong emotion which exalts and quickens the inner life of man at the same time exposes the outer life of accident and circumstance to increased risk. But the theme of tragedy, as conceived by the poet, is not material prosperity or failure: it is spiritual;

fulfilment or failure of a destiny higher than that which is related to the art of getting on in life. To die, under certain conditions, may be a higher rapture than to live.'[26] Barely hidden in the rhapsodic language is a sense that the play magnified for close scrutiny everything that a contemporary sensibility needed in order to understand the complexity of non-tragic life. For these later readers, Shakespeare was still 'our poet' working on their behalf, offering a way to negotiate inescapable contradictions, dilemma-horns, paradoxes and oxymora.

The modern construct

Almost 130 years after Dowden and 200 years after Coleridge, René Girard noticed that oxymora are in fact the *most appropriate* linguistic structures for the situation in which the protagonists find themselves: he calls Juliet 'a living oxymoron: as a lover she blesses Romeo; as Tybalt's cousin, she curses him'. But this simple observation will not do for Girard. 'Is Shakespeare simply trying to break the world record of oxymora? ... [He] must have had something more interesting in mind, something more relevant to the nature of this particular play.'[27] And though he arrives at his conclusion via a different event (Tybalt's death instead of Mercutio's), turn-of-the-twenty-first-century Girard comes to the same conclusion as his nineteenth-century predecessors:

> the oxymoronic style of Romeo and Juliet ... is a realistic representation of how lovers related to each other in a hypermimetic world ... Thanks to Tybalt's death, Juliet sounds as painfully divided against herself as a passionate lover should be, while still appearing serenely united with Romeo ... The fusion of words that apply to the love affair with the words that apply to the blood feud is convincing enough for the whole thing to sound like the splendid

> expression of a love whose depth and intensity are such that to question anything would seem sacrilegious.[28]

Anyone looking for a trans-historical fight here – for evidence that we read very differently today from the way a Romantic or Victorian poet read – might be disappointed. The play's verbal and situational collisions speak to both the earlier sensibility and the later. Girard too brings up multiple instances of oxymora, mainly but not only from Juliet. For Girard, this language expresses the fundamental paradox of the whole play – as he puts it, 'a mutual contamination of the love affair and the blood feud that produces some poetic miracles'[29].

A different kind of oxymoron caught the attention of mid-twentieth-century critics: situational rather than semantic, philosophical more than sociological. Irving Ribner, writing in 1960, traces in *Romeo and Juliet* a dramatic version of the *felix culpa*, the Paradox of the Fortunate Fall (described earlier by Herbert Weisinger),[30] which posits that original sin was 'fortunate' because it made redemption necessary, that evil must be in order for salvation to be. It makes some sense, after all, that this idea gains currency, perhaps even urgency, in the years following the Second World War and the Holocaust, when large numbers of survivors of both catastrophes sought explanations for the inexplicable. Ribner writes:

> Shakespeare in *Romeo and Juliet* poses the question of how man may live in a world in which evil lurks about him and in which the inevitable end of all worldly aspirations must be death. Elizabethan Christian humanism held that although good and evil are in the world together, the entire universe is ruled by a benevolent God whose plan is purposive and just. The paradox of the fortunate fall taught that evil might itself contribute to this plan. Man, bearing the burden of original sin, had evil within him, but as the chosen creature of God he had good also. When evil predominated he was ruled by passion, but he had reason

> which could keep passion under control, and reason was an acceptance of the will of God.[31]

Ribner is interested in the paradoxes inherent in dramatic action and situation, more than in semantic oxymora: 'Out of the self-inflicted deaths of Romeo and Juliet comes a rebirth of good ... In Shakespeare's play we are made to see that through the suffering of individuals the social order is cleansed of evil; the deep-rooted family feud is finally brought to an end.'[32] At the same time (actually a year later), in 'Christianity and the Religion of Love in *Romeo and Juliet*' (1961), Paul N. Siegel suggested a similar reading: 'In *Romeo and Juliet* the medieval and Renaissance concept that sexual love is a manifestation of the cosmic love of God, which holds together the universe in a chain of love and imposes order on it, acts as a nexus between the two doctrines. ... The ideas of the religion of love and those of Christianity not only work together; they also pull in opposite directions, creating a dramatic tension which is relieved only with the transcendence of love at the very end.'[33] For Weisinger, Ribner and Siegel in the mid-twentieth century, the paradoxes governing the action of the play are understood and explained as juxtaposed ethical positions, effecting a compromise between ecclesiastical Christian doctrines and cultural practices regarding sex, sin and death, creating perhaps a clash of ideas for the reader or audience but not, it seems, for the author or his characters. The paradoxes present in the play deny any 'either/or' requirement, insisting instead on 'both/and' as the only authentic reflection of contradictory but equal truths.

Two and a half decades later, Northrop Frye was also interested in the play's contrasts, heard in the contradictory ways language works in this play. He focuses on the spaces inside the oxymora where change actually happens. (The anthropologist Victor Turner called this kind of space *liminal*,[34] and, except for *Hamlet*, there is arguably no play in the Shakespeare canon more concerned with what happens during transitions and traversals.) Frye notes the shift early on, invoking in a very different register the same speech that made Hazlitt's pulse race:

> Before she sees Romeo we hear Juliet making proper-young-lady noises like 'It is an honour that I dream not of' (... her marriage to Paris). After she sees Romeo, she's talking like this:
>
> Gallop apace, you fiery-footed steeds,
> Toward Phoebus' lodging! Such a wagoner
> As Phaeton would whip you to the west
> And bring in cloudy night immediately. (III.ii.1–4)[35]

In Frye's reading, the rhetorical moves we hear in Juliet's speeches and in Romeo's are a kind of metonymy for all the contradictions and clashes at work in the play. Frye too notices the oxymora in Romeo's 'O brawling love, O loving hate', but sees them as part of the play's *action:*

> The figure he is using is the oxymoron of paradoxical union of opposites: obviously the right kind of figure for this play ... From there we go on to Friar Laurence's wonderfully concentrated image of
>
> fire and powder
> Which, as they kiss, consume, (II.vi.10–11)
>
> with its half-concealed pun on 'consummation', and to Juliet's
>
> Too like the lightning, which doth cease to be
> Ere one can say it lightens. (II.ii.119–20)
>
> suggesting that their first glimpse of one another determined their deaths as well as their love.[36]

Frye, it must be said, shows some analytic weaknesses when

he tries to explain things that do not in fact make sense to *him:* he is clearly uncomfortable with the play's suggestions of homoeroticism among the male characters, and he is also uncomfortable with the Nurse. In both cases he feels compelled to explain (away) what he takes to be Renaissance ideas of male bonding and friendship, loyalty and even logic. When he worries about how to discuss what he prefers not to discuss, he dismisses the problem with appeals to genre ('male friendship overrides love of women, but this is tragedy')[37] or to class-bias: the Nurse's speech is 'not very logical, but who said the Nurse was logical?'[38] Frye is not very good on character analysis, but he does very well what he is good at: like Ribner, he traces archetypes and patterns – as we would expect of the author of the *Anatomy of Criticism*:

> The Prologue, even before the play starts, suggests that the feud demands lives to feed on, and that sooner or later will get them ... Romeo and Juliet are sacrificial victims, and the ancient rule about sacrifice was that the victim had to be perfect and without blemish ... One of the first things Romeo says of Juliet is: 'Beauty too rich for use, for earth too dear!' But more than beauty is involved: their kind of passion would soon burn up the world of heavy fathers and snarling Tybalts and gabby Nurses if it stayed there. Our perception of this helps us to accept the play as a whole, instead of feeling only that a great love went wrong. It didn't go wrong: it went only where it could, out.[39]

Despite a shared appreciation for oxymoron and paradox, certain obvious differences emerge in the trajectory from Romantic critics who focus on Shakespeare's use of language and his characterization to their mid-twentieth-century counterparts who have been more interested in interpretation than appreciation. The later group tends to explain things, sometimes even to preach, and to explain away what makes them uncomfortable. Thus Ribner, writing in the late 1950s, invokes 'a Christian view of man's position in the universe'[40] centred in presumably agreed-upon notions of good and evil into which we are born, and 'which affirms justice in the universe and the benevolence of God'.[41]

The orderly system that Ribner longed for and Frye believed in was not available to W. H. Auden, writing a decade before Ribner and immediately after World War II. Lecturing on *Romeo and Juliet* in November 1946, Auden locates 'contradiction' in the very nature of the situation being dramatized, but in ways that lean over into the domains of philosophers like Kierkegaard (*Either/Or*) and Buber (*I and Thou*), whom he invokes several times, and to my thinking calls up echoes of some of the post-war dramatic Absurdists like Ionesco or Genet, or Brecht. Perhaps in the immediate post-war years, a linguistic phenomenon like the oxymoron or the situational paradox might not have seemed unusual enough to warrant notice, as the whole world had become an oxymoron. Auden invokes something like cultural relativism:

> Don't bother about the judgments of the audience contemporary with the author, except in cases where we can't understand why so much attention is paid to something that seems to us unimportant – the scruples of the characters in the blood feud in *Romeo and Juliet*, for example. We do better imagining ideological fights ... Though Elizabethans would have condemned blood feuds, as the Prince does, they were near enough to understand and feel it as a temptation. We must correct for that: otherwise the lovers will seem more unlucky and more reasonable than they are. If you take the Nurse's view that Juliet should marry Paris and have an affair with Romeo on the side, the plot does not make any sense to us.[42]

When Auden comments on the 'love' between Romeo and Juliet, he reaches a very different conclusion from that of his Romantic predecessors:

> In literary tradition there are always obstacles to love. For the intoxicant of romantic love to remain effective it is essential that the relationship not change into something else, dwindle into friendship or domestic, married love, for example, with its ties to the community. No, something must come between the lovers that prevents their union: one of them is already married, there is an interfamily feud, there is a barrier of race, or religion, and should no barrier be present, the lovers themselves must provide one. The purpose of the obstacle is clear: it is to intensify desire by impeding its fulfillment. Now the obstacle that the lovers ideally require must be insurmountable. That is to say, their union must be possible only through their deaths. This is the secret, the religious mystery, of Romantic Love, the mystery that is represented by the suicides of Romeo and Juliet. If people marry on the assumption that love must always overcome obstacles, they will either become unfaithful or they will make things difficult. The better you know someone, the better you can torture him: man and wife become each other's devils.[43]

What might be a post-war cynicism (or perhaps just the poet's own) creeps into Auden's reading:

> Romeo and Juliet don't know each other, but when one dies, the other can't go on living. Behind their passionate suicides, as well as their reactions to Romeo's banishment, is finally a lack of feeling, a fear that the relationship cannot be sustained and that, out of pride, it should be stopped now, in death. If they become a married couple, there will be no more wonderful speeches – and a good thing, too. Then the real tasks of life will begin, with which art has surprisingly little to do. Romeo and Juliet are idolaters of each other, which is what leads to their suicides.[44]

Auden here seems to have fallen into the trap that stymies many undergraduates: taking the characters as real persons who have the will and consciousness required to produce the 'fear that the relationship cannot be sustained and that ... it should be stopped now'. His more deliberative conclusion recognizes that love and death wrap this play in a paradoxical bind.

Though he does not invoke (by name) what a later generation would call a psychoanalytic model, his language and the interpretative thread he follows imply the oxymoronic pull of Eros and Thanatos, which is given perhaps its finest articulation twenty years later in Norman Rabkin's chapter, 'Eros and Death', in *Shakespeare and the Common Understanding*. Simply put, in this play along with *Antony and Cleopatra* and *Venus and Adonis*, 'Shakespeare tells us that love, the most intense manifestation of the urge to life, is ineluctably linked with the self-destructive yearning for annihilation that we recognize as the death wish.'[45] Like those nineteenth-century trail-blazers who lacked the advantage of a post-Freudian vocabulary, Rabkin finds the oxymora of this basic psychoanalytic principle displayed in the semantics his predecessors (as represented above) had examined, for which the play's successive dramatic situations provide externalized, performable equivalents.[46] 'Love between the children of enemies is paradoxical; even more so is a love that finds its marriage only in death. Such paradox emerges not from the inventive mind of a sonnet-fed young man, turned in upon itself and delighting in the ambiguities of emotions simultaneously bitter and sweet, but from the actual confrontation of a reality that destroys in creating.'[47] Again like nearly all of his predecessors, Rabkin locates the true core of the play in Juliet's 'Gallop apace' speech, appropriately placed in the play's temporal and spatial centre in 3.2, which he identifies as Juliet's 'epithalamion'.[48] *Romeo and Juliet*, he concludes, 'is about youth and age' (another paradox, to be sure); 'it stages the internal conflict in love as a tension between the consuming eros of adolescence, which so insists on the complete satisfaction of the ego that it must end in the annihilation of the self, and its polar opposite, that mature social love which insists on the sacrifice of the ego's fulfillment for another kind of good, a world that fosters rather than destroys'; 'the problem is eros; its form is Shakespearean'.[49]

The thirty years since Frye wrote, the fifty-five since Ribner and the seventy since Auden have seen significant changes, critically, politically and socially. In the sixties, iconoclast protests, discontents, traversals and reversals, by and large, asked us to read, hear and perform in (arguably) new paradigms. With the seventies, Shakespearean criticism faced a dilemma. Critics could either reject Shakespeare altogether as elitist, sexist, essentialist, outmoded or irrelevant, or they could come to terms through refocused lenses with Shakespearean models that both challenged and re-inscribed the critical revisions of previous generations' observations. For perhaps the first time in Shakespearean critical history, multiple and dissonant 'readings' of the sort Richard Levin invoked in the material quoted at the start of this essay came to occupy readers, students and audiences. One of the most intriguing features of this newly multifaceted approach to Shakespeare was its capacious inclusion of entirely different perspectives sprung from such foci as gender and social class. Shakespeare was still 'our playwright', but now multiple perspectives claimed ownership, and the referral of 'our' became newly complicated.

The women's view

The most sustained of these lenses – it has been around the longest and shows no sign of abating even now – is the experiential perspective through which women established readings that look different from those of male readers. It should come as no surprise that these approaches by women emerge fully in the late 1970s and early 1980s, during what came to be known as the Women's Movement. I focus on four influential exempla: Coppélia Kahn's 'Coming of Age in Verona' (1978),

Susan Snyder's *The Comic Matrix of Shakespeare's Tragedies* (1979), Marjorie Garber's *Coming of Age in Shakespeare* (1981) and Irene Dash's *Wooing, Wedding and Power: Women in Shakespeare's Plays* (1981). But nearly 170 years before the first of these re-started a revolution in how Shakespeare was read and by whom, the first strike was made by two women: the actress, playwright and author Elizabeth Inchbald, whose twenty-five-volume anthology, *The British Theatre* (1806–1809) includes 'Remarks' on *Romeo and Juliet,* and Anna Jameson, an art historian and literary biographer.

Inchbald broke ground first and firmly, not only by the sheer enormity of her *oeuvre* but also by finding the characters of Romeo and Juliet insufficiently inspiring to excite much sympathy:

> The illustrious author of this drama well knew, that the passion of love, in the young, is seldom constant, as poets describe it, but fickle as violent ... As Shakespeare found those hasty, inconsiderate, lovers, unable in themselves to protect his drama, he provided ample means of support in the additional characters, [combining] the most varied excellence – the mirthful elegance of Mercutio, the comic humour of the Nurse, the sage reasoning of the Friar, together with a whole group of no less natural, though less prominent, persons ... But, with all the genuine merit of this play, it seldom attracts an elegant audience. The company, that frequent the side-boxes, will not come to a tragedy, unless to weep torrents – and 'Romeo and Juliet' will not draw even a copious shower of tears.[50]

It is startling to realize that Inchbald wrote and published these remarks in the same years that the Lambs and the Bowdlers were busy protecting innocent readers from infection by the same passionate impersonations that Inchbald here finds uninspiring, though her preference for the secondary characters aligns her with others of the next decade – Coleridge and Hazlitt, visited earlier in this essay. A theatre professional herself, Inchbald's critical voice is equally interested in male and female characters, and more interested in performance and credibility than in reception and likability.

In *Characteristics of Women: Moral, Poetical, and Historical*, the first systematic published attempt by a woman to analyse Shakespeare's heroines (1832), Anna Jameson echoes nearly *verbatim* fellow Romantic Henry Graves' epithet for Juliet ('all love'): 'All of Shakespeare's women, being essentially women, either love or have loved, or are capable of loving; but Juliet is love itself.'[51] In a few years, Jameson's work could be seen to inaugurate a new critical voice altogether: readings of Shakespeare's characters written by women, and mainly about female characters. One of these Victorian Shakespeareans is Mary Cowden Clarke, the first woman to edit Shakespeare's plays (with her husband Charles) and the author of *The Girlhood of Shakespeare's Heroines* (1850–2). There is no critical assessment in this fanciful compendium of imagined 'backstories'. Cowden Clarke, writing under the banner of Shakespeare, created instead a lengthy narrative for 'Juliet, The Fair Dove of Verona', a 'backstory' longer than the play itself and no more connected to it than the ill-fated 'Romeo and Ethel the Pirate's Daughter' imagined at the start of Marc Norman's and Tom Stoppard's script for John Madden's 1998 film *Shakespeare in Love*.

Such inventions of the unwritten were not uncommon in Victorian assessments of the play, and especially in the hands of women writers. In 'Shakspere Talks With Uncritical People' (1879), Constance O'Brien is particularly vehement about Lady Capulet, whom she finds 'frozen with pride, cold, hard, and stiff; herself a Capulet, her family feelings are her strongest feelings; she comes sweeping over the scene, a determined, unlovable woman … Her child should not have been sweet Juliet, but fierce Tybalt; his haughty and vindictive nature has some family likeness to that of his aunt; both are relentless and unscrupulous.'[52] As we might by now expect, the Nurse is given a slightly better share of critical appreciation, albeit grudgingly: she is 'the one example of her class which Shakespere shows us ... A thoroughly coarse-minded woman, yet she loves her foster-child in her foolish fashion.'[53] Romeo fares better, but only a little: 'He is a graceful, pleasant sort of lover, full of ardour and devotion; but is he quite man enough for Juliet?'[54]

Lady Capulet and her husband both come in for similar scolding by M. Leigh-Noel in *Shakespeare's Garden of Girls* (1885):

> Old Capulet had married a young wife, and Juliet is their only child. It seems to have been a joining of hands rather than hearts. It was doubtless the old man's money and position that was the attraction ... It was an ill-assorted match, as extreme youth and gilded age must always be, and the result in the woman's case was apparently an idle, vain, cold, and calculating existence, in which, though still in the heyday of her life, she had acquired a most mercenary spirit ... Juliet's father was what a father of his age can scarcely fail to be, incapable of sympathizing with his child's feelings or entering into her young life. His dancing days are now a far-off memory, and the festivities he indulges in are attended as functions due to society and not as congenial pastimes. It is his delight to visit the larder, scold the servants, direct the household, and amuse himself with such domestic arrangements as Lady Capulet was too indolent or too superfine to trouble herself with.[55]

As in the hands of O'Brien, the Nurse is dismissed as 'innately vulgar – as her class always have been',[56] but even Juliet, who is clearly adored by these Victorian matrons as a miracle of girlish purity lucky to have escaped such parental incompetence, needed some rewriting. The problem was her age: 'Repugnant as this may be to us, we cannot dispute the fact that under Southern skies the conditions of physical and moral development are vastly different to what they are in the cold North. To represent Juliet on our stage as of the age Shakespeare makes her would be odious and absurd. It would be ridiculous to the British public to see a mere child in years so precocious in feeling and understanding. But we are in Italy, and in a far-back period, when society was less conventional and artificial.'[57]

By the early twentieth century, the critical neglect that had characterized earlier decades gives way to a deliberate, even defiant campaign to redress the gap, starting with Agnes Mure Mackenzie in 1924. In the preface to *The Women in Shakespeare's Plays*, Mackenzie announces her break with the scholarly tradition that required homage to A. C. Bradley and the London theatrical establishment operating at the Old Vic: 'It is a point to be taken for granted in these days that any young critic undertaking serious work on Shakespeare must be heavily in debt to Dr. A. C. Bradley ... But ... directly the major sources of this book are probably in other quarters', by whom she means H. J. C. Grierson and others at the University of Aberdeen where she wrote this pioneering feminist work as her D. Litt. dissertation.[58] Bradley of course could not have been much of an influence on any book concerned with female characters or indeed on any discussion of *Romeo and Juliet*, since he did not write on either subject (except for some notes in *Shakespearean Tragedy* on Lady Macbeth). Mackenzie's evidence is entirely drawn from the plays themselves and built upon a solid exasperation with the critical traditions of the nineteenth century, despite 'the enthusiasts of the Coleridgean school' who produced 'a certain indiscriminateness of outlook'. The problem is that 'in the nineteenth century as in the eighteenth, the opinions of women upon themselves were derived in the main not from their own direct observation of the subject, but from the attitude towards it of the opposite and more articulate sex'.[59] Shakespeare, as 'a man of the pre-Puritan Renaissance ... saw women sharing as fully as men in the life about him, influencing the course of it no less profoundly, yet grasping as it were from another angle, living it in a somewhat different manner of experience'.[60] Even so, 'they are drawn, as a rule perfunctorily enough, with an eye less on women themselves than on what men had written and believed, or believed that they believed of them. There was a good deal of that, as there has always been.'[61]

Nonetheless, Mackenzie admires the portraits drawn in *Romeo and Juliet*, particularly those of Juliet and the Nurse. Juliet is 'incomparably the greatest figure ... There is nothing at all intricate about her, and that, indeed, is where the triumph lies, for this very simplicity made her very difficult for an extremely complex man to draw as she is drawn ... One sees how fatally easy it would have been to make her a sentimental, shallowly impulsive flapper ... There is not a trace of this in her clear depth.'[62] Mackenzie's championship of the Nurse is even more eloquent:

> To set against these beings of fire and air the gross Chaucerian person of the Nurse was a notable dramatic audacity ... She stands, as do so many figures in the later tragedies, to show the prose current of the commonplace sweeping around the fortunes of the tragic pair, and not only making these part of human life, instead of a remote dream-world, but, by their indifference to the deep issues at stake under their noses, filling ourselves with an uneasy consciousness that our own dull life in stalls and pit may have more vital and dramatic elements than we are commonly aware.[63]

Mackenzie opened a door to feminist perspectives in Shakespearean criticism that has never closed. As Lenz, Greene and Neely, editors of the landmark collection, *The Woman's Part*, point out, Mackenzie changed the way we write or speak about her subject; the topic is 'no longer "heroines" or "girls", or "female characters", but "women"'.[64] That collection reprints Coppélia Kahn's essay, 'Coming of Age in Verona', first published in 1978. Kahn augments the conventional reading of the play as a 'domestic tragedy' by noting the difference patriarchy makes, and approaches the play as a tragedy of 'family', specifically of patriarchal family: 'The feud is the deadly *rite de passage* that promotes masculinity at the price of life';[65] it 'constitutes socialization into patriarchal roles in two ways. First, it reinforced their identities as sons and daughters by allying them with their paternal household against another paternal household, thus polarizing all their social relations ... in terms of filial allegiance.'[66] Like Rabkin, Kahn notices the 'antitheses on so many levels, the all-embracing opposition of Eros and Thanatos';[67] unlike him, she finds the play's embodiment of the death wish not inevitably in the love of Romeo and Juliet but in the feud itself.[68] Patriarchal agency, not Freudian predetermination, accounts for the tragedy.

The title of Susan Snyder's 1979 study, *The Comic Matrix of Shakespeare's Tragedies*, announces immediately the paradox of *Romeo and Juliet*. Snyder links the play to *Othello* because both plays are 'Shakespeare's only ventures into the Italianate tragedy of love and intrigue' (56), but there the similarity ends. 'The movement of [the earlier play] is unlike that of any other Shakespearean tragedy. It becomes, rather than is, tragic.'[69] Snyder's binary categories are the two genres of her title; the play's first half participates in all the jocular, playful, celebratory promises of comedy, shifting irreparably to the tragic when Tybalt is killed, but, she argues, we can see the start of that slide from the moment Capulet overrides Tybalt's 'proposed violence' at the feast. From that point forward, the play moves inexorably to tragedy; the game changes, and 'comic adaptability confronts tragic integrity'.[70] There is nothing inevitable about this; Snyder traces in good Aristotelian form what happens, not what should or must happen, and by the end of Act 3, when Juliet rejects the Nurse and her bad advice to choose the 'lovely gentleman' Paris in the absence of the 'dishclout' Romeo (3.5.219–20), the 'possibilities of comedy have again been presented only to be discarded'.[71] Snyder reveals the play's paradoxes not as contradictions but as 'mingled genres'; these are 'not counterpoint but the *fusion* of tragic and comic'.[72]

On the cusp of the 1980s, feminist criticism began to situate its observations in early modern historical, sociological and political contexts and constructs, and in interdisciplinary and multicultural projects. Marjorie Garber's *Coming of Age in Shakespeare* (1981) exemplifies what was then a new approach, and if it now seems inescapable, that is evidence of the reach and purchase of her vision. It soon became less possible, less inviting and less useful for critics to refer to 'our' Shakespeare; criticism no longer acknowledged any univocal group implicated in a single 'our'. In her preface, Garber acknowledges the guiding influence of Margaret Mead's *Coming of Age in Samoa*;[73] in the same year, in *Wooing, Wedding and Power: Women in Shakespeare's Plays,* Irene Dash notes a debt to Simone de Beauvoir's *The Second Sex*. Not only is Shakespeare seen now as culturally contingent; his readers too acknowledge their own contingency in a wide scope of influence and learning that shapes the way we read and see.

Garber's chapter locating *Romeo and Juliet* among other plays, titled 'Women's Rites', immediately announces her interest in matters anthropological, sociological and historical: 'In approaching the predominant patterns of sexual and marital behavior in Shakespeare's plays, it will be useful to consider ... what the playwright might have inherited and observed from his times and how he changed it to conform to his own dramatic purposes.'[74] Garber historicizes such legal prohibitions as 'precipitate early marriage ... between persons less than twenty-one years of age',[75] bigamy (as proposed by the Nurse after Romeo's banishment), and marrying without parental consent, which she identifies as 'the greatest violation committed by Romeo and Juliet'.[76] On this view (following such social historians as Lawrence Stone), communal custom is the antagonist in the tragic action.

In contrast, Dash invokes Samuel Johnson's observation that 'Shakespeare's "characters are not modified by the customs of particular places ... or by the accidents of transient fashions or temporary opinions: they are the genuine progeny of common humanity." ... Although the setting is Verona, the relationship of a teenage daughter with her elders ... has a universality not limited to a particular place.'[77] Dash's emphasis in this chapter is centred in Juliet's effort to separate from childhood and adolescent ties to the structures of the family: 'the decision of the parents to catapult Juliet out of childhood into marriage with little thought of her responses as a person'[78] – their failed project – is the core of this tragedy.

Dash's exemplary critical strand of 'universality' clashes with the historicists' counter-claim of cultural contingency. After this penultimate decade of the twentieth century, such disparate strands seemed less to demand that we choose among them, in a now unappealing and unnecessary 'either-or' of the sort Levin identified, and more to allow an individually respectful 'both-and'. The hunt and trace of paradox and oxymoron come to rest in a room of their own, where paradox and oxymoron seem an appropriate compromise of earlier critical contentions.

The postmodern paradox

This essay began with a notice of inexplicable critical neglect during two major periods of literary history: the Victorian and the Modern, which makes all the more interesting the close interest in the play's contradictions, paradoxes and oxymora by two avatars of the postmodern, Julia Kristeva and Jacques Derrida.

In '*Romeo and Juliet:* Love-Hatred in the Couple' (1987), Kristeva enters the play via her commitment to post-Freudian, post-Lacanian psychoanalytic reading, which, like Rabkin's, also notices the primacy of 'death-mark'd love'. Romeo and Juliet's love is 'transgressive love, outlaw love ... notions that prevail in ordinary consciousness and literary texts as well'.[79] 'The loving couple is outside the law, the law is deadly for it ... [They] mistook love for death ... The story of the famous couple is in fact a story of the impossible couple: they spend less time loving each other than getting ready to die'.[80] Of all the critics I have read for this history, only Kristeva notices that paradox and oxymoron are announced on the title page of the play's second quarto: 'The Most Excellent and Lamentable Tragedie of Romeo and Juliet', which, she says, announces immediately 'a deeply ambivalent text'.[81] Kristeva locates their 'impossibility' in 'the device of an antiquated, tribal law that ... rejects the jouissance of bodies and decrees social incompatibilities'.[82] Layering paradox upon paradox, Kristeva summarized the relationship of the couple (while still alive in the play) in terms reminiscent of Auden's or Frye's, but to quite different effect:

> Either time's alchemy transforms the criminal, secret passion of the outlaw lovers into the banal, humdrum, lackluster lassitude of a tired and cynical collusion: that is the normal marriage. Or else the married couple continues to be a passionate couple, but covering the entire gamut of sadomasochism that the two partners already heralded in the yet relatively quiet version of the Shakespearean text. Each acting out both sexes in turn they thus create a foursome that feeds on itself through repeated aggression and merging, castration and gratification, resurrection and death.[83]

The violence that preoccupies Kristeva here is fundamentally that of the oedipal triad. In her psychoanalytic reading, coherence is only available (if at all) through such de(con)struction and regeneration. 'The alternating love/hatred braids passion's tangle, and its eternal return never produces a "better" couple than the sadomasochistic one' of the 'child-father-mother triad':[84] ('my only') love sprung from ('my only') hate.

Derrida also recognizes the paradoxical failure of a familial structure designed to protect, nurture and securely replicate itself. Explaining in a 1989 interview his interest in *Romeo and Juliet*, he reflects on his adolescent years in Algeria after 1945: 'I thought of literature as the end of the family, and of the society it represented, even if that family was also, on the other hand, persecuted.'[85] Perhaps more than any other literary critic, Derrida's ear picks up nuances and suggestions of contradiction, paradox, impossible possibilities. This attention, he says, is the reason he agreed to write a piece for a production of the play in Paris in 1986: 'This tragedy, I mean this destiny without a strictly assignable destination, is also the tragedy of competence, relevance, truth, etc. ... And this play threatens what it makes possible. The threat cannot be separated from the chance, or the condition of possibility from what limits possibility.'[86] The piece, 'Aphorism Countertime', focuses on the balcony scene, with its dialogic examination of names and naming, metonymically condensing all the paradoxical divisions and alignments implicit in such terminology.

In 'Aphorism Countertime' terminology is the domain in which *Romeo and Juliet* exists. As Derrida immerses us in the play's play of and on language, he opens it to a vortex of reading that seems to have nothing and everything to do with the decade in which he is writing and with the decade in which Shakespeare was writing. Derrida does not engage with the cultural contingencies of language, but he manages nonetheless to extract from the play's oxymora, paradoxes, contradictions, 'the *trompe-l'oeil* depths of its paradigms',[87] a collection of resonances that allow readers to play with the language without committing to any particular interpretative affiliation. It is that range of possibilities, unanchored to any single reading, which marks Derrida's venture as a fitting postmodern terminus for this 400-year survey. 'Aphorism is the name,' he begins[88] – it is the isolating factor that causes and stands for the tragedy of the pair. 'Romeo and Juliet *are* aphorisms, in the first place in their name, which they are not (Juliet: "Tis but thy name that is my enemy" ... Romeo: "My name, dear saint, is hateful to myself" ... for there is no aphorism without language, without nomination, without appellation, without a letter, even to be torn up.'[89] In this vein, Derrida mines the word 'name' in as many of its varied forms and associations in the play as he can think of, identifying it as the poison-and-cure of the couple, their families, their city, the world of the play. He extricates with equal diligence even the grammatical conjunction of the title:

> Romeo *and* Juliet, the conjunction of two desires which are aphoristic but held together, maintained in the dislocated now of a love or a promise. A promise in their name, but across and beyond their given name, the promise of *another name*, its request rather: 'O be some other name.' ... The *and* of this conjunction, the theatre of this 'and', has often been presented, represented as the scene of fortuitous contretemps ... the failed rendezvous, the unfortunate accident, the letter which does not arrive at its destination ... the remedy which transforms itself into poison when the stratagem of a third party, a brother, Friar Laurence, proposes simultaneously the remedy and a letter.[90]

Derrida spends much of the essay sounding out the name *Romeo* and dissociating it from the bearer of the name. This disentanglement is the key to his engagement with the play, every bit as possible and impossible, contradictory and meaningful, as the teasing out of the play's signifying action. 'Yet *the impossible happens* – not in "objective reality", which has no say here, but in the experience of Romeo and Juliet ... They live *in turn* the death of the other, for a time, the contretemps of their death. Both are in mourning – and both watch over the death of the other, attend to the death of the other. Double death sentence.'[91]

For Derrida, the play's semantic switchbacks fascinate as much in what is not said as in what is said. In a brilliant observation near the end of the piece, he points out that whereas Juliet asks Romeo to change his name and renounce his family:

> Romeo does not make the same demand of her. He does not request that this woman who is secretly to be his wife

> renounce her name or disown her father. ... Usually, in our culture, the husband keeps his name, that of his father, and the wife renounces hers ... But this inversion confirms the law: the name of the father should be kept by the son, it is ... the double bind, which ties a son to the name of his father ... [He] can neither efface it or tear it up ... He is doomed ... and she with him, by the double law of the name.
>
> There would be no contretemps without the double law of the name. The contretemps presupposes this inhuman, too human inadequation which always dislocates a proper name. The secret marriage, the pledge (*sacramentum*), the double survival which it involves, its constitutive anachrony, all of this obeys the same law. This law, the law of contretemps, is double since it is divided; it carries aphorism within itself, as its truth. Aphorism is the law.[92]

Derrida's exegesis is necessarily convoluted. Perhaps it could not be otherwise, coming at the end of four centuries of critical attempts to 'explain' pairs and paradoxes in linear terms. For the 1980s, with the millennium looming, simplification had no bearing on the way a play or its language works, and would simply have betrayed it.

2

Performance History

Ian Munro

This chapter explores the performance of *Romeo and Juliet* from its early modern inception to current re-workings of the play for the twenty-first century, both within the Anglophone theatrical tradition and globally. *Romeo and Juliet* is perhaps Shakespeare's most popular play – in the twentieth century, at least, it vied with *Hamlet* for number of stage productions – and is certainly the most adapted of Shakespeare's works, both in terms of sheer numbers and the diversity of these adaptations. As such, any comprehensive treatment of the play in performance and film is impossible in the space available. Nor does this chapter seek to provide a canonical performance history, inventorying the major productions – not least because excellent examples of such histories are available, especially in René Weis's introduction to the *Arden* edition and Jill Levenson's introduction to *The Oxford Shakespeare* edition (both of which I have relied on extensively, especially for the earlier material).[1] Rather, I want to explore the play's reception, performance and adaptation through a particular lens: the iconic nature of the lovers. As the story of Romeo and Juliet has gradually become *the* Western love story, supplanting its predecessors in the cultural imagination, the play has acquired an already-told, mythic quality that necessarily informs the imperatives of theatrical production.

'An ancient receptacle'

To illustrate this point we might look briefly at two very recent adaptations: one reverent, one irreverent. Nancy Meckler's 2006 production of *Romeo and Juliet*, for the Royal Shakespeare Company, enfolded the play in a framing story, in which two warring Sicilian clans come together in the wasteland on the edge of their village to participate in an ancient festival: laying down their weapons collectively, they perform and watch the play together. In this repackaging *Romeo and Juliet* becomes a kind of social parable or morality play, its quasi-sacred status reinforced by the symbolic choreography of the play's violence and the presence of choral chanting throughout. Meckler's inspiration for this framing is surely Bertolt Brecht's *The Caucasian Chalk Circle*, in which the folkloric story of Grusha and the governor's baby is used to adjudicate a present conflict – although Brecht's counterpointing of the heroic tale of Grusha with the comic tale of Adzak, the cynical judge, adds a kind of ironic leaven to the mythic solemnity that is absent here. Instead, *Romeo and Juliet* is made almost scriptural, a repository of timeless truths, a sacred thing in a societal wasteland. At the other end of the scale, we could put the Nature Theater of Oklahoma's 2009 production of *Romeo and Juliet*, at the Kitchen Theater in New York City.[2] The company began by asking numerous friends to recall the plot of the play. Ultimately, these recollections were performed verbatim, no matter how far they strayed from the actual script or how bizarrely they imagined the story – one especially creative recounting culminates with Paris masturbating over the corpse of Juliet. The effect is comic travesty, an impious mocking of Shakespearean *gravitas*. Yet the theatrical traction the show is able to produce from these mis-remembrances demonstrates the status and power of the story. As Charles Isherwood wrote in his review of the production, 'what comes through is a definite sense of how deeply the romantic–tragic ideas imparted in *Romeo and Juliet* have seeped into the collective consciousness of generations.'[3] If hardly a sacred text, this *Romeo and Juliet* is ubiquitous, unavoidable, iconic even in its pluriform disseminations.[4]

The complex iconicity of the play has long operated as a kind of problematic through which productions articulate their relationship to their theatrical context, and to their theatrical inheritance – a process especially visible in non-Western performances, which must negotiate these issues across intercultural terrain. In some ways, this dynamic is cued by the original script, which seems to forecast the archetypal status the play subsequently achieves. In the final couplet of the authoritative second quarto, the Prince announces, 'For never was a story of more woe / Than this of Juliet and her Romeo' (5.3.309–10). The first quarto, perhaps an earlier, acting version of the play,[5] has a slightly different line, 'For nere was heard a Storie of more woe',[6] which connects more closely with the Prince's desire to 'have more talk of these sad things' (5.3.307) – a characteristically Shakespearean gesture, where further discussion of the events of the play is promised at a later point, imagining a persistence of the representational world of the play beyond the threshold of its performance.[7] The second quarto, by contrast, seems to gesture directly out to the audience, acknowledging the already existing fame of Juliet and Romeo – due both to its lengthy pre-Shakespearean history and to the immediate popularity of the play.[8] As the years and centuries pass and the mythos of the lovers increases, so too does the desire of productions either to rectify the play, so that it more closely matches an imagined ideal, or to brush it against the grain by appropriating it for new purposes – or indeed, often both at the same time. Such interplay between iconodulism and iconoclasm (between reverencing a sacred object and seeking its reformation or overthrow) in approaching *Romeo and Juliet* mirrors the countervailing energies of the play itself, an iconic story of iconoclasts.

These countervailing energies are especially present in the tomb scene, always one of the most challenging locations for any production. The tomb is quite literally the space of tradition: 'an ancient receptacle / Where for this many hundred years the bones / Of all my buried ancestors are packed' (4.3.39–41), as Juliet describes it, the place where she fears she will go insane if she wakes before Romeo arrives, 'madly play with my forefathers' joints' (4.3.51), and kill herself with an ancestral bone. Both of the lovers violate tradition in their actions in the tomb: Romeo through his forced entry and spilling of Paris's blood; Juliet through her suicide with Romeo's dagger, which symbolically counterpoints Romeo's eroticized assault on the space of the tomb. Yet as this symbolic consummation suggests, in terms of the plot of the play the actions in the tomb are not violation but fulfilment – yet, to turn things around again, fulfilment that depends on the strange incompletion of the reunion of the lovers, who never see each other alive after the *aubade* scene near the end of Act 3. Dramaturgically, the separate deaths of the lovers are the culmination of the separation inflicted upon them; the separation also bestows unusual agency on Juliet, as I will discuss below. But can such an alienating ending resolve the course of true love? If the Prince's final words have come to seem unnecessary to so famous a love story, unease about the tomb and what happens in it speaks to an anxiety about the theatrical estrangement of the deaths being incompatible with the perfection of the story.

Dramaturgical choices about the ending of the play must also engage with questions about the relation of the love plot to the civic plot: the relation, we might say, between the 'pair of star-crossed lovers' and 'their parents' strife' (Prol. 6, 8). The structure of the conclusion of the play underscores this relation, as the scene rapidly dilates from the enclosure of the tomb to a public, urban setting recalling the start of the action, with the outside world now brought in to observe the spectacle of the dead lovers. In one sense, this spectacle is intended to heal the world, creating peace between the families. In another sense, those who arrive at the conclusion of the play double the theatre audience, as they take in the pathos of the scene and learn the story. There is thus an inherent homology between the staging of the love plot to the civic plot within the final scene and the theatrical performance of the play as a whole. Paul Kottman has recently contended that we do not 'really care whether Capulet and Montague could be reconciled to one another ... Objectively and affectively, it is Romeo and Juliet's sorrow and joy that we have followed and that we continue to talk about.'[9] This is incontrovertible in terms of *reading* Shakespeare's play, but less clearly true in the context of theatrical and cinematic productions, where an increased emphasis on the civic plot and the public world of the play often runs parallel with concerns about the relation of the performance to the real world in which it is performed. This is especially true, as we will see, of modern adaptations and relocations of the play, which characteristically reframe the civic plot in iconoclastic ways while maintaining the iconic character of the love plot.

'Grave-beseeming ornaments'

Given the tenor of these dramaturgical tensions, it is appropriate that the first successful recuperation of *Romeo and Juliet* for the English stage was also a radical adaptation: Thomas Otway's *The History and Fall of Caius Marius*, first published in 1680 and first performed in 1677, with the star actors Elizabeth Barry and Thomas Betterton in the leading roles.[10] Otway integrates Romeo and Juliet into Plutarch's account of the first-century BCE Civil War between Caius Marius and Sylla: Romeo becomes Marius's son, Marius junior (who is given a fictional death), while Juliet becomes Lavinia, the daughter of Metellus, the former mentor of Caius

Marius who now supports Sylla and has offered him Lavinia's hand. Perhaps a third of the play is repurposed directly out of Shakespeare: most notoriously, we hear Lavinia ask 'O *Marius*, *Marius*! wherefore art thou *Marius*?'[11] The events of the play turn less on the love affair than on the machinations of power between Metellus, Caius Marius and Sylla, as the fickle Roman public (whose scathing portrayal is at points cribbed from *Coriolanus*) swings from one leader to the next. As a play in part about banishment and civil strife, *Romeo and Juliet* clearly spoke to the contemporary political moment of the Exclusion Crisis, in which Whig forces in Parliament (led by the Earl of Shaftesbury) sought to exclude Charles II's brother James from succession to the throne because of his Catholicism. This was the most acute political crisis in England since the Civil War, and many feared that the country might fall back into such a state. Otway is thus directly inserting his theatre into contemporary political events; staging political unrest in a historical moment intended to suggest contemporary parallels – both to the immediate crisis surrounding exclusion and the recent past of civil war. It seems probable, as critics have observed, that Caius Marius is to some extent a portrait of Shaftesbury, who introduced the Exclusion Bill, but the play is not merely a Tory attack on Whig challenges to the monarchy.[12] Rather, it uses the idea that 'civil blood makes civil hands unclean' (Prol. 4) to anatomize a corrupt and chaotic society and counsel reformation and reconciliation.[13]

Otway achieves this through a fundamental reframing of the love story as both less subversive and subordinate to the political story. As Jessica Munns has pointed out, 'Unlike Romeo, Marius jr's love for his enemy's daughter never leads him to rethink his position in relation to her family.'[14] Nor does Caius Marius relent once Marius Junior and Lavinia wed: the knowledge that his son is joined to the daughter of his enemy only inflames his rage and hatred. It is only when Lavinia finds Caius Marius starving in exile and succours him that he changes his opinion of her – a brief reconciliation that vanishes as soon as the political calculus changes and Caius

Marius is able to return to Rome and wreak bloody vengeance on his foes. In this way, the civil strife of the play is rendered inexorable: we are never led toward the possibility that love or the lovers could affect it. Relatedly, while the tomb scene is catalysed in the same manner as in Shakespeare – that is, Lavinia takes the potion to avoid marriage to Sylla, Marius Junior believes her dead, and comes to commit suicide beside her in the tomb – the playing out of the scene is fundamentally different. As noted, Marius Junior and Lavinia have an extended dialogue in the tomb, after Marius Junior has taken the potion, an act that makes the reunion of the lovers the central (and sentimental) dynamic: it also subordinates Lavinia to Marius Junior, as she must watch his passing, audience to his final pathos. The scene is then interrupted by the abrupt entry of Caius Marius and his soldiers, who drive in Metellus and kill him in front of his daughter. The subsequent suicide of Lavinia – tellingly, with Caius Marius' sword, not Marius Junior's dagger – is less a declaration of the impossibility of living without Marius than an act of revenge against Caius Marius for all of his cruelties and his forgetting of Lavinia's care for him during his exile. Instead of symbolically re-enacting the sexual consummation of Romeo and Juliet – 'O happy dagger! / This is thy sheath' (5.3.169–70) – Lavinia's demise is linked more strongly to the death of her father and the conventions of feminine complaint, a stinging yet helpless rebuke against the masculine political world.

Otway's play held sway for roughly half a century; between 1680 and 1735 it displaced Shakespeare's play from the public stage, and remained a strong influence on the productions that followed. It is in Otway's play that the idea of a *balcony* scene originates; Shakespeare's encounter takes place at a window. More substantially, Otway inaugurates the idea of a final conversation between the lovers in the tomb. A version of Shakespeare's play finally returned to the English stage in 1744, when Theophilus Cibber mounted a production starring himself as Romeo and his fourteen-year-old daughter as Juliet. Although Cibber rejected the strong political focus of Otway's play – in his version, the strife is domestic and centres on the quarrelling of the two mothers – he nevertheless incorporated much of Otway's final dialogue between the two lovers.[15] David Garrick was inspired to stage *Romeo and Juliet* in response to Cibber's production, which he detested in every respect. Yet his 1750 production followed Cibber in imitating Otway's ending, albeit in very different terms: his Romeo is so delighted at the revival of Juliet that he forgets, for a moment, that he has swallowed poison and the lovers are allowed a period of joy and resolution before his memory and tragic inevitability return.[16] Garrick's insistence on the importance of a final scene between the lovers in the tomb made such a scene a theatrical imperative. Faulting Shakespeare's reliance on imperfect translations of his source, Mateo Bandello's novella, Garrick continued: '*Otway*, in his *Caius Marius*, a Tragedy taken from *Romeo and Juliet*, has made use of this affecting circumstance [i.e., a final conversation], but it is a matter of Wonder that so great a Dramatic Genius did not work up a Scene from it of more Nature, Terror and Distress.'[17] Garrick's new conclusion to the play also solved the problem of the Prince's final words, repointing the moral away from the status of the love story and toward a civics lesson: 'We'll hence, and further scan these sad disasters – / Well may you mourn, my lords, now wise too late, / These tragic issues of your mutual hate. / For private feuds what dire misfortunes flow! / Whate'er the cause, the sure effect is woe.'[18] Garrick's other substantial change to the play, in his revision to his adaptation, was made reluctantly: eliminating Rosaline and making Romeo already in love with Juliet at the start of the play. Garrick clearly resented its necessity: 'The sudden Change of *Romeo*'s love from *Rosaline* to *Juliet*, was thought by many, at the first Revival of the Play, to be a blemish in his Character; an Alteration in that particular has been made more in Compliance to that Opinion, than from a Conviction that *Shakespear*, the best Judge of Human Nature, was faulty.'[19] In this change, too, Garrick followed the path laid down by Otway; as in Otway's play, the pre-existing character of Romeo and Juliet's love also helps contain its energies.

Garrick's play dominated the English stage (and later the American stage) until the middle of the nineteenth century, and persisted as an acting script until the start of the twentieth. Even after its heyday had ended, Garrick's script was sometimes considered a theatrical improvement on Shakespeare's text because of the dramaturgical and thematic challenges it resolved; in 1879, Fanny Kemble, daughter of Charles Kemble, remarked, 'I have played both; my father has played both; and I *know* which is best for the stage.'[20] Garrick's play was the direct inspiration for Hector Berlioz's 1839 '*symphonie dramatique*' and had a strong influence on Charles Gounod's 1867 opera, which likewise incorporated a final duet between the lovers; as late as 1935, Sergei Prokofiev wanted to include a final dance for the lovers in his ballet of the play, but was overruled by the Kirov Ballet.[21] In the theatre, John Philip Kemble altered Garrick's script in minor ways for his 1803 production, but retained all of the major changes: the elision of Rosaline, the final encounter between the lovers, the repositioning of the Prince's final words. The same holds true for other major nineteenth-century revivals, which repositioned the play in various ways through characterization and histrionic style but failed, as Levenson puts it, 'to upset the balance of Garrick's *Romeo and Juliet*, a tragedy uniform and decorous at every level of its composition'.[22] Decorum, the appropriate fitting of matter and situation, is the operative word for Garrick's script, which thus provided a kind of rectification of the iconic love story at the heart of the play. The irony is that Garrick's decorous script owes so many of its changes to Otway's profoundly indecorous script; in important respects this odd adaptation set the parameters of *Romeo and Juliet* for two centuries – and at least indirectly, influenced modern adaptations as well. As James Loehlin has noted, 'In the twentieth century it again became common to have Juliet wake before Romeo's death', citing such notable productions as Michael Langham's 1960 Stratford version and Trevor Nunn's 1976

Stratford production, as well as Baz Luhrmann's 1996 film *Romeo + Juliet*, in which the lovers exchange some anguished eye contact before Romeo expires.[23] In the most successful modern adaptation of the play, *West Side Story*, Tony dies in Maria's arms, as they imagine a better place where they will be able to love. It also falls to Maria to play the Prince, delivering the final moral of the story: despite asking if there is one bullet left for her as she holds the gun that killed Tony, she rejects suicide and throws the gun aside, choosing instead to mourn her love and the hateful state of the world.[24]

Such changes partly derive from a desire to curb the radical agencies of Shakespeare's play, especially when it comes to Juliet. In Shakespeare's script, Juliet's suicide is subversive of her expected gender role in that it is unprompted in any way by Romeo's words or story.[25] The Juliet of Garrick's play, or the Lavinia of Otway's play, or the Maria of *West Side Story*, barred from such destabilizing actions, is thus recuperated to a more traditional gender position, responding rather than acting. Even in Luhrmann's film, where Juliet does not throw the gun aside (pointedly unlike Maria), the violence of her death is tastefully obscured by switching to a long shot and positioning the bodies of the dead lovers so that no blood is visible.[26] Even versions that reject such revisions to the text often find ways to minimize or contain Juliet. The theatrical event that heralded the end of Garrick's reign, as both Levenson and Weis discuss at length, was Charlotte Cushman's sensational 1845 London production, in which she performed the part of Romeo to her sister's Juliet.[27] The transvestite casting was less surprising than Cushman's rejection of Garrick's script in favour of something like Shakespeare's original play: Rosaline was returned to the story, the final dialogue between the lovers was excised and Juliet was again allowed her solo suicide. Nevertheless, in this production Juliet was still overshadowed by Romeo, who through Cushman's textual edits – and bravura performance – was reinforced as the central figure of the tragedy: the dynamic, masculine centre to whom Juliet responds.

'The date is out of such prolixity'

What finally vanquished Garrick's theatrical script was the rise, in the late nineteenth and early twentieth century, of a philosophy of restoring Shakespeare productions to the original text and, more loosely, the conventions and expectations of the original performance. Both Weis and Levenson concur that in the case of *Romeo and Juliet* this project reached its apotheosis with John Gielgud's 1935 production at the New Theatre in London.[28] This was an enormously successful production, due both to its stellar cast – Peggy Ashcroft played Juliet, while Gielgud and Laurence Olivier alternated in the roles of Romeo and Mercutio – and the clarity of its staging: eschewing the complex and overdressed sets of the previous century, the play was performed in continuous action on a simple set, where a central Italianate tower divided the stage into two playing areas.[29] Despite the theatrical innovation of Gielgud's approach, this was perhaps also the high-water mark of an iconodulist framing of *Romeo and Juliet*, both in its fidelity to Shakespearean stage conventions and its view of the lovers as ideal creations: although the costumes suggested an Italian Renaissance setting, Gielgud called the protagonists 'symbolic, immortal types of lovers of all time',[30] and the production insistently focused on the perfection of the love story. Perhaps in response to Gielgud's establishment of a new model of perfection, productions later in the twentieth century tended to be more aggressive in their approach to the play. It might be fair to say that since Gielgud there has been a strong (if not universal) desire to recapitulate the iconoclastic energies of the play in treating the iconic story itself. In 1947, Peter Brook's production for the Shakespeare Memorial Theatre (forerunner to the Royal Shakespeare Company) cut the final reconciliation between the families in order to stress the violence of the play. Franco Zeffirelli's 1960 production at the Old Vic (with Judi Dench and John Stride in the lead roles) retained a Renaissance setting, but turned the focus of the play away from the sentimental perfection of the lovers to the dynamics of generational conflict, a repositioning underscored by having the younger male characters sport long hair: historically accurate, to a point, but also strongly connecting the play with the historical moment of its staging.

Radically cutting the flowery rhetoric of the play in order to increase its immediacy and authenticity, Zeffirelli directed his cast to speak prosaically and naturally, warning them 'verse speakers will be prosecuted'.[31] In Loehlin's verdict, the production managed 'to free *Romeo and Juliet* from lyricism, prettiness, and the weight of the past, and present it as a vivid and immediate play about youth'.[32] Recent British productions have taken this approach to Shakespeare's language even further. In order to ground the play in the present moment, Rupert Goold's 2010 Royal Shakespeare Company production deliberately displaced the unifying sonorities of Received Pronunciation in favour of a plethora of contemporary British accents; to drive the point home, the older characters were in quasi-Elizabethan dress that would not have looked out of place in Gielgud's production, while the younger generation wore hoodies, trainers and other modern teenage wear. Bijan Sheibani's 2013 production at The Shed (a venue of the National Theatre in London) further radicalized the sonic landscape of the play by removing white Britons from its world: the Capulets were South Asian while the Montagues were diasporic Africans, with each group speaking in a wide variety of subaltern dialects and creoles.[33] Such linguistic tactics are common in non-English productions, which often use language as a means of reinforcing the play's conflicts. Robert Lepage's 1989 *Romeo and Juliette*, staged at a theatre festival in Saskatoon,[34] was a bilingual production featuring Anglophone Montagues and Francophone Capulets. Funded by the Canadian government in order to 'celebrate the country's bilingual co-existence',[35] the production has been more commonly read as emphasizing intractable differences – not least through its scenic design, with an asphalt highway dividing both the stage and the house. At the 'Shakespeare in Taipei' festival in Taiwan in 2003, a bilingual *Romeo and*

Juliet was staged in Taiwanese and Mandarin, the effect of which was less establishing a dialogue than 'complicating the experience of artists in the Chinese diaspora and the play's capacity as a national allegory', as Alexa Huang puts it.[36]

Zeffirelli's extraordinarily successful 1968 film of the play worked in the same fashion as his 1960 production: the historical gravitas of the beautiful Renaissance costuming and setting – the film was shot in several well-preserved Italian Renaissance towns – is counterpointed by its energetic portrayal of youth culture, its frenetic violence and bawdiness, and the nakedness of the teenage couple in the *aubade* scene. A generation later, of course, Zeffirelli's film had itself become the icon that Baz Luhrmann sought to topple with *Romeo + Juliet*, which relocated the play to imaginary Verona Beach, a wealthy, multi-ethnic and violent suburb of Los Angeles. If Zeffirelli rebelled against the refined elocution of older productions such as Gielgud's, Luhrmann's young actors (most lacking training in Shakespeare) deliberately flatten their language further, interspersing monotone delivery with histrionic flourishes, creating a new vernacular for the play. Which is not to say that *Romeo + Juliet* rejects beauty: against the elegance of the colonnaded streets and Italian vistas that dominate Zeffirelli's film, Luhrmann's film revels in mundane settings unexpectedly transformed by lighting and mood: a swimming pool lit at night, a ruined seaside theatre at sunset, a glass elevator lifted by a kiss.

Luhrmann's film was notable for foregrounding the homoerotic aspect of Romeo and Mercutio's relationship, a conjecture that had been visible since at least 1973, when Terry Hands's Royal Shakespeare Company production played up Mercutio's misogyny and thwarted affection for Romeo via a life-size female doll that he dismembers.[37] Such elements have since become a standard, even expected, aspect of productions and adaptations – see, for example, Joe Calarco's 1998 play, *Shakespeare's R&J*, in which four teenage boys at a military boarding school stage the play for each other as a vehicle for their forbidden desires.[38] The mood, style and setting of

Luhrmann's film also owes a great deal to earlier theatrical productions which sought to brush the play against the grain by transposing it to anarchic, corrupt and violent settings. Of particular note in this regard is Michael Bogdanov's 1986 Royal Shakespeare Company production, which portrayed a shallow, materialistic society of Armani suits, hypodermic drugs and fast cars – Romeo arrives in the play on a motorcycle and Tybalt's entry in a red sports car earned the production the sobriquet 'The Alfa *Romeo and Juliet*'.[39] Similar stylistic chords are struck (if perhaps not sustained) in the derivative 2013 Broadway production, directed by David Leveaux, in which Romeo (played by Orlando Bloom) again enters on a motorcycle, and the set is dominated by a large Renaissance fresco tagged with graffiti – a symbolic representation, presumably, of the production's imagined relationship to its source material.

Two notable Brazilian adaptations of the play deserve longer discussion, due to the complexity of their social and cultural positioning. In 1992, the company Grupo Galpão ('warehouse group') staged an intercultural adaptation of the play in Rio de Janeiro (a production brought to Shakespeare's Globe in London in 2000).[40] Interweaving Shakespeare's play with elements of street theatre, *commedia dell'arte* and circus acrobatics, the production was firmly grounded in the language and rhythms of Minas Gerais, a highly traditional province in the south of Brazil. As Aimara da Cunha Resende explains, 'Deviation from the rigid norm of classical performances establishes a link with the Brazilian audience, contemporary relationships, and ever-present tribal antagonism.'[41] An even more complicated adaptation was Elza de Andrade's *The Love Story of Romeo and Juliet* (1998), which staged an adaptation by Ariano Suassuna of an early twentieth-century Brazilian popular retelling of the Romeo and Juliet story (*Romance de Romeu e Julieta*), by João Martins de Ataíde.[42] Ataíde had set his version of Romeo and Juliet in the Amazonian backwoods of north Brazil, as a locale distant enough from the metropolitan centres of the country that honour codes similar to those of the play could be found – thus literally mapping the temporal distance of Shakespeare's setting onto the geography of Brazil. As with the Grupo Galpão production, Suassuna's adapting of Ataíde's text incorporated many meta-theatrical and para-theatrical elements, especially puppetry and popular song. What emerges in both cases is a complex web of social, political and cultural tensions: these intercultural productions are energized not only by the local conflicts that frame the retelling but also by power relations between metropolitan and provincial Brazil, and, implicitly, cultural power relations between Brazil and Europe.

'Much to do with hate'

Leveaux's production is notable for casting all the Montagues with white actors and all the Capulets with black actors; although Leveaux has been reluctant to ascribe much weight to this casting decision, it is clearly intended to have some kind of explanatory effect regarding the civil strife of the play. With this manoeuvre, Leveaux participates in a pervasive dramaturgical tactic. 'In the latter half of the twentieth century,' Loehlin has dryly observed, '*Romeo and Juliet* was transformed, in production and perception, from a play about love to a play about hate. Modern productions have tended to emphasize the feud over the love story, and have used it to comment on a variety of social ills.'[43] This sense of the play as contemporary commentary is part of a larger trend in Shakespearean production over the last fifty years, in which explicit settings are chosen that will allow the play to speak to new social and political formations.[44] This tendency is perhaps more evident in the case of *Romeo and Juliet* than other Shakespeare plays. In part this is because of the example set by *West Side Story*: by locating the play in the present moment the love relationship is counterbalanced by what might be understood as the true focus of the musical, the conflict between teenage gangs in New York City. As we have seen, *West Side Story* did not originate this practice – something similar happens in Otway's play, with its subordination of the lovers to civil strife – but it established a pattern that many theatrical productions have imitated. Another reason for the popularity of this approach to *Romeo and Juliet* is surely the play's governing structure, in which division counterpoints unity, and the play's conclusion can offer either a sharp warning or a hope for a peaceful resolution. In such productions, the fateful story of the two lovers becomes a kind of myth, one that plays out in an unexpected time and place; we often are led to imagine the play as happening again, as it were, in a new setting.

Recent examples of such productions abound, as a brief survey will illustrate. In 2000, Clare Stopford set *Romeo and Juliet* in a gang-ravaged sector of contemporary Cape Town in order to address the challenges of post-apartheid South Africa. This celebrated production took place at the Maynardville Open Air Theatre, the longest-running Shakespeare festival in South Africa – a venue significant for having multiracial casts and audiences, even under apartheid. *Romeo and Juliet in China* was a 2012 collaboration between the National Theater Company of Korea and the National Theatre of China, set in China during the Cultural Revolution, with Juliet as a soldier and Romeo as a member of a workers' collective. Organized to commemorate the twentieth anniversary of diplomatic relations between China and South Korea, this production carefully sequestered its political conflicts in the past; it was performed first in Mandarin and then in Korean, ignoring the opportunity to use the two languages within the fiction of the story.[45] In 2005, the Los Angeles company, Native Voices, produced a Native American version of the play called *Kino and Teresa*, written by James Lujan, at the Autry National Center. Set in seventeenth-century Santa Fe, the play revolved around conflicts between the Pueblo Indians and Spanish colonists. As the *Los Angeles Times* describes it, 'Lujan envisions tensions running high in the settlement's plaza, where Spanish colonists and Native Americans openly regard one another as "savages" and engage in bloody free-for-alls.'[46] Although it is unlikely that it was a source for this production, it is also worth noting that one of the earliest film versions of the play was also a Native American adaptation: *Indian Romeo and Juliet* (1912), directed by Lawrence Trimble and set amidst a war between the Hurons and the Mohicans.[47]

A plethora of recent movies complements this theatrical pattern of relocating the story in other conflicts. *Brooklyn Babylon* (2001) sets *Romeo and Juliet* amidst the Crown Heights riot of 1991; the Romeo character is an African-American hip-hop artist, while the Juliet character is a young Lubavitcher.[48] *Romeo and Juliet in Yiddish* (2010) also has Brooklyn as its setting, although here the conflict is between rival Hasidic groups; Ava, a graduate student (and emergency room nurse), has been assigned to update an old Yiddish translation of the play, which catalyses a series of confrontations.[49] *Bollywood Queen* (2003) is set in London, where a Scottish Romeo encounters a British Indian Juliet, to the violent disapproval of both their families; unusually, the film ends with the two lovers escaping together.[50] *Amar te duele* ('Love Hurts') is a 2002 Mexican film that locates the story in the brutal socioeconomic differences of suburban Mexico City.[51] In *Gucha (Distant Trumpet)*, a 2006 Serbian film, a Serbian girl falls in love with a Romani boy.[52] A 2009 Indonesian movie sets the play in the context of soccer fanaticism, between the rival clubs of Jakarta and Bandung; a similar idea animated the Brazilian film *O Casamento de Romeu e Julieta* (2005), in which feuding Paulistano soccer clubs provide dramatic tension, although in this version love ultimately proves stronger than soccer.[53] *Goliyon Ki Raasleela Ram-Leela* ('A Play of Bullets: Ram-Leela') is a 2013 Indian adaptation of *Romeo and Juliet*, set in a small town in Gujarat amidst gunrunning and violent crime; another Indian adaptation of the same year, *Issaq*, puts the action in Varanasi, where local crime families and communist guerrilla groups are at war; and at least two more Bollywood versions of the play (one a romantic comedy with a happy ending, another a controversial gay adaptation) have been released or are in planning.[54] The sheer volume and cultural diversity of these films stands as a useful corrective to the complacent critical perspective that tends to view cinematic adaptations of *Romeo and Juliet* as an Anglophone binary, Zeffirelli versus Luhrmann.[55]

One question that emerges from 'the conflict turn' is the degree to which any production of a play might effectively intervene in the political situation it chooses for its setting. To take one particularly fraught example, it has become especially common to set the play amid the Israeli–Palestinian conflict. Versions of this setting have been recently performed not only in the Middle East but in locales as varied as Brooklyn, St Louis, Winnipeg and Budapest. The setting has also become popular for movie versions of the play, both serious – *In Fair Palestine* (2008), a film produced by Palestinian high school students in Ramallah and subsequently screened worldwide – and satirical: *West Bank Story* (2005), a musical comedy set in competing falafel stands in the West Bank (winner of the 2006 Oscar for Best Live Action Short Film).[56] Whatever might be said about the quality of these adaptations, their sheer ubiquity, and the ease with which *Romeo and Juliet* might be mapped onto this conflict (or other conflicts, for that matter) paradoxically suggests the failure of the story to connect with the political realities it appropriates for dramatic colour.

The original inspiration for these productions was a highly controversial 1994 collaboration between the Khan Theatre and the El-Qasaba Theatre in Jerusalem (although as the trope works its way through regional and local theatres around the world it seems likely that its genealogy has become obscured). The Khan/El-Qasaba production was an unprecedented collaboration between Israeli and Palestinian theatre companies. The script was bilingual, and structured to highlight thematics of conflict and miscommunication: Romeo woos Juliet in Arabic, but she responds in Hebrew. The production, staged shortly after the conclusion of the First Palestinian Intifada, faced extraordinary challenges: the Israeli director received death threats from extremist Jewish organizations for staging a play involving intermarriage, while Palestinian actors in the show were sometimes stopped from entering Jerusalem and attending rehearsal by Israeli security forces.[57] A few months before the show was to open, an Israeli settler massacred twenty-nine Arabs praying at a mosque in Hebron, a catastrophe that almost derailed the production. The production was very popular and generally lavished with critical praise for daring to use current events in challenging ways; it was subsequently staged in Europe as well, in particular at the Festival of the City in Lille, France.[58] Yet some critics questioned the degree to which even this production could operate as an effective political intervention. Freddie Rokem analyses at some length the production's unconscious Israeli biases, starting with the fact that both Palestinian and Israeli characters mostly speak in Hebrew to each other: an accurate representation of the linguistic reality of Jerusalem, perhaps, but one that the production did not critique in any way.[59] The complexity of the play's relationship to its actual scene of performance – visible, I have suggested, in all productions, but especially so here – reinforces Rokem's analysis. Noting that the play was performed in a hall formerly owned by the Israeli Electric Corporation, Rokem asks, 'Take for example the associations which the hall ... has for a Palestinian' – referring especially to the frequent use of blackouts as a means of political control – 'what does it say with regard to power, in particular here in Jerusalem'.[60] The point to emphasize here, I would suggest, is the porousness of the production: the setting, in Rokem's estimation, overwhelms the ability of the play to control its own narratives and theatrical space. One might say that this production attempts in real life what Nancy Meckler's production merely playacts – and despite Rokem's overall dismissal, the failure of the production to transcend the political dynamics of its staging sounds more interesting than a production that can submerge its political realities beneath a mythic narrative (as Shakespeare rescues the world yet again).

'Who set this ancient quarrel new abroach?'

Bearing this production in mind, as well as many other issues this chapter has touched on, I want to conclude with a longer discussion of an especially noted, recent adaptation, *Romeo and Juliet in Baghdad*.[61] As the title suggests, this is a rewriting of Shakespeare's story in the context of contemporary Iraq; it was commissioned by the Royal Shakespeare Company as part of their 2012 World Shakespeare Festival, which sought to cultivate new and especially intercultural approaches to Shakespeare. The play was translated and adapted by its director, Monadhil Daood, an Iraqi-born actor and playwright who left Iraq in the 1980s after producing a play about the Iran–Iraq war that angered the government. As befits the title, the play was first performed in Baghdad, in Arabic; it was subsequently mounted at Stratford and in London, still in Arabic but with English surtitles. To summarize the terms of the adaptation, Capulet and Montague are brothers – Sunni and Shiite, respectively – who are feuding over control of their family inheritance, a pearl-fishing boat. The lovers, not especially young, actually fell in love nine years ago, before the invasion of Iraq; they are reunited when Romeo, having returned home, attends a party at Capulet's house. Both families object to their open desire to marry; in particular, Capulet has promised his daughter to Paris, a middle-aged, foreign-born Al Qaeda operative who exacerbates the feud between the brothers. At the end of the play, Paris, now turned suicide bomber, destroys the church in which Romeo and Juliet have taken sanctuary.

Romeo and Juliet in Baghdad touches on many of the themes of this chapter: linguistic issues, the framing of female characters, iconicity versus iconoclasm, the use of conflict settings – and above all, the question of how to take possession of *Romeo and Juliet* and use it for new purposes. As an intercultural performance, the idea of tradition plays an especially complicated role in this production. Calling himself, and by extension the Iraqi people, 'a legitimate son of tragedy', Daood makes it clear that he is appropriating the story of the play for Iraq and its recent history, reframing the play with elements of Arabic theatre: music, dance, spectacle and especially narrative, as the Queen Mab speech is replaced by an Iraqi folktale.[62] At the same time, the story that he tells is less about Romeo and Juliet as a couple than what their love story might say to his country. In the programme notes Daood writes, 'I forgot the first scene ... where their eyes meet for the first time ... I forgot the shy glances, the trembling first touch ... I'll have to leave all of that to your imagination.'[63] Despite the apology, it is clear that our interest in this Romeo and Juliet is supposed to be less in their 'sorrow and joy', in Kottman's terms, than in their subversion of traditional social structures. The battles of Romeo and Juliet against social and religious traditions are reinforced by a new character, 'The Teacher', who operates as a kind of amalgam of the Prince and Friar Laurence, and who continually offers advice to other characters that functions as commentary for the audience: 'Teach your children your ways, and they will live in the past'; 'If tradition fosters hatred, we are better off without it'; and similar comments throughout.[64] The greatest audience-pleasing moment of the show – both in England and in Iraq, according to multiple accounts – is when Capulet turns on Paris after the killing of Tybalt, rescinding his betrothal to Juliet and planning to reconcile with his brother.

This rebalancing of the love story and the civil story contributes to the interpenetration of the production's space of representation and space of performance, separated less by a 'fourth wall' than by a fluid, shifting boundary. Deborah Shaw, the director of the World Shakespeare Festival (and Daood's spouse) observed in an interview that they lost two actresses in rehearsal 'because there's the pressure for women to cover up and for Juliet not to be touched by Romeo', and several reviewers of the London show remarked on the courage shown on this point by Sarwa Rasool, the actress who ultimately played Juliet.[65] The new part of the Teacher was played by 84-year-old veteran Shakespearean actor Sami Abdulhameed, an iconic figure in Iraqi theatre but one whose specific history perhaps cast an ambiguous tone on the part. One review declared, 'No more fitting role could have been cast for a man who survived the brutality of Saddam's regime while many of his contemporaries were exiled or killed', while another described him as 'one of the complicated intellectuals who played the difficult, not wholeheartedly admirable game of surviving and continuing to produce art under a dictatorship that killed or exiled many of their colleagues and friends'.[66] All these issues apply in different ways to the final location of the play, the Christian church where the Teacher proposes the lovers reunite. In Katherine Brokaw's account of the production, 'knowing audience members cringed' when this was announced, as the setting 'evoked Our Lady of Salvation, the church where terrorists killed fifty-two people during Mass in October 2010'.[67] With this final setting, the play's sense of fatal inescapability comes not from its events but from something that happened in the real world, before the adaptation existed. Nor are Romeo and Juliet suicidal; rather, when they finally find each other in the church it is a moment of unqualified joy and pleasure – interrupted by the arrival of Paris wearing a bomb, and a blackout and explosion. A brief, unspoken coda shows the two families mourning, reunited in grief.

The church that replaces Shakespeare's tomb is thus less an 'ancient receptacle' of tradition or the play itself than a liminal space that leads out of the realm of the play – or rather, that lets the world invade and occupy the realm of the play. A different sort of real-world 'invasion' happened in the London staging of *Romeo and Juliet in Baghdad* on 27 June 2012, when an activist (a member of 'The Reclaim Shakespeare Company') climbed on stage just before the start of the play and used a parody of the opening of *Romeo and Juliet* to attack British Petroleum (a principal sponsor of the festival) for lobbying in favour of the 2004 invasion of Iraq, suggesting as well that the World Shakespeare Festival had made itself complicit in the destruction visited upon the country: 'Two households, BP and the World Shakespeare Festival, both lacking in dignity, in befouled Iraq where we lay our scene / For oil feud breaks to new hypocrisy where civil blood makes their money unclean.'[68] What is most interesting about this political intervention is that it was effectively an extension of the theatrical philosophy of *Romeo and Juliet in Baghdad* and indeed, the entire World Shakespeare Festival: the fundamental desire to join play world to real world. In a striking echo of Rokem's critique of the 1994 Khan/El-Qasaba production, the festival's exposure of Shakespeare to contemporary politics allowed a further exposure of the politics of the festival, perhaps making that London audience ask themselves what, exactly, they were endorsing with their participation.

The specific adaptive strategy undertaken by Daood in bringing Romeo and Juliet into the contemporary moment owes most to *West Side Story*, where the death that concludes the play similarly comes not from the lovers' own hands but from an ancillary party – making the sacrifice of the lovers entirely a matter of unclean civil hands instead of a demonstration of the depth of their love. In this change, a certain agency is removed from the lovers – especially Juliet, who loses the opportunity to demonstrate the depth of her commitment to her lover. But its dramaturgical strategies and its complex relation to Shakespeare as a mythic figure also take us all the way back to Otway's *Caius Marius*, the first play to attempt to refashion *Romeo and Juliet* for other times, other mores. If the immediate political impetus behind Otway's adaptation is clear, his choice of *Romeo and Juliet* is less so: why not choose a more explicitly political Shakespeare play to illustrate the crises of his time? Given the play's general absence from the Restoration stage – Samuel Pepys saw a production in 1662 which he thought was terrible – we might understand Otway as not only intervening in the Exclusion Crisis but finding a way to negotiate his own relationship to Shakespeare's play.

Matters of inheritance and the anxiety of influence are much on Otway's mind in the Prologue to the play, which begins by linking Shakespeare to Ovid and Horace as a poet who lived in a time 'When Empires flourisht' and political authority supported the arts:

Our *Shakespear* wrote too in an Age as blest,
The happiest Poet of his time and best.
A gracious Prince's Favour chear'd his Muse,
A constant Favour he ne'r fear'd to lose.
Therefore he wrote with Fancy unconfin'd,
And Thoughts that were Immortal as his Mind.
And from the Crop of his luxuriant Pen
E're since succeeding Poets humbly glean.[69]

Calling himself (or rather, having Betterton call him) 'the most unworthy of the Throng' of latter-day poets, he apologizes for his thefts:

You'll find h' has rifled him of half a Play.
Amidst this baser Dross you'll see it shine
Most beautifull, amazing, and Divine.
To such low Shifts of late are Poets worn,
Whilst we both Wit's and *Caesar*'s Absence mourn.[70]

'Caesar's Absence' refers to Charles II's temporary absence from court due to serious illness, and the prologue concludes by prophesying a rejuvenation of the arts once the king returns. But it's clear that the real point is the decline of an age, and the fundamental severing of its historical connection to *antebellum* England: for Otway, there are stronger parallels between Shakespeare's time and distant Augustan Rome than between his own time and Shakespeare's. Otway is twice referred to as 'This-day's Poet',[71] which seems to carry a double meaning: both the poet of this specific day, when the play is being performed, and also a poet of the present, forced to glean the work of happier times because of the political corruption of his own. This age must steal its poetry from Shakespeare because it can produce nothing comparable, but at the same time, the easy symbiosis of politics and poetry that Otway fantasizes as the source of Shakespeare's plays means that they ill suit the times: the work demands adaptation. Performing Shakespeare in the modern world requires a means of reclaiming Shakespeare.

Otway's play is thus the earliest experiment in what has become a standard approach to Shakespearean performance. In a way, this is less about the particular problems that the play presents for a new age – language that must be excised or rewritten to suit contemporary mores, characters and dynamics that seem problematic in various ways – than about the fame and universality of the story. Otway does do much to render Lavinia conventionally feminine, to restore to the play a sense of normative gender roles and to take out most of the liberatory sexuality associated with Juliet. More importantly, he takes the fame of the story as license to reposition it for other times, other places. As with *Romeo and Juliet in Baghdad*, this repositioning involves imagining theatre as a radically public and political space, where the boundaries between representation and performance are permeable. If the Prince and the other citizens are proxies for the theatre audience in Shakespeare's play, as I suggested at the start of this chapter, the violent entry of Caius Marius might be understood as the audience violating the space of the play, precipitating the conclusion, demanding attention. And while there is no record of any event comparable to the appropriations of the Reclaim Shakespeare Company, the play certainly acknowledges that the world outside may take notice and intervene. The epilogue, spoken by Elizabeth Barry, asks:

> May I believe this Play of ours shall thrive?
> This Drumming, Trumpetting, and Fighting Play?
> Why, what a Devil will the People say?
> The Nation that's without, and hears the Din,
> Will swear w'are raising Volunteers agen.[72]

Although the narrative of the play pleads against a return to the catastrophe of civil war, the performance of the play risks being taken as a sign of such a return by 'The Nation that's without', that hears the drums without understanding (or caring about) their intended meaning. Nor, it seems, in a time of such political instability can a powerful theatrical performance be entirely separated from political recruitment. Unlike Otway's dream of the Age of Shakespeare, where theatre might revel in an uninvolved aesthetic perfection, in an age of violence *Romeo and Juliet* inevitably enters the conflict.

3

The State of the Art

Rebeca Helfer

Is *Romeo and Juliet* a timeless tale of young love? In 'The untimeliness of youth', Marjorie Garber debunks the myth of the play's universal appeal, demonstrating instead how our current interpretation of the play is time-bound: historically and culturally specific.[1] We have made this story modern in our own image, she suggests, as indeed each generation has created its own version of *Romeo and Juliet*. Garber's wide-ranging essay spans a variety of media – theatre, ballet, film, musical, rock song, cartoon and even advertisement – to highlight the different ways that the play has been interpreted over time. In contrast to earlier interpretations that focused less exclusively on the two young lovers, or saw them as romantic rebels against adults and society alike, Garber argues that our current view of *Romeo and Juliet* emerged with the rise of 'theories of youth culture and subculture' in the 1950s and 1960s; as she notes, one critic described the Zeffirelli film of *Romeo and Juliet* as '*The Graduate* set in Renaissance Verona'.[2] Garber admits that 'it may be too strong a claim to say that *Romeo and Juliet* has *produced* youth culture, but nonetheless the composite idea Romeo-and-Juliet does function, today, as a recognizable signifier ... of young love, obstructed passion, "star-crossed lovers"', 'parents who just-don't-understand' and 'peer pressure'.[3]

Garber's insight applies broadly to this chapter, which explores how the most recent generation of scholars (from 1990–2014) have understood what is arguably Shakespeare's most popular play. The generational divide that marks *Romeo and Juliet* finds a reflection in scholarship about the play – indeed, Garber's essay itself now appears to be 'of a time' for this particular kind of cultural criticism – though the broad trends that I track also reflect Shakespeare studies, as well as literary studies, as a whole. Much scholarly work of the early to mid-1990s extended the theoretical, cultural and historical approaches of the 1980s on such subjects as language, sexuality, gender, identity and power. By contrast, much *Romeo and Juliet* criticism of the new millennium increasingly has focused less on social issues *per se* than on new kinds of historical approaches, including those that emphasize the material conditions and practices of the early modern theatre. At the same time, the critical pendulum has also swung back to more traditional fields of inquiry, such as aesthetics and ethics, yet newly conceived for the present in theoretically and historically informed ways. To consider the most recent generation of *Romeo and Juliet* scholarship, I have divided this chapter into six broad critical categories: page and performance; language and literature; love and sexuality; death and violence; space and time; body and soul, mind and matter. However, my aim is to trace lines of dialogue in a critical conversation that has changed over time, and which continues to evolve in response to new approaches to literary and humanistic study.

Page and performance

Where can the real Shakespeare be found? On the page – and if so, which version? – or in production – and if so, how faithful must a performance be to the original text? These questions have absorbed Shakespeare scholars of the past generation, who have responded by dismantling the assumptions that underwrite these very questions, and by posing new questions that have inspired new answers. *Romeo and Juliet* has proved an important test case in debates about authenticity and authority, as Wendy Wall demonstrates in 'Editors in Love?: Performing Desire in *Romeo and Juliet*', which examines the intersection of page and performance in the context of such debates.[4] Throughout the '90s, scholars increasingly challenged the conclusions of editors and bibliographers about earlier printed versions of *Romeo and Juliet*, particularly the so-called 'bad' quarto of 1597, Q1, which was thought to be a memorial reconstruction of a performance, and thus suspect. In so doing, scholars worked to reverse the assumption that the written text always precedes performance, rather than vice-versa, and therefore matters more, as well as the assumption that a unified text exists. 'Today we commonly think of performances as mutating, while the text remains stable', Wall writes, but argues that this is a 'fantasy of textual production ... at odds with the realities of theatrical practice in the Renaissance'.[5] Wall surveys this critical shift, based on the work of critics such as Stephen Orgel, Jonathan Goldberg, Barbara Hodgdon and W. B. Worthen, who have disputed the primacy of the play text in the context of *Romeo and Juliet*. 'The written text ... belatedly takes its meaning from theatre', Wall asserts and 'since the text is *of* a performance (rather than the other way around), the simple question "is a modern performance faithful to *the* text?" appears to be inadequate at best.'[6]

Wall's essay is indebted to Jonathan Goldberg's '"What? in a names that which we call a Rose": The Desired Texts of *Romeo and Juliet*', which reflects upon the differences between Q1 and Q2 *Romeo and Juliet* and the ways that editors and bibliographers have responded to them.[7] Goldberg traces the editorial and bibliographic reception of Q1, deemed the 'bad' quarto in part because of its differences from Q2, versus that of Q2, deemed the 'good' quarto because it was thought to represent Shakespeare's 'foul papers' (or unedited draft) of the play. As Goldberg argues, however, this narrative reflects the desire of editors to 'clothe an interpretation with authority'.[8] Instead of seeing Q1 as a performance text and Q2 as an authorial work, he contends that Q2 is 'an anthology of a number of productions of *Romeo and Juliet*', from which editors make their selections.[9] Goldberg reconfigures the relation between page and performance, and in so doing exposes fantasies of authority as a product of our own desire.

Wall's essay also draws on the work of Barbara Hodgdon, who explores issues of performance in her seminal essay, 'Absent Bodies, Present Voices: Performance Work and the Close of Romeo and Juliet's Golden Story'.[10] Hodgdon contends that performances of *Romeo and Juliet*, on both stage and screen, inevitably bespeak 'loss': whereas in traditional productions, 'audiences ... mourn' for Romeo and Juliet's lost youth and love, in unconventional adaptations, 'reviewers and critics mourn' for the loss of the traditional text and context.[11] This longing for an original authorial text against which the fidelity of a production must be judged is itself a historical fiction, Hodgdon argues. Shakespeare 'wrote within ... a system of performed representations, which was at least as privileged, if not more so, than the published (literary) text of the play', she writes, yet 'today ... scholars tend to measure performances against a peculiarly obsessive brand of Shakespearean quality control – the extent to which the performance successfully (or unsuccessfully) competes with the printed text or, more significantly, with each reader's private, ideal construction of that text, for authority'.[12] Hodgdon points the way to a 'more historically and culturally engaged model of performance criticism', or 'performance work', which challenges the 'opposition between a so-called authoritative text and performance' and instead seeks to negotiate between them.[13]

W. B. Worthen exemplifies such cultural performance work in '"What light through yonder window speaks?": The Nature Theater of Oklahoma *Romeo and Juliet* and the Cult(ure) of

Shakespeare.'[14] Less a production than a deconstruction, the 2010 performance by the experimental group Nature Theater of Oklahoma consists of remembered fragments of the play, though 'very few lines of *Romeo and Juliet* are actually spoken', and 'when they are, they are routinely spoken as quotations, usually misremembered quotations at that'.[15] Worthen nevertheless proposes that this production allows us to reconsider what Shakespeare means today, asking 'how does this *Romeo and Juliet* understand Shakespeare at the intersection between literary drama and the embodied work of performance?' and replying that it 'stages an ambivalent regard for the literary drama'.[16] Despite the production's radical and revisionist elements, it ultimately romanticizes an idea of an 'original' *Romeo and Juliet*, Worthen argues, by staging *Romeo and Juliet* as 'loss': the loss of an authoritative Shakespeare, which the production mourns.[17] As Worthen suggests, this production of the play ironically exposes, and indeed dramatizes, a continued desire for an idealized authorial text or private reading experience.

In *Shakespeare and World Cinema*, Mark Thornton Burnett considers issues of performance from the perspective of film adaptations of *Romeo and Juliet*, which span the globe from China to Brazil.[18] The play lends itself easily to narratives of cultural change and issues of social justice, Burnett demonstrates. '*Romeo and Juliet* repeatedly forms a partnership with societies caught on the cusp of transition, arguably because the play itself is concerned with a coming of age', he writes, particularly in 'cultural systems and nation-states characterized by an uneven relation to modernity'.[19] The importance of global film adaptations lies not only in what they import from Shakespeare, Burnett contends, but also what they bring from home, so to speak. 'The breadth and depth of the global fascination with *Romeo and Juliet* confirm the play's status as a mobile representational resource', and in turn this alters the lens through which Western cultures see the play: 'through its global instantiations, we are encouraged to see more creatively this canonized romance'.[20]

In *Negotiating Shakespeare's Language in Romeo and Juliet*, Lynette Hunter and Peter Lichtenfels approach the language of *Romeo and Juliet* in an innovative and holistic way: through the triple lens of criticism, editing and performance.[21] Conceived as a companion to their textual edition of *Romeo and Juliet* on DVD, which also contains a performance of the play, the book divides into two parts: Part 1 explores *Romeo and Juliet*'s language in relation to 'Reading, Acting and Editing' and Part 2 considers 'Transdisciplinary Work' on 'The Family', 'The Humours' and 'Governance'. This combining of fields, which they call 'transdisciplinarity', represents an 'attempt to integrate disciplines or at least to make the borders between them more porous'.[22] Their experimental treatment of the play's language 'from the perspective of a reader, a critic, a theatre practitioner, [and] a bibliographer' serves as an invitation for more such experiments in disciplinary line-crossing: 'a modest foray into what could become a much more complex interchange'.[23] Hunter and Lichtenfels's linking of page and performance at once builds upon the critical movement of the past generation and looks to future innovations of this kind, from within the platform offered by questions of editing.

Language and literature

Whether on the page or in performance, *Romeo and Juliet* is clearly *about* language and literature, and the last generation of scholars has continued to explore its linguistic and literary aspects from a range of perspectives: from Petrarchism, to patriarchy, to performance. The importance attached to names in the play has been a perennial source of scholarly fascination, particularly the extent to which language defines reality. In *Shakespeare's Names*, Laurie Maguire deconstructs Juliet's famous question, 'What's in a name?', exploring the disjunctive relationship between words and meaning, and culminating with a cultural history that – much like Marjorie Garber's – illustrates the stakes of translating *Romeo and Juliet* for new places, times and contexts.[24] Maguire analyses the play's extensive use of paradox in linguistic and thematic terms, describing *Romeo and Juliet* writ large as a paradox: a play of 'contradiction, contrast, and clashes'.[25] Indeed, the play is also a generic paradox: it begins with the trappings of a comedy only to turn tragic (though when and to what degree is the subject of debate). Yet Maguire's essay takes a sharp turn from treating the play as 'a tragedy of language' to considering issues of translation and adaptation in both theoretical and practical terms, shifting into cultural and performance criticism.[26] This leads her to Canada, where Maguire considers an English–French production that illustrates how the linguistic and familial tensions of Verona translate to new places and times with rival clans and competing languages.

William N. West similarly begins with the premise that '*Romeo and Juliet* seek a language of transcendence', but in order to reflect upon 'Mercutio's Bad Language', the title of his essay. As West suggests, Mercutio's language both thwarts our desire for linguistic transcendence and paradoxically enables it.[27] 'Mercutio's presence disrupts' the course of true love thematically and linguistically, West contends, yet Mercutio's cynical and complex use of words ironically produces the liberating language that the lovers seek, by breaking down 'the binaries that structure *Romeo and Juliet*'.[28] Mercutio's 'bad language' functions doubly in *Romeo and Juliet*, at once demonstrating the power of words to create new places and times and testing the inevitable limits of language.[29]

Madhavi Menon, by contrast, focuses exclusively on the failure of the lovers' linguistic transcendence in *Wanton Words: Rhetoric and Sexuality in English Renaissance Drama*.[30] Menon poses the question, 'What makes *The Tragedy of Romeo and Juliet* tragic?' and replies that it should be considered a 'tragedy of *rhetoric*, in which a malign fate and crossed stars are but the external manifestations of a rhetoric gone awry'.[31] Her argument turns on the morning-after 'scene of love's consummation', in which the lovers together produce the lyric form known as *aubade* or morning song.[32] Although Romeo and Juliet unite in the creation of this poem, Menon argues that their duet instead signifies the rupture of intercourse and discourse, or love and language, locating the tragic source of the play in the failure of words.

Relatedly, scholars since 1990 remain fascinated by *Romeo and Juliet*'s meta-literary language, particularly its radical transformation of the sonnet's language of love: the Petrarchism that the play both satirizes (especially through Mercutio) and takes seriously in turn. Kiernan Ryan's 'The Murdering Word' examines this literary language of love in a social context, arguing – contra some feminist scholars, who see Petrarch's poetry as a tool of patriarchal oppression – that Romeo and Juliet's mutual love emerges through their rejection and reformation of the conventional language of the sonnet.[33] 'Romeo's Petrarchan bondage' creates a radical inequality with Juliet, Ryan contends, binding the lovers 'to a set text dictated by the sexual conventions of their society, which forbids them to invent their own script, create their own roles or speak lines of their own devising'.[34] Such prescriptiveness defines and confines the lovers, yet by 'transmuting ... the old Petrarchan diction, with all that it implies', they achieve 'the innovative character of their love'.[35] For Ryan, Romeo and Juliet's genuine love story resides in the transformation of clichéd Petrarchan language into an original language of mutual love, by which they free themselves from Verona's social and sexual norms.

David Schalkwyk's *Speech and Performance in Shakespeare's Sonnets and Plays* reconsiders the role of the sonnet in *Romeo and Juliet* from the perspective of performance, responding to earlier critics such as Diana Henderson, whose exploration of Petrarchism and gender in the play remains influential.[36] 'Critics may differ in their views of the degree to which *Romeo and Juliet* is contained by or transcends the Petrarchan tradition', Schalkwyk writes, but rather than entering into this critical debate, he considers the performance of this lyric form, the act of turning verse into theatre through 'the player-poet'.[37] He situates the sonnet in a political context, framing the sonnet as 'a form of social action' that is already 'public' rather than made that way through performance.[38] Schalkwyk thereby reverses a critical tendency to read the sonnet in *Romeo and Juliet* as a lyric form that is superseded by performance, bringing literary and theatrical modes of experiencing the play together.

Love and sexuality

In terms of critical generations, some of the best-known studies of love and sexuality in *Romeo and Juliet* emerged from debates in the early 1990s about desire, gender, ideology and culture. In her seminal article, 'The Name of the Rose in *Romeo and Juliet*,' Catherine Belsey affirms that '*Romeo and Juliet* is a play about desire', but she then radically complicates what desire means in psychoanalytical terms.[39] For Belsey, *Romeo and Juliet* dramatizes the paradoxical nature of desire, as both an absence and a longing for presence that, by its very definition, can never be satisfied. This notion of sexual desire as a lack finds a parallel with the desire for meaning that language can never completely fulfil. '*Romeo and Juliet* suggests the degree to which the lover is always only a stand-in for something which cannot be embraced', Belsey concludes, thereby reframing the lovers' particular tragedy in terms of the universal if paradoxical structures of the human psyche.[40]

Like Belsey, Lloyd Davis pursues 'the link between lack and love' in '"Death-Marked Love": Desire and Presence in *Romeo and Juliet*', but from a historical perspective that complicates psychoanalytic notions of desire as lack or absence. While acknowledging that the play 'stages the outcome of unfulfillable desire', he contends that it represents a shift between earlier and later conceptions of desire, arguing that the play 'marks a complex intersection between historical and emergent discourses of desire'.[41] *Romeo and Juliet*'s explorations of links between love and death articulate a scepticism about desire that points toward modernity. The play moves beyond 'a narcissistic poetics of desire as self-loss and death' toward a 'reciprocal presence', Davis argues, and 'anticipates the tension between romantic and skeptical visions of desire ... [in] later literary and theoretical works'.[42]

Whereas Davis's account affirms the presence of mutual and reciprocal desire in the play, Dympna Callaghan's 'The Ideology of Romantic Love: The Case of *Romeo and Juliet*' offers a feminist critique of just such notions of desire and equality. Callaghan argues that romantic love in the play should be seen as 'a classic instance of false consciousness', observing that 'among its oppressive effects, the dominant ideology of (heterosexual, monogamous) romantic love ... secures women's submission to the asymmetrical distribution of power between men and women'.[43] Offering a 'materialist history of desire', she argues that *Romeo and Juliet* participates in forming patriarchal ideology at a pivotal moment in history and further that 'Shakespeare's text has been used to perpetuate the dominant ideology of romantic love.'[44] Rather than viewing Juliet's forthright and fervent desire as proof of her liberation or equality, as Davis does, Callaghan sees it as the product of an inescapable patriarchal system.

Jonathan Goldberg also sharply attacks the ideology of romantic love in '*Romeo and Juliet*'s Open Rs', not as Callaghan does from the perspective of feminist studies but from that of queer studies.[45] Indeed, his essay highlights the tension between feminist and queer approaches to *Romeo and Juliet*, exploring 'the forbidden desire named sodomy' partly to suggest how the 'heterosexist order' has been perpetuated by feminist critics.[46] Goldberg argues that *Romeo and Juliet* has become the seminal Shakespeare work assigned to high school students because 'the idealization of the lovers ... serves an ideological function', and he partly blames feminist scholars for this, who understand the play as a 'coming of age story' in which homosocial bonds are inevitably broken for heterosexual ones.[47] Goldberg instead 'queers' *Romeo and Juliet*, reinterpreting it as a transgressive play about same-sex desire, witnessed by Romeo's relationship to Mercutio. Goldberg concludes that 'the open arse and the open grave of transgressively (un)productive desires', visible at the play's end, fundamentally 'structure the trajectories of desire imagined in the play'.[48]

In '"Standing to the Wall": The Pressures of Masculinity in *Romeo and Juliet*', Robert Appelbaum argues that Goldberg and others have ignored 'the regime of masculinity' in the play, 'constituted as yet another system from which there is no escape'.[49] Appelbaum sees the pressure to perform masculinity as the source of the play's tragedy, making it less about men than 'masculine performance'.[50] He thereby emphasizes compulsory masculinity in *Romeo and Juliet* as an important 'ideological prejudice' ignored by feminist and queer critics alike, but which 'nevertheless determined the drama of social and political order in the Shakespearean world'.[51]

Paul Kottman reframes the critical debate about love from a philosophical perspective in 'Defying the Stars: Tragic Love as the Struggle for Freedom in *Romeo and Juliet*'.[52] He first explicitly responds to 'feminist scholars ... as well as their critic Jonathan Goldberg, [who] argue that the idealization of "love" in Shakespeare's play is an ideological construct (patriarchal, heterosexist, homosocial, and so forth) and hence "social" through and through', not as 'a transcendent state of otherworldly bliss but a worldly predicament'.[53] Instead, Kottman sees 'individual desires as irreducible to the social norms by which they are shaped', and offers another approach: a philosophical meditation on freedom in *Romeo and Juliet*, which asserts that lovers paradoxically discover their individuality in relation to one another and within the social constraints of Verona.[54] Against the notion that the '"tragic" core of our modern subjectivity is rooted in a conflict between individual desires and the reigning demands of family, civic, and social norms shaping those desires',

Kottman reads the play as 'the story of two individuals *who actively claim* ... their own freedom, in the only way that they can—through one another'.[55] Kottman's approach swings the critical pendulum back to more affirmative approaches (like Davis's) on the topic of love, but also suggests the need to interpret the play dialectically by incorporating the important critiques of critics like Callaghan and Goldberg.

Death and violence

While *Romeo and Juliet* scholarship of the 1990s evinces a fascination with love and sexuality, a similar interest in violence and death marks more recent criticism of the play. In '"*Alla stoccado* carries it away": Codes of Violence in *Romeo and Juliet*', [56] Levenson examines the play's 'encounter with early modern codes of violence,' arguing for both its dramatic and political implications.[57] On the one hand, Levenson links the play's violence to its language of love, arguing that the 'implements and acts of combat ... provide the dialogue with metaphors' related to the poetic conventions of the Petrarchan sonnet, and which reflect the play's representation of desire and death, as well as ambition and power.[58] On the other hand, Levenson places the play's depiction of aggressive acts in the historical context of early modern England, arguing that 'allusions to violence at every level of the text reflect ... a reality of late-sixteenth-century England', and citing the 'proclamations against fighting in public [that] had been issued by Henry VII, Henry VIII, and Elizabeth' as proof.[59] These constraints on the 'capacity for violence', Levenson further contends, were political attempts to limit the power of the aristocracy: 'with its feud, street fights, dueling, casualties, and deployment of combat imagery, *Romeo and Juliet* offers a panoramic view ... of violence in Elizabethan England'.[60] Such historicizing approaches to violence and death are the hallmark of *Romeo and Juliet* criticism of the new millennium.

Chris Fitter addresses the issue of violence in *Romeo and Juliet* from a popular perspective, taking issue specifically with Levenson's exclusive focus on aristocratic violence.[61] In '*Romeo and Juliet*, Dearth and the London Riots', Fitter complains that '*Romeo* criticism to date ... has addressed only *aristocratic* bloodshed', which fails to account for the overwhelming violence of contemporary London, which Shakespeare represented in the play: 'At the heart of a war-torn, over-taxed and now hunger-threatened nation, London in the mid-1590s was a congested, polarized and angry city, in which the crown and its officials had become hated, and the Lord Mayor made to fear for his own life.'[62] Arguing for *Romeo and Juliet*'s 'populist sympathies', Fitter calls it a 'play of political protest' rather than, as Levenson argues, a play about the taming of an unruly aristocracy.[63]

In 'Wherefore Art Thou Tereu?: Juliet and the Legacy of Rape', Robert Watson and Stephen Dickey examine the play's representation of sexual violence, which they provocatively argue has been wilfully ignored by critics.[64] As they contend, 'the seemingly exhaustive commentary on Shakespeare's *Romeo and Juliet* has contrived to ignore a cluster of allusions linking the hero to the most notorious rapists of classical culture: Tereus, Hades, Tarquin, and Paris'.[65] After illustrating the play's wide array of intertextual allusions to classical literary rapes, Watson and Dickey engage with the issue of rape in *Romeo and Juliet* from both historical and meta-critical perspectives. Attempting to 'historicize the crime of rape' and 'our discussion of it', they wonder why this subject failed to be addressed 'thirty years ago, when feminist scholars began excavating analyses of sexist violations from the depths of Shakespearean drama'.[66] In the response to what they perceive as a critical silence on the subject of rape in the play, Watson and Dickey assert 'it is time we moved from silent censorship to an open confrontation with the[se] issues'.[67] This shift away from focusing on male-on-male violence reframes its significance in *Romeo and Juliet*, illustrating how sexual violence saturates (rather than competes with) the romance plot.

In 'Romeo's "Death-markt" Imagination and its Tragic Consequences', William McKim finds another important absence in *Romeo and Juliet* criticism: a lack of attention to 'the differences between the ways the two protagonists imagine themselves as being in love and the tragic significance of those differences'.[68] Rather than arguing for the mutuality of Romeo's and Juliet's love (as Kottman, Davis and Schalkwyk do), McKim emphasizes the lovers' different views of love; and rather than blaming Verona society for the violence and tragic events in the play (as Levenson and Kitter do), McKim focuses on Romeo's romantic fixation with death. McKim depicts Romeo's 'death-marked imagination' as 'directed toward violent encounters and self-enhancement through self-sacrifice', as 'already formed, even scripted, before the action of the play begins and [which] does not significantly change during the course of the play'.[69] McKim gives new weight to the old saw that Romeo is in love with love – especially the language of love. 'Romeo's poetizing persists throughout the play and reaches its grand climax in his dying speech', McKim writes, when his death wish is finally fulfilled.[70]

Ramie Targoff's 'Mortal Love: Shakespeare's *Romeo and Juliet* and the Practice of Joint Burial' offers a revisionist interpretation of love and death in the play, through a historical and historicist account of early modern burial practices.[71] Whereas Shakespeare's sources sweetened the lovers' death with the promise of a shared afterlife, Targoff argues that 'Shakespeare removed any such transcendent vision of posthumous love from his play' and, paradoxically, 'in doing so, he created his most potent expression of what it meant for love to be mortal'.[72] Targoff's argument turns on Reformation theology, specifically Calvinism, and the separation of conceptions of marriage from the afterlife. This religious transformation is expressed in *Romeo and Juliet* as the denial of posthumous love, though ironically because of this very denial, Targoff concludes, *Romeo and Juliet* becomes 'Shakespeare's greatest expression of *carpe diem*'.[73]

Hugh Grady's *Shakespeare and Impure Aesthetics* marks a departure from such historicist readings by taking a 'presentist' approach, a playful term for a return to more theoretically and aesthetically engaged Shakespeare scholarship.[74] Grady examines the play 'as a crucial instance of Shakespeare's treatment of death and its links to the aesthetic and to desire in Western culture', and he considers the play in a number of contexts, including psychoanalysis; the history of death; the concept of love-death, or *Liebestod*; and a broad critical history of death from the Restoration to the present.[75] Grady's wide-ranging take on death and aesthetics answers contemporary critics who focus on the negative aspects of desire in *Romeo and Juliet*. Such interpretations 'inevitably diminish [the play's] impact with an imposition of moralizing judgments and insensitivity to the play's utopian spirit', which discloses 'a space in which love and desire persist even when they are represented as defeated by larger forces'.[76] Grady's work shifts the conversation about death and violence in the play to the realm of aesthetic possibility, dramatically and critically.

Space and time

Grady's pursuit of the liberating possibility of aesthetic space marks a larger trend in *Romeo and Juliet* studies, which has long considered the tension between freedom and constraint within the play's space-time continuum. In '"There is no world without Verona walls": The City in *Romeo and Juliet*', Naomi Conn Liebler explores the importance of the city, in both theoretical and historical terms.[77] Liebler reorients the play around the city that the lovers represent: '*Romeo and Juliet* performs an indictment of the civic institutions and structures of authority represented in the play, shifting the focus off the protagonists who serve as the agents for that performance, and on to the collective city for which they stand.'[78] Calling Verona 'the collective protagonist of the tragedy called *Romeo and Juliet*', Liebler suggests that the characters cannot be separated from the space of the city or its double, the space of the stage, and that the private and public worlds of Verona are inextricably intertwined.[79]

Paul Kottman's *A Politics of the Scene* similarly positions *Romeo and Juliet* as 'a play about the impossibility of rigorously separating public from private, city square from household orchard', but unlike Liebler, he pursues the liberating implications of these overlapping boundaries.[80] To illustrate that 'the space of politics is not reducible to the walls of Verona', Kottman focuses on the balcony scene as one of ostensibly '"private" discourse between two lovers ... removed from the public sphere of brawls and civil strife', arguing instead that an ostensibly 'apolitical sphere of private intercourse' collapses into the public sphere of Verona, and indeed is never truly separate from it.[81] For Kottman, the personal is political in *Romeo and Juliet* and the 'politics of the scene' relates to the lovers' freedom to interact in ways that aren't circumscribed or determined by the civitas.[82]

Julia Lupton likewise dwells upon the space of possibility in 'Making Room, Affording Hospitality: Environments of Entertainment in *Romeo and Juliet*'.[83] Lupton explores how Shakespeare's play sets the stage, so to speak, for potential and promising interactions through a theory of affordances: an interdisciplinary approach to space and objects, and the possibilities they present, which draws upon psychology, ecology, semiotics and design theory, as well as literary criticism. Beginning with the masked ball where Romeo and Juliet meet, she examines how party-planning in the play highlights the opportunities that such 'environments of entertainment' afford; such scenes test 'the scripts of hospitality for the risks and resistances they harbor, the leftover times and spaces they generate, and the chance for unexpected encounters that they court'.[84] Lupton's concern lies less with performance *per se* than with phenomenology: how the experience of a space's possibilities has 'the power not only to illuminate Shakespeare's world but also to link his to ours'.[85]

The ways in which *Romeo and Juliet* also dwells upon the pressures of time, starting with the Prologue's characterization of the play as the 'two hours' traffic of our stage', has been an abiding source of scholarly fascination. David Lucking's 'Unkind Hours and Timeless Ends: Uncomfortable Time in *Romeo and Juliet*' treats it as 'a play about time'.[86] Despite the lovers' desire for transcendence – to stop time, or at least slow it down – they 'fail to take into account their own enslavement to the time whose tyranny they implicitly reject'.[87] Lucking highlights their ironic end: Romeo and Juliet find transcendence as art, as gold statues frozen in time, forever young lovers who seek (in vain) to stop time.

In 'Shakespeare's Time-Riddles in *Romeo and Juliet* Solved', Steve Sohmer proposes a calendrical solution to the many puzzling elements of time in the play.[88] Sohmer contends that 'Shakespeare set his story in 1582', the year that Pope Gregory XIII reformed the Julian calendar, condensing the year by extracting ten days from October.[89] Queen Elizabeth I did not adapt the reformed calendar for religious reasons, which meant that England was ten days out of step with the continent until the mid-eighteenth century, when the Gregorian calendar was finally adopted. Explaining that 'throughout Shakespeare's working lifetime, Europe lived by not one but two rival calendars', Sohmer asserts that 'the key to Shakespeare's ... time-play in *Romeo and Juliet*, lies in the ... discrepancy between the English Julian and Catholic Gregorian calendars'.[90] As Sohmer contends, Shakespeare's obsession with time in *Romeo and Juliet* is not 'merely poetical', but also historical, relating to the time warp in early modern England.[91]

In 'Between Idolatry and Astrology: Modes of Temporal Repetition in *Romeo and Juliet*',[92] Philippa Berry considers how the play 'puts the putative singularity and linearity of time and history into question' by emphasizing its contradictory trajectories, both circular and linear: as combining 'frantic temporal acceleration' with the 'turning backwards of time (in the form of the repetitive and cyclical timing of calendrical and festive modes of memorialization)'.[93] She places this double rhythm in historical context, arguing that through Juliet, Shakespeare remembers the pre-Reformation calendar (the old Julian calendar that had a 10-day gap from the reformed Gregorian calendar), in order to highlight a tension between Catholic and Protestant time-keeping. Berry points to the lovers' meeting in July (versus December, in Arthur Brooke's *Romeus and Juliet*) and its role as a personification of Juliet, whose birth, marriage and death all take place in this month. Berry concludes that *Romeo and Juliet*'s complex temporal 'imagery encapsulates the perceived multi-faceted character of time in the late sixteenth century'.[94]

Body and soul, mind and matter

The most recent generation of scholars have taken up these interrelated subjects with increased interest, approaching them from historicist, cognitive, materialist, philosophical, ecological and performative perspectives. In 'Comedic Form and Paschal Motif in the First and Second Quartos of *Romeo and Juliet*', Beatrice Groves considers the mingling of comedic and tragic elements in this play from a temporal and religious perspective, arguing that 'Easter allusions are one, unrecognized, part of the comedic theme.'[95] She places Juliet at the centre of 'the comedic strand of the tragedy', not only because she is a 'witty female who is the instigator of her own marriage, passionate in her desire for sexual fulfilment, and whose language is alive with double meaning when she banters', but because, from a religious perspective, 'she is also at the heart of the paschal imagery in the play'.[96] Exploring the play's varied registers of comedy, satirical and salvific, Groves illustrates how *Romeo and Juliet* combines diverse forms of comedy.[97]

Tanya Pollard's '"A Thing Like Death": Sleeping Potions and Poisons in *Romeo and Juliet* and *Antony and Cleopatra*' also explores the thematic of resurrection: specifically, how Shakespeare's 'ambivalent drugs' represent potions that hover between poison and cure. Pollard connects these potions with the ambiguous representation of genre in *Romeo and Juliet*, as containing elements of both comedy and tragedy.[98] 'Juliet's artificial sleep' exemplifies a theatrical moment that hovers between the possibilities of comic and tragic outcomes, between life and death, and which suggests the alternative possibilities always present in the play. Pollard extends this consideration of potions to the ambiguous status of literature and theatre itself, seen throughout history as both harmful and curative.

Karen Raber's 'Vermin and Parasites: Shakespeare's Animal Architectures' raises questions about the nature of humanity from the perspective of ecocriticism.[99] Raber begins with the premise that 'Montagues and Capulets fight like cats and dogs', in order to explore the relationship between animal and human, as well as issues of gender and space. Observing the play's paradoxical treatment of masculinity, Raber writes that 'establishing a distinction between masculine and feminine requires an act of bestial violence that then defeats the human/beast distinction'.[100] She connects this elision with the space of the play, arguing that 'each time the young men of the play enter a public place, they reveal the instability of the human–animal divide that underwrites the civil actions and civilized self-control upon which social interaction in the crowded city relies'.[101] Raber's argument exposes the interdependence of human and animal in the play, the ways in which '*human* society is in turn dependent in many ways, materially and ideologically, on *animals*'.[102]

In 'Feeling Dreams in *Romeo and Juliet*', Matthew Spellberg examines the sensory connection between mind and body in dreaming.[103] Starting with Mercutio's dream of Queen Mab, Spellberg asks, 'what does a dream actually feel like?'[104] He suggests that the 'felt experience of illusion is uncannily close to the felt experience of reality' in *Romeo and Juliet*, and that 'the dream-world that runs parallel to the real world in this play presents itself as unusually open to being experienced'.[105] This emphasis on sensory experience leads 'away from the metaphysical tradition, and toward a materialist one'.[106] Spellberg engages the history of philosophy, focusing particularly on Lucretius, to argue that 'it is the simultaneous reality and impossibility of bringing together fantasy and carnality – mind and body – that destroys Romeo and Juliet, who finally experience being as nothingness'.[107]

Daryl Palmer explores physics and philosophy in 'Motion and Mercutio in *Romeo and Juliet*'.[108] '*Romeo and Juliet* takes up an ancient conversation about motion' that it extends in innovative ways, Palmer argues, writing that 'Juliet wants to know what is in a name' and that 'Shakespeare … might well have answered, *motion*.'[109] The figure who 'embodies' both ancient and early modern conceptions of the universe as motion and change is, naturally, the mercurial Mercutio.[110] Palmer points to Mercutio's philosophical physics in the Queen Mab speech, but also in his discourse about fencing. 'Mercutio aims to dazzle his auditor with a discourse as applicable to life as it is to fencing', Palmer explains, and with his lessons as well as his death by duel, 'Shakespeare … teases us with the possibility of making motion answerable'.[111]

Lina Perkins Wilder pursues the performance of memory in '"I do remember": The Nurse, the Apothecary, and Romeo'.[112] Wilder first describes *Romeo and Juliet*'s broad concern with memory and widespread use of 'mnemonic structuring', such as recapitulation and reportage, but her focus lies specifically with how this manifests as performances within the play. 'Two of Shakespeare's clearest examples of memory theatre occur in *Romeo and Juliet*', Wilder argues: 'the Nurse's recollection of Juliet's weaning and Romeo's recollection of the contents of the Apothecary's shop'.[113] In both cases, mnemonic spaces are not physically present on the stage but instead constructed verbally in performance: 'Romeo and the Nurse create memory theatre … which for the most part [is] not staged' except through their recollections.[114] As Wilder reveals, Shakespeare's treatment of memory is dramaturgical, creating a theatre at 'a crossroads of the physical present and an absent, immaterial, but inescapable past'.[115]

The state of the art?

The works examined here represent a cross-section of the vital and fascinating *Romeo and Juliet* criticism of the past generation. Nevertheless, *Romeo and Juliet* scholarship – like that of Shakespeare studies and, indeed, literary studies as a whole – is also at something of a crossroads. Hugh Grady's conclusion to *Shakespeare and Impure Aesthetics* offers a useful reflection upon the current state of Shakespeare studies and beyond.[116] Observing the apparent decline of theory and the rise of historicism, Grady argues that 'studies from the 1990s to today ... [are] couched in the theoretical concerns of the broad poststructuralist theory of the 1980s, with its emphases on deconstructing gender, race, class, sexuality, and colonialism ... the terrain opened up by the critical revolutions of twenty to thirty years ago'.[117] In response to scholars who now see themselves as 'traditionalists' or 'post-theory', especially 'new materialists', Grady proposes a theoretically informed aestheticism (or 'impure aesthetics') and new formalism as a link between the past and 'the "presentist" movement'. He conceives of presentism as 'a "big tent" for a large array of contemporary critical practices that share the assumption that the critic's own situation in our cultural present is a resource for, rather than an impediment to, a productive and insightful reading of Shakespeare'.[118] Grady's shift from historicism to presentism not only marks a return to theory, it also returns us to Marjorie Garber's insight earlier in this essay: that Shakespeare criticism has been defined by generational conflict, as it were. Albeit in different ways, both Grady and Garber explore these meta-critical issues through *Romeo and Juliet*, as a play that reflects on these very matters. Are such conflicts inevitable? Can the generational divide that separates the past from the present and the future be bridged? Are there ways to speak with each other despite changes in time and language itself? Consider a few of the most famous lines in the play:

> O Romeo, Romeo, wherefore art thou Romeo?
> Deny thy father and refuse thy name,
> Or if thou wilt not, be but sworn my love,
> And I'll no longer be a Capulet.
>
> (2.2.33–6)

The question of Romeo's identity – and by extension, that of *Romeo and Juliet* – turns on a pun about being, 'art' that questions the status of art and its place in the world, its relationship to language and love, to time and generations, to politics and power, to meaning and reality itself. Juliet answers her own innocent question with fantasies of both patricide and potential, voicing the simultaneous possibility and impossibility of making and remaking the world anew with only words to play with. As the following 'New Directions' chapters confirm, *Romeo and Juliet* continues to ask such questions, and to offer new answers.

4

New Directions: Why No One Hears Lord Capulet's Line

Robert N. Watson

Weary of bloodshed after the fatal swordfights, Verona's Prince asks a potentially conciliatory question: 'Romeo slew him, he slew Mercutio, / Who now the price of his dear blood doth owe?' Seizing the opportunity to protect his son, Romeo's father answers, 'Not Romeo, Prince, he was Mercutio's friend. / His fault concludes but what the law should end, / The life of Tybalt' (3.1.184–8). Or at least that's who seizes the opportunity unless you happen to be reading the 1963 Signet edition of the play, which – unlike every other modern edition I can find – gives that answer to Juliet's father instead.[1]

Otherwise a reader can traipse back through the entire Hall of Fame of Shakespeare editors without finding that little speech attributed to Lord Capulet. Try the great Dr Johnson (1765), Capell (1768), Malone (1790), the lavish Steevens/Boydell editions (1802), the infamously proper Bowdler (1820), Collier (1842), Furness's Variorum (1871), Dowden (1900), Dover Wilson (1955), George Walton Williams (1964), the controversial Rowse (1968), Kittredge with or without Ribner's updates (1936, 1978), Harbage's Pelican collection of the works and the new version by Orgel and Braunmuller (2002), Raffel for Harold Bloom's series (2004), the old and new Folger editions (1959, 2004), or Bate and Rasmussen's RSC *Complete Works* (2007). Dig through all three Arden editions, both the traditionalist old Oxford version and Wells and Taylor's professedly revisionist new Oxford *Complete Works*, the New and updated-New Cambridge editions and the Cambridge School edition, the Bedford editions, the Norton Shakespeare, the Bevington editions, the G. B. Harrison that sat as a treasure on my mother's desk, and the Riverside Shakespeare that sits treasured on mine. Also the three most prominent online texts: MIT, Project Gutenberg, and No Fear Shakespeare by SparkNotes.

Even in what is supposedly a facing-page transcript of Q1 and Q2 for textual scholars, Jay Halio felt obliged to replace Q2's '*Capu.*' speech-heading with Q4's '*Moun.*,' despite the fact that there is no indication that Q4 has any independent authority.[2] The prompt-books of the famous actor-managers I have found – David Garrick's adaptation for Drury Lane (1750) and Kemble's revision of it (1814), for example – do the same;[3] from Garrick onward, some actually transfer Lady Capulet's vengeful speeches to her husband. A Theatre-Royal production in 1773–4 gave a paraphrase of the line to Montague. The widely taught 1979 BBC/Time-Life video, and the hugely popular 1968 Franco Zeffirelli and 1996 Baz Luhrmann films, also erase Lord Capulet's concession.[4] Everybody agrees that the line is Montague defending his son; I have never heard Capulet speak it, on stage or screen, although the reactions of other characters to him doing so could be fascinating. Two of the most recent studies even make 'Capulet Father's complete silence' in this scene a meaningful clue for actors.[5]

The only major figure who steadfastly disagreed with this consensus was apparently William Shakespeare, because in all the early editions of the play (except the controversial first quarto, which omits this speech entirely), the speech-heading gives Capulet the lines. This is hardly conclusive – some other speech-headings in this play seem clearly erroneous – but neither should it be presumed negligible, especially since it remains through quartos and folios while other oddities are corrected.

Usually Montague is inserted without comment. The latest and most scholarly edition, René Weis's impressive Arden third series, simply remarks that this speech is 'attributed mistakenly to Capulet in Q2' – as if it were not the same in Q3 and the early folios. Jill L. Levenson's generally excellent Oxford *Romeo and Juliet* (2000) pauses only long enough to dismiss the original speech heading as 'an obvious mistake', and Brian Gibbons's no less excellent Arden second series (1980) calls it 'an obvious error'.

So it seems. With the play so focused on the binary family feud, and that feud at a fatal height at this instant, one would hardly expect the head of the Capulet clan to plead on behalf of the young Montague who has bereaved them.[6] In Shakespeare's principal source, Brooke's 'Romeus and Juliet', it is only the Montagues who 'plead their Romeus void of fault'.[7] Similarly, Painter's translation of Bandello's 'Rhomeo and Iulietta' has the Montagues 'declarying the innocencye of Rhomeo, and the wilfull assault of the other', with 'witnesses heard on both partes'.[8]

But Shakespeare's play is hardly on the side of the feud against human freedom and against the depth and complexity of human experience. From the micro to the macro level, *Romeo and Juliet* – in a characteristic Shakespearean move – invites us to attach ourselves to simplistic, formulaic assumptions and then exposes their costs and limitations. It offers us neat binary oppositions, only to teach us that a seemingly opposed two can converge toward one, and thereby liberate an almost infinite set of possibilities. In other words, it becomes a love story.

This emendation is so nearly universal, and also, I think, so consequentially mistaken, that – especially as it persists in our current era of first-do-no-harm 'un-editing' of Shakespeare – it seems to cry out for explanation as well as correction. Why have editors and directors been so quick to conclude that Shakespeare and/or his printers had this wrong?[9] My theory is that Shakespeare gambled by signalling so compelling a binary logic on so many levels of the play that cognitive-dissonance mechanisms block out the alternative he wanted us to glimpse.

That Lord Capulet would defend Romeo against Tybalt is otherwise hardly implausible. The Capulet of 3.1 has recently undergone what must have been an extensive admonishment by the Prince toward reconciliation (1.1.97) and his vows of peace have been convincing enough to allow Paris to speak of the feud in the past tense (1.2.4–5). What seems most germane is the fact that Capulet has already praised Romeo while trying to restrain Tybalt from attacking him:[10]

> 'A bears him like a portly gentleman
> And, to say truth, Verona brags of him
> To be a virtuous and well-governed youth.
> I would not for the wealth of all this town
> Here in my house do him disparagement.
>
> (1.5.65–9)

When that message falls on deaf ears, Capulet demands, 'Am I the master here or you?' and calls Tybalt 'a saucy boy' who will 'make a mutiny'. He even threatens to betray Tybalt someday – 'This trick may chance to scathe you' (1.5.83) – for his impudent tendency to 'contrary me'. By the time of the street-brawl, Capulet has every reason to suspect the hot-headed Tybalt instigated it, and to be glad Tybalt is out of his household (his wife's fervour on Tybalt's behalf, often sexualized in production, may add another motive). Romeo has only made good on Lord Capulet's warning to Tybalt: 'I'll make you quiet' (1.5.77–87).

Capulet's three brief public comments interspersed with these private reprimands to Tybalt, apparently spoken as Romeo (whom he has just been watching) approaches Juliet for the first time, encourage us to see him as potentially endorsing their connection: 'Marry, 'tis time, / Well said, my hearts ... More light, more light! ... What, cheerly, my hearts!' (1.5.84–7). This genial Capulet, who even urges the Montague lads to stay longer for a banquet (1.5.120–1), is capable of eclipsing the irascible one; his comment that 'our whole city is much bound to' Friar Laurence (4.2.32) suggests a broad endorsement of the Friar's civic project, not just gratitude for Juliet's daughterly penitence; and Capulet is the one who initiates the closing reconciliation (5.3.296). I am not convinced that Shakespeare intended to signal that Capulet was seeking a Montague son-in-law, but such a claim would be bolstered by the fact that Shakespeare shows us Capulet trying to defer any marriage to Paris (for 'two more summers') before the fatal brawl (1.2.8–13), but then hastening that marriage once the blood-feud is renewed and Romeo exiled (3.4; 4.2.24). Frustration with the failure of an earlier, grander plan would amplify his exasperation with Juliet's rejection of that renewed Paris match, and thus could explain exactly the violent reaction that has prevented readers from imagining him as a conciliator.

Some may object that if Capulet speaks these lines, the feud and hence the play would end. But in fact neither house speaks ill of the other from that moment forward. The only trace of the feud is the assumption of Paris – whose dramatically ironic misapprehensions are a running joke – that Romeo intends to defile the Capulet tomb, and the Prince's reference to the families' 'hate', which need not refer to any recent events. The embittered Lady Capulet, while vilifying Romeo for killing Tybalt, says nothing further against the Montagues; and the servants, formerly present mostly as carriers of the feud in its crudest form, make no further mention of it. All that matters thereafter is the banishment, which the Prince presumably saw as a calming compromise, and would hardly therefore seek to revoke when it seemed to be working.

Restoring the speech to Lord Capulet, and thereby recognizing that he might actually have approved of Juliet's choice as a way of ending the feud (as in Monadhil Daood's *Romeo and Juliet in Baghdad*),[11] adds another compelling instance to the dramatic irony that drives the play: '*Romeo and Juliet* is a play that trades freely in near misses', as Will West writes elsewhere in this collection, and several opportunities for a happy ending are missed because characters fail to communicate. While I focus on a specific lost opportunity for painless reconciliation and on a hint that the lovers transcend their painful exit from this world, West focuses – compatibly, and no less legitimately – on the infinite variety of unpredictable possibilities Shakespeare sustains within this world.

From the play's overarching themes of polar opposition down to the microscopic level of the play's persistent euphuistic verbal pairings and Petrarchan oxymora (fading fashions in Elizabethan literature), Shakespeare elides the love-story with an over-determined Hegelian mode of tragedy driven by contradictory imperatives. The triumph within the tragedy of these young lovers, however, is the conversion of life-denying antitheses into more generous and generative syntheses that express the real intricacy of human experience. The emended speech heading is both a result and a reinforcement of a tragic assumption. Editors and directors cannot hear Capulet's conciliatory voice because Juliet fatally fails to hear it, and the result is that readers and audiences do not even know what she missed or what we are therefore missing.

The key question the play keeps raising, in many areas and at many levels of scale, is whether symmetry can be converted into synthesis. Do the pairs merge in some expansive way, or do they instead remain separate (and hence double), or reflexively antithetical (and hence cancelling each other into a zero)? Shakespeare proposes and reinforces many opposed pairings in this play, only to break them down. But these invitations to facile binary distinctions can provoke editors and readers – as they provoke many of the play's characters – to overlook a more complicated and potentially redemptive blending of the seemingly paradoxical juxtapositions.

Binary themes

As editors all feel certain that the line is Montague's, so critics generally concur that this play is structured around irreconcilable contraries that determine the tragic outcome. *Romeo and Juliet* signals thematic tensions so broadly that it seems written for adolescent English essays as well as lovesick English adolescents. Shakespeare flaunts at least a sonnet's worth of anti-couplets:

A	/	B
Romeo	/	Juliet
Montague	/	Capulet
male	/	female
sexual violence	/	sexual affection
hate	/	love
Thanatos	/	Eros
age	/	youth
death	/	life
tragedy	/	comedy
reality	/	dreams
waking	/	sleeping
light	/	dark
public	/	private
Protestant	/	Catholic

Harry Levin has concisely traced some further counterpoises and complementarities: along with oxymora and other antitheses, the play features feuding families with metrically identical names, whose elderly patriarchs rush into brawls despite the efforts of their wives to block them, and whose children each have an alternative mate (Paris and Rosaline) and a gender-matched advisor (one devoted to the personal life-experience of the body and the other to the conventional wisdom of the soul).[12]

When erotic drives become tainted with murderous violence in the opening scene (through paired threats against men's heads and maidenheads), and again when Romeo's loving embrace turns the fight between Mercutio and Tybalt fatal, it seems clear that love and hate cannot be profitably reconciled. The failures of the lovers to live up to their hyperbolic assertions – Romeo's 'stony limits cannot hold love out' (2.2.67) and Juliet's 'follow thee my lord throughout the world' (2.2.148) ring hollow after Romeo is banished – suggest the same problem: a failure of love to unify the pair, persisting right through the unlucky timing in the Capulet tomb and the paired statues that are all that visibly remains of the hopeful lady and gentleman on our earth. Reason enough to picture the story in two-point perspective (see fig.1).

But the most persistent and pervasive theme of the play could be described as an effort – almost alchemical – to use erotic heat to reconcile bluntly opposed and thus mutually exclusive elements into a mysterious compound that converts

FIGURE 1 *Romeo and Juliet in two-point perspective. Illustration drawn by John Gleb, based on the Torre dei Lamberti in Verona, Italy*

two into a one that amounts to more than two ones could be, with a goal of immortality. That this is also the usual structure of sexual reproduction is probably more than a mere coincidence. This numerology of romantic transcendence will recur emphatically in 'The Phoenix and Turtle' (lines 25–52). By this measure, what marks the failure of Verona to learn the key lesson of this story is less the opulent monumentalism of

FIGURE 2 *Romeo and Juliet in single-point perspective. Illustration by John Gleb.*

the statues than the simple fact that there will be two of them (Bandello at least leaves the lovers entombed together under 'a high marble Piller').[13]

Especially under the spell of this play, we may overall prefer to value column B over the less romantic column A, but in fact the columns cross-affiliate erratically: love enjoys darkness but creates light, for example, and hatred seems sharpest among the youth, who do more tragic dying, partly propelled by their privacy and their dreams. The only hope for a coherent meaning lies in the convergence of all these pairs (as it does in the binaries of *The Merchant of Venice* and *The Winter's Tale*). Since the parallel lines do not converge in two neat sets, perhaps we should picture the play as instead conceived in single-point perspective – a perspective that the play's ending cuts off just short of the vanishing-point where a full convergence may occur and implicitly continue invisibly into eternity (see fig.2).

By the end, Romeo has proven that the stony limits of Verona and the Capulet tomb cannot keep him out, while Juliet proves she will follow him even beyond this world. Juliet's ecstatic suicide suggests (as her 'Gallop apace' speech had hinted) that the risks and violence of sexuality can actually combine with the tenderness and devotion of romantic love, each magnifying the other, rather than cancelling each other as they did in the dirty jokes that permeate the first half of the play.

This brinkmanship concerning the resolution of binaries may also explain why Shakespeare chose to remove the moment in the Bandello source when Juliet awakens before Romeo expires – a moment so dramatically juicy that it has regularly been reinserted in production, including in films from Theda Bara's 1916 silent through Luhrmann's 1996 extravaganza, and in Garrick's rewrite that gave the lovers over fifty lines of sweet parting sorrow before the poison overcomes Romeo. Shakespeare also removes the extended display of the two bodies at the end of Brooke's poem from which he otherwise drew so heavily. The point where Romeo and Juliet (re-)meet occurs within a vanishing-point: the parallel lines may appear doomed (as standard geometry would dictate) to remain endlessly apart; but the lovers' perspective, as they leave us behind and disappear from our view, may be a convergence to a single shared point that implicitly continues beyond what our vision allows. If the lines were to intersect any earlier, within our field of view, then we would see them begin to diverge again, as necessarily happens by the end of such stagings.

A crucial value of literary consciousness, beginning at the small scale of metaphor, is its ability to break down a culture's facile binaries (which sell themselves as realism), including the binary of self and other, into something new, generative, and potentially more fully human. This seems to me the deepest pattern of *Romeo and Juliet*, and in fact of the Shakespearean 'negative capability' famously lauded by John Keats: it negates a destructive pairing that threatens to confirm a mere antithesis, offering in its place – through the (creative or illusionist) magic of art – an exciting and aesthetically pleasing synthesis, even if the transcendence of contradictions defies rational explanation. Such artworks can suggest both the dangers and the opportunities of pairings, which usually either merely repeat or cancel each other by conflict, but can sometimes become a mysteriously generative union. By 1594 Shakespeare had already written some tragedy and much comedy, and (as the ending of *Love's Labour's Lost* suggests) he must have seen the limitations – artistic, spiritual and commercial – of those genres as binary opposites. *Romeo and Juliet* shows that he saw some possibilities in super-colliding the opposed formulas to create a new kind of substance.

If Montague and Capulet can converge in this loving couple, allowing the personal world to shape a public world that now honours what had been private, and if male and female can combine also, as light and dark do imagistically around them, then perhaps we should look for the hopeful merging of the other binaries as well. Suicidal romantic fantasy may become the sanest path to immortality, imaginative language becomes reality and the dreams that you dare to dream really do come true.

The romantic idealist can suppose that the 'strange dream' Romeo narrates in the opening lines of Act 5 is both prophetic and optimistic (the ominous one at 1.4.50 seems so by then), given its mysterious foreknowledge that Juliet will soon be kissing the lips of his corpse, and the fact – which Romeo himself remarks is mysterious – that he was conscious of this revivifying passion while apparently dead. If the dream is paranormal precognition, then perhaps it constitutes 'joyful news' after all, because somewhere beyond the field of our overly realistic vision, there may be a magic resurrection of these two people by the intense power of their love. In fact, everyone who has ever seen this play has seen Romeo revive. The persistence of *Romeo and Juliet* itself affirms the play's most romantic reverie about Romeo and Juliet. For centuries adults have sat in theatres lamenting the way these lovers have allowed their passions to condemn them to an early death and yet, every day all over the world those same young lovers spring back into life precisely because they indulged those passions, and millions who have headed home maturely lamenting that indulgence lie forever cold and silent in their graves. It all depends on how we understand what Romeo calls 'a dateless bargain' and Juliet calls a 'timeless end' (5.3.115, 162).

Shakespeare – certainly interested, his sonnets show, in this idea that love can overcome death if it earns perpetually renewed attention from human eyes and ears – offers at least a faint suggestion that Romeo and Juliet have somehow slipped out of the frame of the picture. Just as love could never pull itself completely free from death in this play, here their mortality cannot entirely exclude the power of their mutual devotion. The difference between what the immature Romeo called 'love-devouring death' and love devouring death is remarkably minimal. Romeo conceivably awakens to Juliet's last kiss on a comic stage at the back of the tragic looking-glass, where *amor vincit omnia*. As in Romeo's oxymoron, this sleep is and is not a perpetual awakening. Like Balthasar in the graveyard, we are left wondering whether we have seen, or merely dreamed, the ultimate death-defying fulfilment of romance. Have they counted down from two to one to zero, or instead to something like infinity – a real *Liebestod* in an imaginary garden?

I don't believe it for a minute. Sometimes I do, however, for a whole precious second. Teachers are likely to remain – unlike some of their adolescent students – stuck back on this side of the glass, clinging to the accommodationist common sense that long life has bred, and that has bred long life, in an associated pair: the Nurse and Friar Laurence. My notion, that Capulet might have been amenable to the marriage Juliet craves but conceals, supports Hugh Grady's observation that critics who read the play as Aristotelian tragedy overlook 'the play's strong assertion of the reality of other possibilities, of the role of chance and accident in the fatal denouement'. My hyper-sentimental insistence on a comic possibility, even after the lovers die, pushes toward and maybe beyond Grady's broader observation that moralizing readings overlook 'this play's *aesthetic* qualities, its status as *other* than reality, its creation of a counter-factual space in which ... love and desire persist even when they are represented as defeated by larger forces'.[14] Is that hope really 'counter-factual', or just outside of the universe we can see as factual? Are we not given a little encouragement to believe that (as Juliet puts it, anticipating their first passionate embrace in the darkness) our 'eyes may wink, and Romeo / Leap to these arms, untalked of and unseen' (3.2.6–7)?

A happier Verona could easily have happened (and a better world as well, according to deconstructionist readings of race, class, gender, etc.), if people stopped granting dominion to the binaries. The play explicitly ends with the reconciliation and cross-recognition of the Montague and Capulet clans, which implies some kind of ultimate union for Romeo and Juliet – either complete or imminent – after many provisional attempts, and of female and male identities (including attitudes, appetites and verbal styles)[15] within that merger. They therefore have reconciled Eros and Thanatos as well, and thereby merged conventionally opposed genres. They even reconcile the deadly feud that was ravaging Christian Europe: Juliet and Romeo's initial sparring about what the physicality of spiritual life (pilgrimages to shrines that reflect the power of touch and of saints) has to do with language (the power of private prayer to replace despair with a saving faith) raises a possibility fulfilled only when Catholic iconophilia, in the form of the penitent statues, becomes compatible with a Protestant emphasis on the power of faith, hope and charity, embodied only in the word, to confer resurrection. That resurrection takes place when an ultimate darkness the Prince attributes to hate is somehow permeated with the light produced by love. By proposing immortality, this moment erases any opposition between youth and age. It also entails the triumphant absorption of sexual violence into erotic love, completing Juliet's revision of the Lucrece story.[16]

The witness for Romeo's defence should of course be Lord Montague: symmetry demands it. But symmetry demands lots of things that creative artists – and humane societies – are rightly reluctant to grant. My least favourite emendation of Shakespeare – the understandable mistake of calling the Lord Capulet speech heading 'an obvious mistake' – makes every kind of sense but Shakespearean sense. Remember that *lectio difficilior potior* has been, for nearly three centuries, a fundamental precept for deciding which reading of an old text probably matches the original: favour the more difficult reading over a simple, easy, comfortable one, since the latter is more likely to have been introduced by intervening scribes, typesetters, or editors, all just trying to be sensible.

Binary rhetoric

What the cellular structure of *Romeo and Juliet* – the fibrous material with which it is built – keeps telling us is that the world consists of pairs and they are either identical or opposite: echo or chiasmus, but never merger. Shakespeare converts the Euphuistic rhetorical fad of the early 1590s, which was mostly a running joke on the characters' formulaic pretentions in *Love's Labour's Lost*, into a vehicle for smuggling the play's themes of collapsing binary division into the very fabric of the play's language. In *Romeo and Juliet*, the poetics reflect the long struggle of two to become something more as well as something fewer.

Shakespeare begins the play with the word 'Two' and reinforces the twinning twice more ('both alike') in that first line of the opening Prologue:

> Two households, both alike in dignity,
> In fair Verona, where we lay our scene,
> From ancient grudge break to new mutiny,
> Where civil blood makes civil hands unclean.
> From forth the fatal loins of these two foes
> A pair of star-crossed lovers take their life …
>
> (Prol.1–6)

After counterpoising 'ancient' and 'new', and doubling 'civil', Shakespeare reminds us that two couples (with two 'loins' each) created our protagonists, inviting subliminal attention to 'forth' as 'fourth', the more so since we are about to hear, twice, 'parents' – a word that echoes 'pair'.[17] He then gives us 'two' balanced across the enjambment with 'pair' – the singular version of the matching plural – and ends the line with the seeming solecism 'their life', paired two lines later with 'their death' and again signalling (as the singular/plural slippages of 'doth' and 'is' in lines 8 and 12 arguably do also) the possibility of two lives merging into one (or into none). This renders birth and death – the two senses of 'take their life': conception through those parental loins or suicide – indistinguishable, as I have argued the play's ending does also, leaving us wondering whether the 'passage' of the love of the two children of the two families was a passing away or a passage away. If Shakespeare then called the story 'the two hours' traffic of our stage' to reinforce the numerical pattern here rather than as an accurate estimate of the duration of a Renaissance performance, then much scholarly energy has been wasted speculating about cuts and pacing. After a request that each one of us lend our pair of 'ears', we are cued to hear the concluding 'strive to mend' echoing 'strife' and 'end' from a few lines earlier: another pair of pairings, but this time slightly askew instead of matched with their originals, with their destructive force converted into reparative force – the crucial move this article will be tracing in the play.

Shakespeare launches into an opening scene of sharp oppositions, with the symmetry of the feud permeating the syntax of the conversations, through the culminating cries from both sides: 'Down with the Capulets, down with the Montagues!' (1.1.72). At that moment the Prince, exasperated with the binary feud, steps in to condemn it with his own antonymic devices, calling the brawlers 'you men, you beasts' whose neighbours must use their hands, 'Cankered with peace, to part your cankered hate' (1.1.81, 93).

Oppositions in feelings and of families are relentlessly expressed in oppositional rhetorical forms, as in Juliet's 'My only love sprung from my only hate, / Too early seen unknown, and known too late!' (1.5.137–8). Soon she will twice in quick succession ask the Nurse whether the news from Romeo is 'good or bad' (2.5.35–7). It is hardly surprising that audiences and editors are unprepared to believe that Lord Capulet breaks that pattern of divisive doubles, when it has just been so systematically reinforced by his Lady: 'For blood of ours shed blood of Montague. / O cousin, cousin! ... Affection makes him false; he speaks not true', followed in the next two lines by her double use of 'twenty' (3.1.151–2, 179–81).

There seemed to be more doubling of words and phrases in *Romeo and Juliet* than in any other Shakespeare play I could think of. As a quick sample, I studied the use of 'Alack' and discovered that it is doubled in three of eight uses in this tragedy, but only six of seventy-three uses elsewhere in Shakespeare's works. Fortunately, it has become relatively easy to evaluate that kind of impression more extensively, so I worked with Dave Shepard at UCLA's Center for Digital Humanities to develop a Python-based program to calculate how many doubles – words or phrases spoken twice, and no more than twice, in immediate succession – each play contained. We excluded instances fewer than four characters in length, to avoid over-weighing common brief words unlikely to register with audiences as significantly repetitive.[18]

The results gratifyingly verified my impression. *Romeo and Juliet* is the only Shakespeare play where such pairs constitute more than 1 per cent of the word-count (it also led all the rest when we re-tested counting doubles separated by no more than one word, where it rises to nearly 2 per cent, and also across any two lines). The peak is 4.4, the brief scene of preparations for Juliet's forced wedding to Paris, with over 3 per cent simple pairings; no other scene reaches even 2 per cent. By useful contrast, the final scene of the play virtually erases this mode of unreconciled pairs. Every other scene in the play runs over 0.1 per cent, but that scene plummets to 0.04 per cent. What we hear – aptly if subliminally, and most clearly in the language of the lovers themselves – is the demise of the play's burdensome two-ness.

The other statistical trials I attempted – this time with the excellent assistance of Craig Messner, a UCLA doctoral student – suggest that the pattern is even more pervasive than Harry Levin estimated, and also more artfully configured. In lines containing antonyms, *Romeo and Juliet* outpaced all thirty-five other Shakespeare plays tested (415, with *Cymbeline* a distant second at 364). A similar dominance emerges in lines containing immediate doubles followed by an antonymic line: *Romeo and Juliet* again leads, with 12 such sequences; *Troilus*

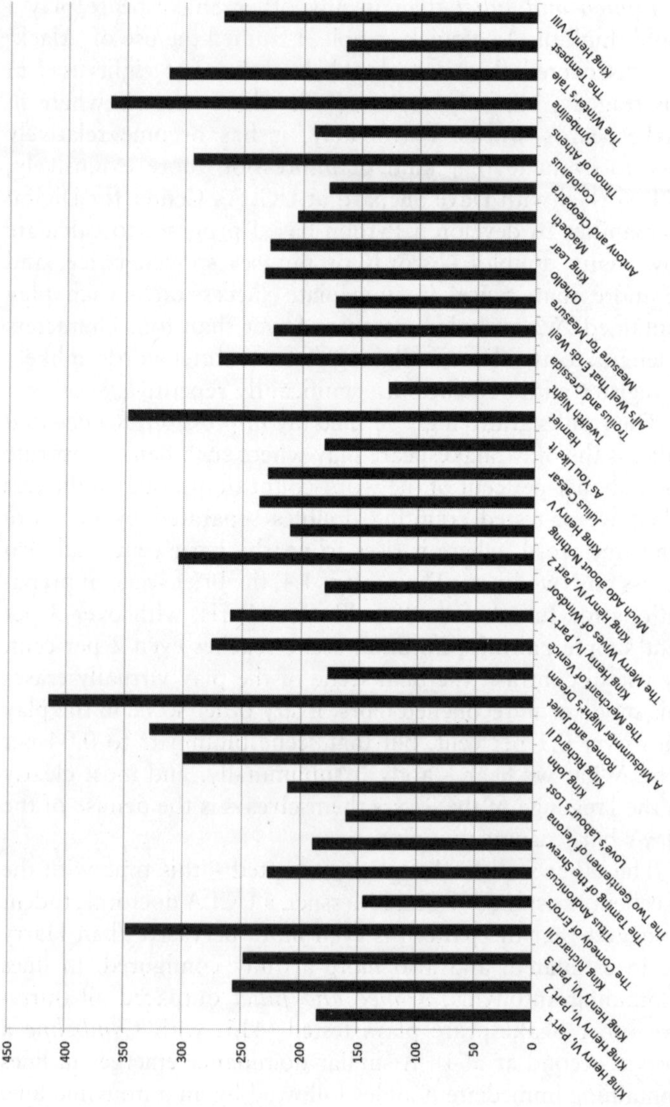

FIGURE 3 *Instances of a word and its antonym in the same line.*

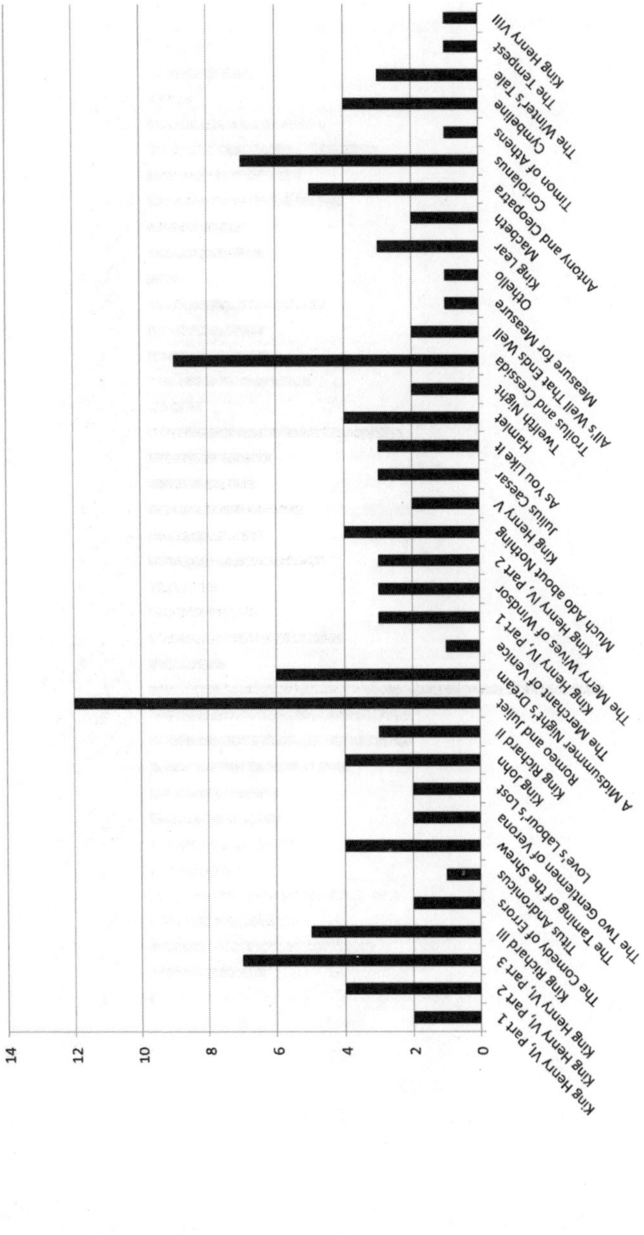

FIGURE 4 *Instances of a word-and-antonym-line following a line with a doubled word or phrase.*

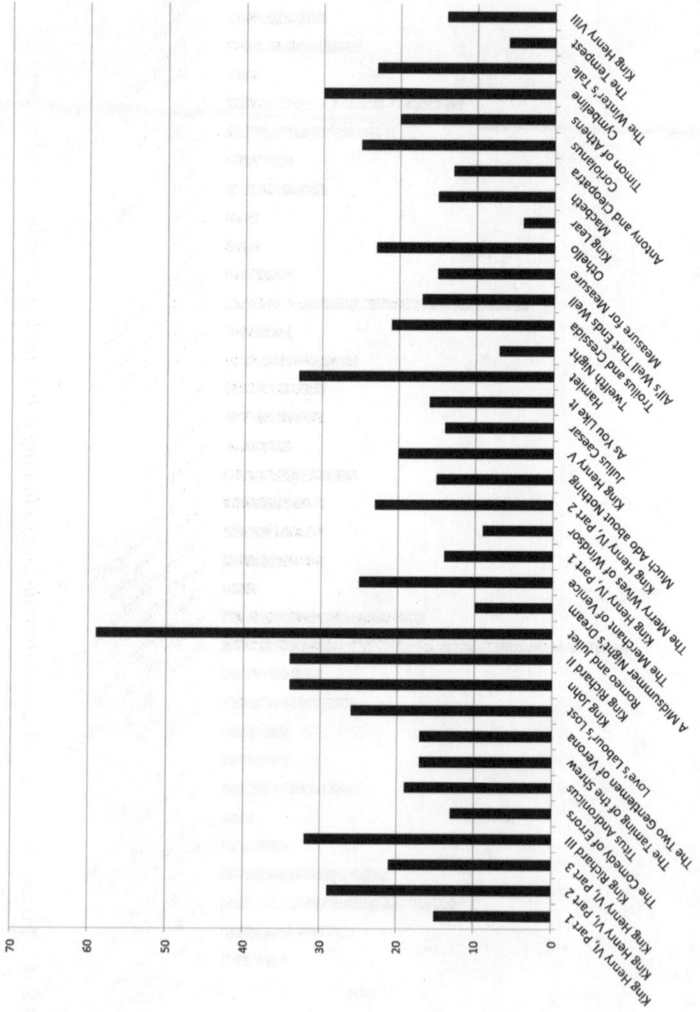

FIGURE 5 *Instances of a doubled word or phrase with its antonym in the same line.*

and Cressida is next, with 9. Intriguingly, *Troilus* – another play largely about uneasy matches at the boundary of the personal and the political – also finishes second in the number of immediate doublings in single lines, and narrowly edges out *Romeo* for the highest number of such doublings over two lines. If we cease to demand that the doublings be immediate, the results are no less compelling. *Romeo* has the most repeated words within single lines and within pairs of lines, and is second only to *King John* in antonymic lines following lines with doubled words. The most decisive lead in any of our half-dozen trials – and these are the complete results; I have not cherry-picked among trials to omit results less supportive of my theory – is in doubles with antonyms in same line: *Romeo and Juliet* has fifty-nine, more than three times the median, and no other Shakespeare play has more than thirty-four.[19]

Friar Laurence's introductory soliloquy, set on the boundary between night and day, relentlessly breaks apparent binary oppositions, despite the way his couplets and zeugmatic syntax structurally resist that project. He seems the right man to cure Verona, since the essence of his wisdom and his project, even before Romeo reports falling in love with Juliet, is bringing opposites together (2.3.1–22). He is also therefore an apt audience for Romeo's plea for a surprising match: 'As mine on hers, so hers is set on mine, / And all combined, save what thou must combine / By holy marriage', because, unlike Rosaline, Juliet 'Doth grace for grace and love for love allow' (2.3.55–7, 82). The second act ends with two rhetorical pairs that rhyme with each other and channel themselves directly into the plot's chief project of pairing:

JULIET
I cannot sum up sum of half my wealth.

FRIAR LAURENCE
Come, come with me, and we will make short work,
For, by your leaves, you shall not stay alone
Till holy church incorporate two in one.

(2.6.34–7)

'Half' prepares us for 'two in one', the two are forbidden to stay 'alone', and the double 'come' sets up the antonymic meaning of 'leaves', which lingers in tension with 'stay'.

Romeo's first substantial speech – an extended overture of the play's themes of paired Petrarchan oxymora – shows how badly Romeo needs a cure for contradictions:

Here's much to do with hate, but more with love.
Why then, O brawling love, O loving hate,
O anything of nothing first create,
O heavy lightness, serious vanity,
Misshapen chaos of well-seeming forms,
Feather of lead, bright smoke, cold fire, sick health,
Still-waking sleep that is not what it is.
This love feel I that feel no love in this.
Dost thou not laugh?

BENVOLIO
No, coz, I rather weep.
(1.1.173–81)

Much of the play will be spent showing that love and brawls can intensify each other, even if sprung from seemingly nothing, and can make heavy spirits banter lightly with weighty implications. Eventually the play shows (taking off from Romeo's assertion that love is 'A madness most discreet, / A choking gall and a preserving sweet' [1.1.191–2]) that the madness of the lovers can be discretion, and the discretion of their mentors can be madness; and that a poison can sometimes be the cordial a heart most craves, and possibly one that preserves by killing.[20]

This transition from Romeo's set-piece to Benvolio's response (**is not/is**, **love/no love**, laugh/weep; I will put echoes in bold font while underlining antonyms) typifies a symptomatic pattern in the play's rhetoric: a balanced pairing, or often a pair of such pairings, that devolve into a more explicitly antagonistic symmetry. This movement, which the statistics show to be exceptionally persistent in this play, is the anti-climax, the failed merger that tantalizes its audiences and characters, in large ways and small. We keep being deprived of the reconciliation that Lord Capulet's forgiveness toward Romeo could have produced.

In fact, we have already been intensely sensitized to this pattern – echoes yielding to opposition – in Romeo's life before we even meet him. His father laments,

> **Many** a **morning** hath he there **been seen**,
> With tears augmenting the fresh **morning**'s dew,
> Adding to **clouds** more **clouds** with his deep sighs.
> But **all** so **soon** as the **all**-cheering **sun**
> **Should** in the farthest east begin to draw
> The **shad**y curtains from Aurora's bed,
> Away from light steals home my heavy son,
> And private in his chamber pens himself,
> Shuts up his windows, locks fair day**light** out
> And makes himself an artificial night.
>
> (1.1.129–38)

Later in this opening scene, Romeo tells Benvolio, 'A sick man **in sadness** makes his will; / A word **ill** urged to one that is so **ill. / In sadness**, cousin, I do love a woman'; and adds, 'She is **too fair, too wise, wisely too fair,** / To merit bliss by making me despair' (1.1.200–2, 219–20). Romeo is complaining here about Rosaline, whose name matches his but then veers off, as does her understanding of where their love should lead.

Consider another instance of this collapse: Benvolio says, 'We'll **measure** them a **measure** and be gone' and Romeo replies, 'Give me a torch. I **am** not for this **ambling, / Being** but heavy I will bear the light' (1.4.10–12). Matching becomes violent opposition again when Tybalt asks the Montagues for 'a **word with one of** you', Mercutio replies, 'And but one **word with one of** us? Couple it with something, make it a word and a blow' (3.1.37–9).

After Romeo kills Tybalt, Juliet struggles with a Petrarchan paradox that seems to resolve into a chiastic balance headed in a positive direction, but again it veers off into a mere uneasy contradiction:

> **My husband lives that Tybalt would have slain,**
> **And Tybalt's dead that would have slain my husband.**
> All this is comfort. Wherefore weep I then?
> (3.2.105–7)

A different version of this doubling of words (some of which are simultaneously antonymic) appears when Juliet pairs two senses of 'long' before bringing 'speak' into direct collision with itself, framed by the repetition of a pair of rhyme words that ended the previous scene: 'Be not so **long** to speak. I **long** to die, / If what thou speak'st speak not of **remedy**' (4.1.66–7). In keeping with the thematic, and I think subtly optimistic, tension (about whether passionate love imposes mortality or instead confers immortality) that culminates the opening chorus and finally the entire play, Juliet had first moved from 'remedy' to 'die', but now instead moves from 'die' to 'remedy'. Eventually she explicates this idea by hoping that kissing Romeo's poisoned body will 'make me die with a restorative' (5.3.166).

The ominous version of this pattern permeates the newlyweds' parting at dawn:

> JULIET
> **Some say the lark** makes sweet **division;**
> This doth not so, for she **divideth** us.
> **Some say the lark** and loathed toad **change** eyes.
> **O, now** I would they had **changed** voices too,
> Since **arm from arm** that voice doth us affray,
> **Hunt**ing thee **hence** with **hunt's**-up to the day.
> **O, now** be gone! **More light and light** it grows.
>
> ROMEO
> **More light and light, more dark and dark** our woes.
> (3.5.29–36)

And twenty-three lines later, the same couple produces a double double that leads to a split double that launches the paradox:

ROMEO
Adieu, adieu! *Exit*

JULIET
O **Fortune, Fortune**, all men call thee **fickle.**
If thou art fickle, what dost thou with him
That is renowned for faith?

(3.5.59–62)

Three lines later, the pattern of pairing lost to opposition continues: 'Who **is't** that calls? **It is** my lady mother. / Is she not down **so** late, or up **so** early?' (3.5.65–6). Lord Capulet's attempt to force an unwelcome match on Juliet then generates a crescendo of this pattern in less than seventeen lines: '**take** me **with** you, **take** me **with** you ... **Doth she not** ... **Doth she not** ... Unworthy ... **worthy** ... Not **proud you have, but thankful that you have.** / **Proud** ... what I hate, / **But thankful** even for **hate** that is meant love ... **How, how, how, how** ... '**Proud**' and '**I thank you**', and '**I thank you not**', / And yet '**not proud**'? ... **Thank** me **no thankings** nor **proud** me **no prouds** ... **Out, you** ... **Out, you** ... **Fie, fie**' (3.5.141–57).

In fact, a similar tendency is discernible from the beginning of this forced pairing, with Lord Capulet telling Paris:

One **more**, most welcome, makes my number **more**.
At my poor house look to behold this night
Earth-treading stars that make dark heaven light.
Such comfort as do lusty young men feel
When well-**apparelled April** on the heel
Of limping winter treads, even such delight
Among fresh fennel buds shall you this night
Inherit at my house. **Hear all, all** see,
And like her **most** whose **merit most** shall be;
Which, on **more** view, of **many mine** being one,

> May stand in number, though in reckoning **none**.
> Come, go with me.
>
> (1.2.22–33)

The middle syllable of 'inherit' echoes in 'hear', and – with the tension between hereditary and earned social rank so prominent in the Renaissance – the word both echoes and opposes 'merit', which echoes in 'more', which echoes the echo from nine lines earlier.

As soon as the wedding plan is in place, Lord Capulet tells Paris, 'it is so very late that we / May call it early **by and by**' (3.4.34–5; Q1 and the folios also double the 'very' here). Paris follows the pattern on his own bitterly anticlimactic wedding-day: 'By **cruel, cruel** thee quite overthrown. / **O love, O life, not life** but **love** in death' (4.5.57–8). Capulet's reply works the same kind of collapse into a single line: **'O child, O child, my soul** and **not my child**!' (4.5.62). Romeo receives an acute version of this disappointment from the same misleading report:

> ROMEO
> **How doth my lady**? Is my father **well**?
> **How doth my** Juliet? That I ask again,
> For **nothing can be ill** if she **be well**.
>
> BALTHASAR
> Then she **is well** and **nothing can be ill**.
> Her body sleeps in Capel's monument,
> And her immortal part with angels lives.
>
> (5.1.14–19)

The project of bringing-together seems further off than ever, death having reportedly parted her (by Christian dualism) as well as them. Romeo then tells the apothecary, '**The world** is not thy friend, nor **the world's** law; / **The world** affords no law to make thee rich, / Then be not poor' (5.1.72–4). The rhetoric of *Romeo and Juliet* thus leads us to expect nothing when pairings break down except a collapse into unhappy opposition.

After Romeo leaves for Mantua, Juliet shows her wit by choosing words that simultaneously satisfy her mother's expectation that she too would want to murder Romeo, and her own need to express a different sort of desire for him (3.5.74–102). She must somehow match her mother's vengeful speech while finally saying the opposite: a piece of verbal tightrope-walking that is possible only because the line between death-wishing and love-desire is so thin in this play's opposing passions. So, within three lines of which they share the middle line, Juliet matches Lady Capulet's 'feel', 'loss', 'friend' and 'weep' with 'Feeling', 'loss', 'weep' and 'friend', to opposite effect (3.5.75–7; see similarly 3.5.114–17).

Many of the things that bothered Samuel Johnson about this play make sense as aspects of Shakespeare's strategy. Romeo may not yet 'deserve all this antithesis' in his first big Petrarchan speech; perhaps '*Juliet's* equivocations are rather too artful' in fending off her mother after Tybalt's death; and one may reasonably ask, 'But why does *Shakespeare* give *Romeo* this involuntary cheerfulness just before the extremity of unhappiness?' as he recounts his paradoxically optimistic dream on his way toward the Capulet tomb.[21] As an Enlightenment rationalist fond of neat judgements based in zeugma and other antonymic forms, Johnson would not have been inclined to see the rhetorical doublings as designed to fail, nor to see transcendent value in their ultimate failure. Wit can yoke some opposites together, but judgement dismisses that as a reckless accomplishment of fantasy. Johnson therefore overlooks the possibility that Shakespeare was deliberately overachieving on his verbal pairings as a symptom of his play-world – and (perhaps consequently) the possibility that Lord Capulet might have sought to mitigate the feud.

More recent editors of *Romeo and Juliet* have understood what Dr Johnson did not. Levenson's introduction suggests that: 'Several well-known passages labour devices as if they were inviting a critical assessment of both the schemes and their effects.'[22] Frank Kermode's no less wonderful introduction to the play in the *Riverside Shakespeare* similarly observes that

Shakespeare has 'the Capulets vie with Paris' conventional outcries and the absurd lamentations of the Nurse over Juliet's body' to increase the appeal of the more authentic-sounding speech the lovers develop.[23] I suspect that Shakespeare was inviting mistrust of the formative consciousness underlying the feud and its analogues by provoking mistrust of, and impatience with, the rhetorical antitheses used to express it. This fulfils another of Romeo's early oxymora: 'Misshapen chaos of well-seeming forms' (1.1.177).

All this is enough to make me question some other generally accepted emendations of Q2 that erase what look like accidental doublings in the text of *Romeo and Juliet*: the nearly identical four-line speeches given to Romeo and the Friar in 2.2 and 2.3 respectively, and especially Romeo's doubled doubling, the first two lines of which are generally now omitted (and were therefore omitted from my statistics), but could express mounting indignation, like the repetitions in Mark Antony's eulogy (*Julius Caesar* 3.2.74–108):

> [This may flies do, when I from this must fly,
> And sayest thou yet, that exile is not death?]
> But Romeo may not, he is banished.
> Flies may do this, but I from this must fly;
> They are free men, but I am banished:
> And sayest thou yet that exile is not death? (3.3.40–2)[24]

What Shakespeare finally hints is that death may not actually be exile, or at least that an eternal exile from the world might bring Romeo more fully together with Juliet than would otherwise be possible.

Lord Capulet seems quite aware that pairing Juliet off requires bringing together various opposites: 'Day, night, hour, tide, time, work, play, / Alone, in company, still my care hath been / To have her matched' (3.5.177–9). What he doesn't know is that a marriage to Romeo was ever emotionally feasible, let alone factual, and that this marriage to Paris would be what the Nurse calls a 'second match'.

This proposed (re-)marriage – seemingly near but fundamentally impossible – is aptly couched in a series of lurking oppositions:

CAPULET
And too **soon** marred are those **so early married.** [made, Q2]

(1.2.13)

LADY CAPULET
And see how one another lends content;
And what obscured in this fair volume lies
Find written in the margent of his eyes.
This precious book of love, this unbound lover,
To beautify him only **lacks** a cover.
The fish lives in the sea, and 'tis much pride
For **fair without the fair within** to hide.
That book in many's eyes doth share the glory
That **in gold clasps locks in** the **gold**en story.
So **sha**ll you **sha**re all that he doth possess,
By having him, making yourself no less.
(1.3.85–95)

JULIET
I'll **look to like**, if **looking liking** move,

(1.3.98)

NURSE
seek **happy** nights **to happy** days.

(1.3.106)

PARIS
These **times** of woe afford no **times** to woo.

(3.4.8)

This pattern becomes acutely visible when Juliet symmetrically parries Paris's verbal advances at 4.1.18–36 – itself a negative double of Juliet's initial word-duel with Romeo (1.5.92–109), which is paired on the love/hate axis with Tybalt's double duel with Mercutio and Romeo, which is itself another instance of Shakespeare's relentless pairing, since Brooke did not provide any slain Mercutio to balance against a slain Tybalt. And when that marriage does fall direly short of completion, Lord Capulet's rhetoric, in a dark double of the Friar's introductory speech, stresses broken pairs:

> All things that we ordained **festival**
> Turn from their office to black **funeral**:
> Our instruments to melancholy bells,
> Our wedding cheer to a sad burial feast,
> Our **solemn** hymns to **sullen** dirges change;
> Our bridal flowers serve for a buried corse,
> And all things change them to the contrary.
>
> (4.5.84–90)

The persistence of weak doubling and strong opposition in the verbal life of Verona, in a closing scene where the lovers have evicted that pattern from their speech, shows that their world has missed – and perhaps thereby caused future editors and their readers to miss – the potential for harmonious union. Friar Laurence says:

> I will be **brief**, for .... short **date** of **breath**
> Is not so long as is a tedious tale.
> Romeo, **there dead**, was husband to that Juliet,
> And she, **there dead**, that's Romeo's faithful wife.
> I **married** them, and their stol'n **marriage day**
> Was Tybalt's dooms**day**....
>
> (5.3.229–34)

After a couplet from Lord Capulet that balances 'rich' with 'poor', the Prince closes the tragedy with a rhymed sestet that uses 'more' twice, thus doubling the paired 'more' exchanged by Capulet and Montague as an awkwardly identical rhyme just a few lines earlier, matching the unsatisfactory compensation of dual statues. The Prince, who had convergently asserted, 'All are punished' just thirteen lines earlier, reverts to the pattern of doubling followed by opposition: '**Some** shall be pardoned and **some** punished' (5.3.295, 308).

It need not have been so. Hidden in the line stolen from Lord Capulet is another reality that could have been: another of the play's tantalizing near misses, lost in a disastrous loyalty to symmetry. That lost chance represents another strand in the string-theory of multiverses, to which literature has always been our best access. But editors and directors have taken the words right out of his mouth. Capulet's attempted exoneration of Romeo shows how the textual history of a play can limit interpretation, and how studying that history can liberate interpretation. Perhaps this example also offers a meta-critical refutation of the binary that sets close reading and textual editing against distant reading, thematic analysis and critique of socio-political dysfunctions.

It took the twenty-first century's most popular songwriter of failed love affairs, Taylor Swift, to recognize a possibility in the most popular sixteenth-century love-tragedy that scholarly commentators in the centuries between have consistently overlooked:

Romeo save me I've been feeling so alone
I keep waiting for you but you never come
Is this in my head? I don't know what to think
He knelt to the ground and pulled out a ring
And said, marry me Juliet, you'll never have to be alone
I love you and that's all I really know
I talked to your dad, go pick out a white dress
It's a love story baby just say yes[25]

Even the movement away from the paired placements of 'alone' at the start of the stanzas, and the progress from slant rhymes to a full rhyme, make this a suitable affirmation of the

Shakespearean project. Perhaps this is just a dying fantasy: that the lost loved ones reunite in the light at the end of an endless tunnel. But the music video of Swift's 'Love Story' suggests it is instead (another) reincarnation of the Renaissance lovers all these centuries later, and now they can be happy ever after within this world.[26] Perhaps all Romeo had to do was talk to Lord Capulet, and perhaps all Juliet had to do was what the Nurse repeatedly recalls her doing as a toddler: 'leave crying and say "Ay"' (1.3.52). The love story goes on, if we let it. Let's at least say – as Lord Capulet might have – 'maybe'.

5

New Directions: *Romeo and Juliet*'s Understudies

William W. West

There are no small parts, only small actors.
KONSTANTIN STANISLAVSKI[1]

In the film *Shakespeare in Love* (1998), the character Shakespeare finds the heroic romance-adventure he sets out to write becoming more and more saturated in his blossoming love affair with a gentlewoman. He gradually pares down the vaunting part of lead player Ned Alleyn's to make more room for the lover's role Shakespeare identifies with, finally deciding to kill off Alleyn's character in the third act, thus transforming the play into a love story that turns out to be *Romeo and Juliet*. *Shakespeare in Love* comically proposes a zero-sum theory of theatre, in which the substitution of Shakespeare's Romeo for Alleyn's Marlovian Mercutio marks a hinge between different epochs of theatre: writers' and actors', tragic and heroic, emotionally true and bombastically stagey, between, in a word, Shakespearean and pre-Shakespearean. Life to Mercutio would be death to Romeo, the film insists, and so Mercutio must die.

This account of Mercutio's demise follows the claim of Restoration critic, playwright and gossip John Dryden that 'Shakespear ... was forc'd to kill [Mercutio] in the third Act, to prevent being killed by him.' [2] Since Dryden Mercutio has seemed to many other interpreters to be the play's edgy breakout star, and a whole new world.[3] His abrupt disappearance has also looked suspiciously like a case of the authorial murder of a scene-stealing second fiddle.[4] But although Mercutio is exceptional – 'a man possessing all the elements of a Poet: high fancy; rapid thoughts; the whole world was, as it were, subject to his law of association ... a perfect gentleman', concludes Coleridge – in *Romeo and Juliet* he is not an exception.[5] I would liken parts like Mercutio's to the play's understudies. *Romeo and Juliet* is full of them.

The understudy waits in the play's wings, shadowing the more prominent parts, for his or her opportunity to take, or take over, the stage, any instant the play allows it. Mercutio, for instance, dies of a double displacement. First, he takes Romeo's place in the fight with Tybalt, then he is stabbed when Romeo tries to re-take Mercutio's place and steps between Tybalt and Mercutio. The nineteenth-century Romantic Samuel Taylor Coleridge argues against Dryden that the fascination of Mercutio and his death are both necessary to the lovers' plot; this unlucky juncture alone can explain why Romeo forgets himself, kills Tybalt in his fury, and sets the catastrophe of the plot in motion. But Coleridge misunderstands the danger in Mercutio that Dryden recognized – it was not Shakespeare who was threatened, but *Romeo and Juliet* as the story of two lovers rather than of one swashbuckling dreamer. And while Coleridge thought that Mercutio's story was only part of Romeo and Juliet's larger one, he repeatedly found his attention drawn away from the play by the Nurse, who threatens to take over the stage whenever she begins to speak.[6] Other figures like Tybalt, Friar Laurence, even the textually insignificant part of Peter, a servant of the Montagues whose speech-prefixes in the 'bad' first quarto show that the part was played by the great improviser Will Kemp, are no less lethal, in that they lead us to forget the plot they repeatedly wander from. The play is torn between two impulses, the lovers' single-minded pursuit of moving in love beyond the power of words to name or describe, and everything else in it. In this chapter I want to make the case for everything else.

Before everything else, though, *Romeo and Juliet* is a play of monumentalization, of the falling into ruin of quick bright things (love, hope, human bodies) and their settling into something more stable and less lively (détente, memory, civil institutions).[7] It would be monumental even if it were not for its long history by the time Shakespeare came to write his version, and even if it were not for its subsequent crystallization into *the* emblematic story of embattled young love.[8] The play's bid for stillness begins with the opening lines of the Prologue, which introduce the enmity of 'Two households, both alike in dignity' (Prol. 1), then inform its audiences that:

From forth the fatal loins of these two foes
A pair of star-crossed lovers take their life,
Whose misadventured piteous overthrows
Doth with their death bury their parents' strife.
(Prol. 5–8)

The rage and desire that set the plot in violent motion are equally planted in the earth at the end of the play.[9]

The Prologue to *Romeo and Juliet* is a sonnet, a conspicuously written poetic form that declares the Prologue's fixity in a tradition unlike the mobile, musical, performative ones rehearsed daily in playing.[10] It lies before the action of the play like a headstone, its grave and graven status anticipating the statues that at the end of the play will be pledged to stand in place of the lovers. The Prologue's static prescriptiveness – formally as an example of the most regular kind of poem in ordinary Elizabethan use, diegetically in its balancing synopsis of the play's opposing voices and forces, dramaturgically in the promised end it points to – insists on the inevitability of what it calls: 'The fearful passage of their death-marked love' (Prol. 9). It reminds its audiences, past and future, that what 'the two hours' traffic of our stage' (Prol., 12) is about to show has nevertheless been written down in advance like an oracle.

When the Prologue concludes, 'What here shall miss, our toil shall strive to mend' (Prol. 14), 'toil' has something of the sense of *a snare*: performance will be a trap that catches anything that might escape the fatality that the Prologue predicts.[11] The stage's 'traffic', not yet begun, will be a 'passage' that is from the perspective of the Prologue already complete. But from another perspective, one that the Prologue itself names, this line limns a struggle between the story of the Prologue and the unfolding of the play. '[H]ere' suggests a particular deictic accessibility, achieved and shared, whether in space or time (the time of the Prologue? the space of the playhouse? and what of Afghanistan, Sarajevo or Baghdad, spaces that also name particular times when the social world is unmade?). The 'toil' then contrasts with the immediacy of 'here', anticipatory, incomplete, a process of working out or working through, a sort of 'passage' that need not arrive where it is directed, a journey that may differ from its destination. Even more aptly, the 'toil' may allow a 'continuance' (Prol. 10) that does not conclude anything, but simply prorogues (a word Romeo tellingly rejects below Juliet's window) the action, unfinished, into the future. Between 'here' and 'toil' lies the difference between the centripetal force of the narrative and its centrifugal extension and diffusion across the bodies and actions of the players who, as the Prologue speaks, are about to enact it. '*What* here shall miss', and how could the 'toil' of performance 'mend' it? What are the differences, in other words, between the story the Prologue tells and the working out of the play that follows it?[12]

'Patient ears attend[ing]' (Prol. 13) to *Romeo and Juliet*, rightly or wrongly, usually take the Prologue at its word: the play is about true lovers, star-crossed, death-marked, love and death equally inevitable in this story. As fates, love and death do not seem intertwined as if by sheer bad luck.

By pre-scripting or prescribing the story of its protagonists, the Prologue seeks to immunize its audiences against coming down with hopes of a happy ending that performance will, in its two hours' traffic, repeatedly raise and repeatedly discourage.[13] The protagonists, too, seem ready, even eager, to make the passage from love to death, as if death were love's necessary destination.[14] Just after meeting Romeo for the first time, before she knows his name or family, Juliet predicts, 'If he be married, / My grave is like to be my wedding bed' (1.5.133–4); under her window later that night, Romeo refuses to flee from the danger of her family discovering him there: 'My life were better ended by their hate / Than death prorogued, wanting of thy love' (2.2.77–8). Even the play's grammar concurs in discovering death in love: the same lines that describe the lovers' births – 'From forth the fatal loins of these two foes/ A pair of star-crossed lovers take their life' – also announce their suicides – 'A pair of star-crossed lovers take their life.' To receive new life, as a gift that cannot be refused, from the love-making of one's parents and to choose death rather than continued life are both forms of life-taking.

There is of course a long habit by which surpassing love conjures the spectre of its opposite, or perhaps its double: death. Love seems driven to confront death as if in a mirror, as its fiercest test and inevitable end, as detailed meticulously in Denis de Rougement's cultural history of tales of love or recorded more offhandedly in the well-known puns on *dying* in Elizabethan plays.[15] Although it certainly did not invent this relation, over the four hundred years of its reception, *Romeo and Juliet* has become one of the most culturally influential expressions of the uncomfortably pleasurable interlacing of love and death. Certainly when couples are baptized Romeos and Juliets in Baghdad, Sarajevo, on the West Side or in Afghanistan, it is not just because of their love but because death is weighed against it. This is not to say that the play embraces de Rougement's influential description of erotic love as a compulsion towards death, or even Friar Laurence's slightly different fear that, 'These violent delights have violent ends' (2.6.9), although these outlooks certainly have a part in the play. Self-destructive *Liebestod*, that kisses and consumes 'like fire and powder' (2.6.10), does not seem adequate to Romeo and Juliet, who would much rather not die in each other even if they foresee their deaths in each other.[16] Almost the last words that Juliet hears Romeo speak express his desire that 'all these woes shall serve / For sweet discourses in our times to come' (3.5.52–3), salvaging present pain with hopes of a future, earthly sweetness. It is not that Romeo and Juliet's love initiates 'a race towards death', as Julia Kristeva forcefully but, I think, incorrectly asserts.[17] Instead the play seems to show that death must be the condition of any love so single-minded that it considers nothing but its own fulfilment. Transcendent love, axiomatically enough, transcends everything else, and in worldly terms this surpassing of things is called *death*.[18] *Romeo and Juliet were born for one another* and *Romeo and Juliet cannot live without one another* are almost logically entailed statements. For Romeo and Juliet to pursue their desire as far as death as a limit of worldly experience, and to find themselves forced to do so in the peculiarly coincidental way the play leaves them, seems a further demonstration of the inevitability of both their love and of love's tragedy.

For all its insistence on the inevitabilities of 'fatal loins', 'star-crossed lovers' and 'death-marked love', though, *Romeo and Juliet* is a play that trades freely in near misses.[19] What if – to note only a few of those missed opportunities – Friar John had not visited his contagious friend and thus had not been quarantined in Verona, and thus Friar Laurence's letter had reached Romeo in Mantua? 'O true apothecary, / Thy drugs are quick' (5.3.119–20), says Romeo as he dies. What if the apothecary had not been true (certainly Romeo considers this possibility when he approaches him), or his drugs even a little less quick? What if Juliet's potion had been a little weaker and she had revived in the tomb a few minutes earlier, or if Paris had been a better swordsman, and delayed Romeo for the space of some seventy lines longer outside the tomb?

But the very improbability of the series of unfortunate events that fall out to realize Romeo and Juliet's 'death-marked love' seems to confirm the necessity of the play's ending. 'Star-crossed' and 'misadventured' sound as if they are opposing categories, inevitability and randomness hemming in each other's sway. In fact, they provide different but homologous horizons for the events of the play. In *Romeo and Juliet* apparent necessity and apparent accident combine to reinforce the impression that the lovers' story must be as it is and end as it does. In *Poetics*, Aristotle said that the most wonderful plots of tragedies take place neither through what he called *automaton* nor by *tukhē* (1452a). Although in English both words are sometimes translated as *chance*, in Greek they distinguish two different kinds of occurrence without agency or intention. What occurs by *automaton* is spontaneous and unconditioned, as if happening by itself; Aristotle might offer the example of the gradual decay and collapse of a statue. What occurs by *tukhē* is happenstance, accident, fluke, as when that statue falls on a passer-by. What is *automaton* is so ordinary that it thwarts ideas of agency; *tukhē* is literal coincidence, impossible to foresee. Of each, one could say that that is just the way it is. The plot that most evokes wonder hooks these two kinds of consequence together, actively mediating them, so that they show 'an excess of *seeming* purpose that is coupled with a known absence of purpose'.[20] Aristotle's example of this is when the falling statue kills the man who was responsible for the death of the person it commemorates (1452a). W. K. C. Guthrie, commenting more broadly on Aristotle's theory of *automaton* and *tukhē* in his *Physics* and *Metaphysics*, explains such events this way: 'Their result is such that it would have been recognized as a purpose and determined the action *had it been anticipated*.'[21] In *Romeo and Juliet*, the action is not anticipated, only its endpoint in the tomb.

I am not considering Aristotle's theory of what makes causality tragic and wondrous as one of Shakespeare's own sources, but because it helps explain how in their very unlikeliness *Romeo and Juliet*'s 'misadventured ... overthrows' may seem to support rather than contest the Prologue's fatal claims. The very improbability of the *coincidence*, literally the *coming together*, of the actions of the play gives them a strange purposiveness, by which every seeming misstep can be recuperated as part of a necessary causal chain that leads to the lovers' deaths. Everything that happens seems anticipated in the Prologue's lapidary account of its outcome. We can see the play – if we follow the Prologue – as an intricate clockwork that counts down the lover's lives and renders them – contrary to everybody's plans and through a string of events that feel too consequential to be nothing but bad luck – dead at the climax. The protagonists' 'misadventured ... overthrows' are so calculated that they seem anything but misadventures. They are perversely perfect in their wrongness, careful plots that bad execution – or poor performance? – turns awry with astonishing consistency. The well-laid plans of the characters make a marked contrast to the stony certainty of the Prologue, which the end of the play proves not to have erred.

That inevitability and singularity is at least one story that the play tells, or maybe the only story it tells, but it is not its only story. The title roles of *Romeo and Juliet* are such charismatic juggernauts that they tend to roll over everybody else in the play; the Prologue confirms – or more accurately, predicts – the central place of their story and the inevitability of its outcome. However, as Dryden hinted, Shakespeare's play is also remarkable for all the other stories it contains, or suggests. I do not just mean later adaptations to opera or ballet or other genres, or applications to Puerto Rican immigrants in New York or lovers in Baghdad or Ireland, although I think these signal the play's openness to transcending its particular instantiations in medieval Italy or early modern England. Nor do I mean the fact that the ending must always have felt quite as certain as the Prologue implies, since during the Restoration *Romeo and Juliet* was rewritten as a tragicomedy, and the two versions then 'Play'd Alternately, Tragical one Day, and Tragicomical another'.[22] I mean the way the play is seeded with other figures, stories, possibilities, like those of Mercutio, which the story of the two lovers undoubtedly overshadows but never entirely obscures.

Consider Paris. He is not really Romeo's rival for Juliet's affections (not as Rosaline is for Romeo's!), but he and Romeo share the same role in the plot (whether we recognize it as first or second *inamorato*, lyric tenor, or 'gentleman caller') and are characterized in the same metaphors. When Lady Capulet first proposes Paris as a suitor to Juliet, the Nurse calls him 'a man of wax' (1.3.77); Laurence tells Romeo 'Thy noble shape is but a form of wax' (3.3.125) after he has killed Tybalt. Lady Capulet urges Juliet to 'Read o'er the volume of young Paris' face ... This precious book of love, this unbound lover', (1.3.82, 88); when Juliet learns Romeo has killed Tybalt, she asks, 'Was ever book containing such vile matter / So fairly bound?' (3.2.83–4). They are, as it were, bound together finally when Romeo kills Paris and recognizes him as 'One writ with me in sour misfortune's book' (5.3.82). Why wax, why books? Because both are metaphors for things that can be like anything, that are nice but unspecific, with no positive qualities other than their capacities to take any shape or content. Wax is easily molded and takes what shape we like, and the books that Romeo and Paris are like cannot be judged by their covers, at least until Romeo signs off on the last page of Paris. Romeo and Paris are alike, or indifferent, exactly in their aptitudes for likeness.

The readiest way to read the insistent likening of Paris and Romeo is to understand Paris as a kind of foil to Romeo. There is something to this, as there is to take Rosaline as a kind of foil to Juliet: instances of love that fall short of the surpassing love of the title characters and so throw it into higher relief. However, unlike the counterpoint of contemplative Hamlet and active Fortinbras, *Romeo and Juliet* seems at some pains to insist on how little different Romeo and Paris are, more like the nearly interchangeable Lysander and Demetrius of *A Midsummer Night's Dream*. Both love Juliet, and both die for her, even if Paris gives his life with less premeditation than

Romeo. At Juliet's death, Paris does exactly what a luckier Romeo would have done had he been in Verona, showing up to strew flowers on her tomb (5.3.12–17). When Romeo kills him there, Paris' last words are a plea to 'Open the tomb, lay me with Juliet' (5.3.73), a place-sharing to which Romeo, astonishingly, assents (5.3.74–83).[23] Earlier, the Nurse had urged Juliet to consider swapping Paris for Romeo when Romeo is exiled; her new enthusiasm for Paris ('Romeo's a dishclout to him. An eagle, madam / Hath not so green, so quick, so fair an eye / As Paris hath' 3.5.220–1) echoes her earlier praise of Romeo ('Though his face be better than any man's, yet his leg excels all men's; and for a hand and a foot and a body ... yet they are past compare,' 2.5.39–42). This exchangeability is a two-way street. In the estimation of the Nurse, Romeo replaces Paris, who then again replaces Romeo. Capulet invites Paris to his feast explicitly as one possible suitor among many ('you among the store / One more, most welcome', 1.2.21–2), like, by accident, Romeo; at the feast it is Romeo whom Capulet speaks well of (1.5.65–9). Men of wax indeed! Is there no more to Paris than that he reached Capulet first? From one perspective, the substitution of Paris for Romeo, or Romeo for Paris, would radically change the play, from another – indeed, from all others but one, it seems – not at all.

Romeo has other foils as well, if we choose to think of this kind of place-holding or understudying in that way. Mercutio, who rejects any kind of romanticizing or sublimation of love, or Tybalt, wedded to violence, or Benvolio, everyone's equal well-wisher, show three courses that differ from Romeo's much more materially than Paris'. Other characters, maybe all other characters, likewise have foils of this kind. Lady Capulet has the Nurse as another maternal figure, and also Juliet, still unmarried when Lady Capulet was already a mother (1.3.72–4). Juliet has Rosaline, but also, resonantly, Susan. A test of how closely one character's life follows another's, how easily one character's life could be imagined as another's, and how much (and how little) of a difference this would make to the play, is how easily one can imagine one character speaking for another. In fact something like this has happened in the reception of the text, as Robert Watson shows: all early sources agree that Capulet intervenes to save Romeo from execution after he kills Tybalt, rather than Montague as editors have repeatedly decided, and Watson brilliantly develops how the import and the concomitant invisibility of this change are related.[24] But contra-factual examples are also easy to come by: imagine Lady Capulet telling the Nurse, 'Susan and she, God rest all Christian souls, / Were of an age. Well, [Juliet] is with God' (cf. 1.3.19–20), instead of the reverse; imagine the Apothecary as the future of the play's other herbalist, Friar Laurence, contempt and beggary hanging upon his back, the world not his friend, nor the world's law (5.1.71–2); imagine, in another vein, what the extemporal wit of 'that most Comicall and Conceited Cavaleire *Monsieur du Kempe*' might have made of the thin part of Peter, assigned to him in some speech prefixes of Q1.[25] Imagining still further afield, Arden editor René Weis finds in the unmoored recollection of Susan a refracted picture of Shakespeare's autobiography and his own lost and surviving children, names and years shuffled but persisting, transformed.[26]

But the familiar device of the foil figure, in the sense of an example that serves by contrast to call another figure's particularities into sharper relief, does not fully explain figures like Paris or Susan, much less Shakespeare's colleague Kemp or his son Hamnet, in whom we make out something that exceeds what we can credit to authorial prescription. The alternatives offered by Susan or Paris or the many other understudies in the play are neither as bright nor as pointed as foils. Neither Paris nor Susan, for instance, really represents roads not taken for Romeo or Juliet. Paris travels too far along the same path as Romeo; Susan and Juliet diverge too early. The understudies offer, more simply and less symbolically, *alternatives*. The device of a foil implies a binary structure, which the play certainly abounds in, most prominently the conflict between transcendent and mortal, worldly loves.[27] But the play is just as full of non-binary alternatives, *other ways* in which a life or a situation like Romeo's or Juliet's – or Lady Capulet's, or Friar Laurence's – might be undertaken and lived. These other ways do not simply invert a given form into its matched (or outmatched) opposite, as Tybalt's sexualized aggression inverts Mercutio's aggressive sexuality. *Romeo and Juliet*'s understudies multiply and vary their forms unpredictably, from similar points lighting in unanticipated directions.[28] In a play that calls so forcefully upon fatal, star-crossed destinies, the mere potential for things to be other than they turn out is a powerful counterargument against the inevitability of love, of death.

In naming these other ways *alternatives*, I am thinking about a fairly specific kind of potential for otherness materially within the archive of the play as we have it, not in what we might call rewritings. I am thus excluding the adaptations of fan fiction, which provide characters with new futures or off-scene (and often obscene) engagements, as possibilities that may be adumbrated by the play but are not realized in it.[29] I also am not considering the exercises of method acting that encourage modern actors to fill in motives, histories and subtexts to round out the lives of characters, although some of the other lives in *Romeo and Juliet* have been made perceptible by actors' choices, like the possibility that Lady Capulet's early marriage has not been happy, sometimes played as a coolness towards Capulet, and sometimes as an excessive interest in Tybalt.[30] Though it be method, sometimes there's madness in it. Nor do I consider – in this chapter! – the alternatives offered by certain textual doublings, which Weis characterizes as 'the pattern of first and second thoughts in Q2' (s.v. 1.2.14), for instance a pair of lines of which Weis cuts the first as redundant:

CAPULET
Earth hath swallowed all my hopes but she,
She is the hopeful lady of my earth.
(1.2.14x–14 [*om.* Weis])

nor how the cue for both Juliet and Lady Capulet in the Nurse's speech about the earthquake, 'say [or said] "Ay"' is repeated, which might have produced overlap and hesitation in the lines.[31] I am, however, interested in how all these kinds of alternative become resources for the play in the traffic of its playing to present other possibilities for all its characters, even as the text repeatedly asserts that Romeo and Juliet are bound by fate, 'star-crossed' by destiny and the singularity of their love. The best way, I think, to trace these alternatives as parts of the play, that is, in the play and not somehow superadded to it, is to confine this chapter to the play in a narrower sense, to its words as they are given in the text (itself hardly fixed), although a more expansive notion of what *Romeo and Juliet* includes will reveal even more other ways. To acknowledge the existence of the alternatives is, I think, neither to accept nor reject them, but to notice that there are – within the play, in the course of the play as traffic – a multiplicity, even an infinity, of ways a future can come into being from the past and the present, not simply as the fulfilment of its promises or the realization of its possibilities, but as actualizations of a cloud of incommensurable virtualities.[32]

As in *As You Like It*, a figure named Rosaline is the entry point to this garden of forking paths. I take this description from Jorge Luis Borges' story of that name, which describes a labyrinthine novel in which a character, confronted with alternative courses of action, does not eliminate every other by choosing one, but follows all simultaneously.[33] Alternatives multiply and ramify, but they also converge and cross, so that the same figure may in a single action be both a friend and an enemy. At the beginning of the play, Rosaline looks like destiny to Romeo: 'She hath forsworn to love, and in that vow / Do I live dead that live to tell it now' (1.1.221–2). Benvolio sees her instead as one possibility among many and encourages Romeo to make her impossibility an opportunity: 'Compare her face with some that I shall show ... Examine other beauties' (1.2.87, 1.1.226). Rosaline ends up, of course, a road not taken by Romeo. She herself follows a road not taken by Juliet, like her a young and eligible woman of the Capulet family. What makes Rosaline one of the genii of virtuality in *Romeo and Juliet* is that, like those of Paris and of Susan, and of other understudies, the roads Rosaline takes, and represents, within the fiction of the play, *are real*.[34] This is what makes *Romeo and Juliet* a garden of forking paths and not just, say, an array of varied figures like those in the *Canterbury Tales* or a sprawling nineteenth-century historical novel, in which every possible social position seems to be present, but not accessible to each other. They are not alternatives *for us*, as are the pilgrims on the Canterbury road or the populations of Middlemarch; the understudies of *Romeo and Juliet*'s characters are alternatives *for the characters*.

On a lesser scale but closer in form and time, plays like *Much Ado about Nothing* or *A Midsummer Night's Dream*, or many Elizabethan double plots, present matching figures that mirror and contrast, but these do not overlap, as they do in *Romeo and Juliet*. Theseus' love and Lysander's and Bottom's all comment on each other but neither interfere with nor speak to each other. They belong, in fact, to worlds that do not really communicate, and although a character may move from one to another, he or she can inhabit only one at any time, Athens or the wood.[35] This idea of a second world that reflects upon the real world is a powerful key to many fictions of the Renaissance.[36] *A Midsummer Night's Dream* is an example, for instance, of how *Romeo and Juliet* could have ended differently, as the mechanicals' *Pyramus and Thisbe* presents a tragic alternative to the main plot of *A Midsummer Night's Dream*, the lovers' antics in the woods outside Athens. But the potentialities of *Romeo and Juliet* are not set – as they are in *As You Like It* or *A Midsummer Night's Dream* – in a sheltered green world of dreams or the forest. They are not utopian. They inhabit the same dimensions as the 'red and white world' of the rest of the play.[37]

Take the scene in which the Nurse talks about her daughter Susan, by talking about Juliet. Lady Capulet's cloudiness at the possibility of Juliet marrying prompts the Nurse to recollect vividly 'her age unto an hour' (1.3.12). The Nurse's memories of Juliet braid with those of her daughter Susan, 'of an age' with Juliet (1.3.20), now dead, dead perhaps even before the events the Nurse tells, for the Nurse does not remember Susan in this story as she does Juliet. The sharpness and perplexity of its details:

> For I had then laid wormwood to my dug,
> Sitting in the sun under the dovehouse wall.
> My lord and you were then at Mantua.
>
> (1.3.27–9)

The toddler's tetchiness with the bitter breast, the dovehouse shaking in the earthquake conjure a buzzing, blooming life-world brighter, solider, and more ordinary than anything else in the play's Verona, full of insignificant but evocative details that seem to point only to their own concreteness.[38] This, like Mercutio, is a whole new world. But Juliet's story here is also, and from another perspective, what Susan's story could have been. For the Nurse tells not only another world, but another, shorter passage through this one, which Susan took while Juliet took another. In the Nurse's telling, Juliet takes Susan's part, being weaned by her mother, teased by her father for falling (1.3.42), getting a bump on her head 'as big as a young cockerel's stone' (1.3.54). The Capulets were away in Mantua (1.3.29), and why not their daughter, too, so that it might have been her own child whom the Nurse bustled from the teetering dovehouse? The Nurse's concrete memories of Juliet are what she has of Susan, too, who is named at the opening of the story and then passed over in silence so Juliet can understudy her. The Nurse's memory renders a vibrant, fleshed world for the play's audience, but it does something else as well. It discloses a world in which there are parts for Juliet or Susan other than those they have taken, coincident with the present world in which Susan is with God and Juliet with the Nurse.

We can see this simultaneity of multiple alternatives in *Romeo and Juliet* in how other ways of inhabiting the same world shadow almost every character, but perhaps most strikingly at the moments when, as in Borges' story, some of these other ways converge in a single scene. It is not simply that characters speak at cross-purposes; rather, the words they share form different meanings for each of them. After Tybalt's death, Juliet must doubletalk her grieving, furious mother about the cause of her own unease:

> Indeed, I never shall be satisfied
> With Romeo till I behold him, dead
> Is my poor heart so for a kinsman vexed.
>
> (3.5.93–5)[39]

Shakespeare uses the trick of artfully unpunctuating a sentence to change its meaning in Quince's comic prologue to the tedious brief tragedy of Pyramus and Thisbe. Here it does something perhaps more serious: it lets Juliet speak her truth to her mother while her mother hears something different. More exactly, Juliet allows her mother to understand a different world than the one Juliet keeps open for herself. It is thus a kind of intentional deception. A more disorienting, and provocative, moment occurs earlier, when the Nurse brings somewhat incoherent news of Tybalt's death to Juliet:

> Ah weraday, he's dead, he's dead, he's dead!
> O Romeo, Romeo,
> Whoever would have thought it – Romeo!
>
> (3.2.37, 41–2)

Juliet hears her saying that Romeo has been killed, not that he is the killer, at least insofar as she understands her at all. But no deception is being practised. Instead, two different worlds come momentarily into contact. The Nurse's description of Tybalt's 'bloody piteous corse' (3.2.54) is, for Juliet, Romeo's. When finally Juliet demands, 'What storm is this that blows so contrary?' (3.2.64), she is not only talking about the storm of bad luck that overwhelms her and the Nurse together, but recognizing that they are driving in different directions. Then these alternative worlds come back into alignment, and Juliet comes to learn that it is Tybalt who is dead, just as we come to learn that Romeo does not *really* love Rosaline or that Susan has survived childhood like Juliet. But for a while, the single scene presents Juliet and the Nurse mourning together the worst loss that each can imagine, but in fact inhabiting two different, equally real worlds, one in which Romeo has killed Tybalt and one in which Tybalt has killed Romeo, or Romeo has killed himself.

The playhouse itself remains a green world, to be sure, a place apart where potentialities like *Romeo and Juliet* can be acted as real, which is to say, as fictions. Within the play's fiction, the alternatives that are repeatedly presented are represented as being virtual: possible in reality and effective in reality. *Romeo and Juliet* includes these alternative potentialities in the same space as that of what happens in the play – neither as dreams nor as dramas, but as events that can be, and often are, actualized simultaneously with those of the main plot. Curiously, in *Romeo and Juliet* dreams are not the fantasies that Coleridge so admired. They seem to reflect reality accurately, indeed almost literally. While Mercutio's Mab is an explosive *tour de force*, the dreams Mab brings are boringly close to their dreamers' day jobs:

> Sometime she gallops o'er a courtier's nose,
> And then dreams he of smelling out a suit;
> And sometime comes she with a tithe-pig's tail,
> Tickling a parson's nose as 'a lies asleep;
> Then he dreams of another benefice.
> Sometime she driveth o'er a soldier's neck,
> And then dreams he of cutting foreign throats,
>
> (1.4.77–83)

At their last meeting Juliet has an image of Romeo 'dead in the bottom of a tomb' (3.5.56), in Mantua Romeo dreams 'my lady came and found me dead' (5.1.6); outside the tomb of the

Capulets, his servant Balthasar dreams 'my master and another fought, / And that my master slew him' (5.3.138–9).[40] Dreams show, we might say, a reality of limited possibility, in which the relation of the future to the present seems to be exclusively one of fulfilment. They represent a utopian alternative as, perhaps counter-intuitively, much more *limited* than the world of alternatives that the play enacts.[41] The small parts of the understudies, in contrast, show us not just that things could always be otherwise, but that in fact they already are.

It is possible that the presence of these alternatives to what happens in *Romeo and Juliet* still reinforces our sense that, whatever else might have happened, the end of *Romeo and Juliet* was inevitable and that its leading lights, Romeo and Juliet, were star-crossed. With all these other ways before or alongside them, the fact that they chose, or found, or were compelled towards, the tomb as their destination (as well as the fact that they arrive there every time the play is performed) shows us that the ending could not have been otherwise. I do not want to foreclose that powerful sense! I want instead to offer the alternative of alternatives, the understudies' other ways. If the play tells us powerfully of fatal love, it also shows that Romeo and Juliet's love is no more star-crossed than, say, Peter's meeting with the musicians, Susan's early death or the second Susan, Susan Grindstone's, admission to the Capulet's party. Also no less.

I want to speak not against love, and not beyond love, but beside or besides love – all there is in the play besides the transcendence promised in love and death. *Romeo and Juliet* suggests, I think, something richer and stranger and, perhaps paradoxically, closer to and more fully caught up in life, than a glorious hope of transcending the present by negating or fulfilling it. It suggests the limited power of transcendence when compared to the virtuality and potential and infinite, inexplicable, unpredictable variety of immanence, all the things that are here in all the ways they are. *Romeo and Juliet* measures the force of 'There's a place for us' (which turns out to be not this place, a utopian no-place) against 'there are other ways', ('passage', a resolved working-through or 'toil', in 'traffic' if need be, of the course one finds oneself in, recognizing that any road actualizes at every step multiple tracks, paces and destinations). Against, or besides, the completed vision of the lovers' tragedy, it sets the infinite potentiality of how things may turn out.

6

New Directions: Dancing Will: The Case of *Romeo and Juliet*

Joseph Campana

Imagine the scene: a Shakespeare scholar attends his first story ballet; the dance critic, his umpteenth one. The work in question was Rudi van Dantzig and Toer van Schayk's archetypal *Romeo and Juliet,* in a 2003 staging set by both original creators for Boston Ballet. The lights went down, the action unfolded, Juliet twittered about her bedroom and one (you can guess which) leaned over to whisper, 'What on earth is this? There's no Shakespeare without words!' Later that evening, the other wrote in a review published the next day in the *Boston Herald*: 'Boston Ballet offered such a full-out performance ... that one felt entirely involved in Shakespeare's tragic tale. It was one of those rare occasions when intellect and emotions resonate at the same frequency.'[1] Perhaps it comes as no surprise if I say that I am the aforementioned scholar. The dance critic is my partner, Theodore Bale.

Perhaps it would also come as no surprise if I say both of our critical assertions might be worth reconsidering.

Clearly, it is not the case that 'there's no Shakespeare without words'. In fact, there is plenty. Not only has Shakespeare been 'danced', but he's been 'painted' and 'sculpted', rendered 'silent' in early cinema. Even more innovative forms – like Punchdrunk's 'Sleep No More', an immersive theatre experience of *Macbeth* – need not involve language at all.[2] Moreover, some translations of Shakespeare possess language aplenty, but leave us with plenty of questions. Thomas Adès's operatic *The Tempest* (2004), for instance, witnesses an extreme yet, to my ears, neither rich nor strange sea change of Shakespeare's exquisite text into a series of clumsy couplets.[3]

But the real issue is this: what is it we conjure, Prospero-like, when we invoke the name 'Shakespeare' for works only partly overlapping with the Shakespearean stage or page?

In other words, what *is* in a name? While Juliet's memorable question might evoke myriad replies, it is safe to say that Shakespeare's name remains one to conjure with in the worlds of opera and ballet. The profusion and history of choreographies alone based on his plays is daunting, to say the least. When classical ballet was developing in the French court, the Swan of Avon (or, Upstart Crow if you prefer) was penning his famous lines. And when Louis XIV made his final appearance in the 1669 *Ballet de Flore*, there must have been those who could remember a time when Shakespeare was alive. Since that thrilling moment in history, how many Romeos have roused with a splendid *rond de jambe* and how many Juliets have sailed through their *jetés* without uttering a word? The celebration of the 450th anniversary of Shakespeare's birth has encouraged ballet companies around the globe to recognize the occasion by choosing from an enormous repertory of dances based on his works, from choreographers both living and deceased, and from a wide variety of balletic and other traditions. The combination of the two seems obvious, at least at first glance. Recently a *New York Times* column by Alastair Macaulay was subtitled 'Shakespeare's plays are a natural fit with dance.'[4] Many of his plays do feature, or refer to, dance, Macaulay points out, and, after all, ballet is deeply theatrical. Macaulay becomes a latter-day Mercutio, who, on the way to the Capulet ball, insists, 'Romeo, we must have you dance' (1.4.13).

And yet one might argue just the opposite, remembering that Juliet identifies the as yet, to her, unknown Romeo as he 'that would not dance' (1.5.131). Shakespeare's translation to the balletic and operatic stages remains a speculation, a kind of perpetually unsolvable mystery. So what is it that makes 'Shakespeare' or 'Romeo and Juliet' what they are? Powerful and alluring language? Not by itself alone. Compelling narrative? To be sure, *Romeo and Juliet* is the iconic example of the story that just won't stop being told over and over again, but Shakespeare's plots were rarely his own, though his transformation of sources is as notable as his capacity to make some stories classics because of his participation in their transmission. For some, character endures. The choreographer Neumeier insists, 'It's why we can play Shakespeare in a parking lot or outer space. The characters live so vividly they can be transferred.' And yet as characters become iconic or mythic they may shed the particularity that rich characterization affords, rendering them more and less than characters.

While language alone may not be sufficient to describe what is singularly Shakespearean, narrative and character, theme and expression are also insufficient grounds. Opera and especially dance provide opportunities to consider these questions – what is 'Shakespeare' and what is '*Romeo and Juliet*' – as both are, like Bottom in *A Midsummer Night's Dream* strangely translated across the arts. That process might be best described as a series of re-materializations, as a work both theatrical and literary phases in and out of shades of materiality and embodiment. The process begins with a dramatic script, written to be staged, which thus re-materializes as performance in the bodies of actors. That performance perhaps then impacts the publication of that 'original' text, which then becomes available to be rematerialized in a variety of bodies and media. The paradox of the choreographic Shakespeare is that it silences Shakespeare in order to speak. Ironically, should we attend only to language and plot, character and emotive force, we might not hear what Shakespeare has to say to us.

Many critical conversations, especially those conducted under the rubric of adaptation, tend to reify narrative, character and emotional expression as the singular and stable 'Shakespearean' elements of a work. To be sure, many operatic and balletic iterations of Shakespeare do the same, leaving us to ask about plot (what differs regarding the sequence or nature of events from one version to another?), character (what is emphasized or de-emphasized about particular characters; who is added or cut, minimized or accentuated in any given version?) or emotional expressiveness (how do we find equivalencies for, say, Romeo's desire or Juliet's despair in the techniques of a given medium, whether in the language of choreography or of musical style as opposed to language or theatrical gesture?). All of these are critical questions for composers, choreographers and other artists as they contemplate creating something based on an iconic work such as *Romeo and Juliet*. But they are overly familiar questions as well, ones that direct us more to the appreciation of *Romeo and Juliet*'s legacy than to the analysis of how that legacy has played out in various artistic forms.

Scholars have been attentive to certain coordinates of the Shakespearean afterlife. Shakespeare in film and on television, Shakespeare in popular culture, global Shakespeares, Shakespeare in new media and on the web, Shakespeare restaged in a dizzying array of times and places: all have received ample consideration and have added considerably to the documentation of Shakespeare's powerful temporal and geographic reach. And while there exists a small body of commentary on Shakespeare's legacy in seemingly more traditional arts, such as opera and ballet, these media have proved less popular with scholars, although not with audiences, even as the dissemination of Shakespeare's works in balletic and operatic forms reflect the same complex crossings of time, space and media of interest elsewhere in both Shakespeare studies and adaptation studies.

Most iterations of *Romeo and Juliet* in opera and ballet have exhibited strong tendencies to re-situate narrative and to search for ideal media equivalence between the distinctive traits of a particular medium and given interpretations of the emotional situations of the play.[5] My interest here will be in iterations of *Romeo and Juliet* that significantly move past familiar narrative, characterological and emotive frameworks and require us to come up with more invigorating language for what happens when 'Shakespeare' struts and frets across the arts. For reasons that will become apparent, this results in an emphasis in this essay on choreography. However, I will start by reviewing some of the language scholars have used to describe what happens when literary works of one era are remade according to the urgencies of another and often in other media, which most refer to as either adaptation, appropriation, intertextuality or intermediality. After considering the way dance historians have addressed Shakespeare and the way Shakespeare scholars have addressed opera and dance, I turn to the choreographic legacies of *Romeo and Juliet* to answer that fundamental question – what is in a name like *Romeo and Juliet*? Rather than 'true love', 'young love' or 'tragic circumstances', we might find, in a name like *Romeo and Juliet*, less comforting qualities: velocity, brutality, anonymity and interchangeability.

While influence and intertextuality have been watchwords for the afterlives of literary works, providing language for describing the networks of allusion, influence and conversation that surround the circulation of texts and authors, including the works of William Shakespeare, adaptation and appropriation have more recently seized the day. The last decade especially has witnessed a veritable boom in adaptation studies evident in a burst of essays, monographs, edited collections and journals dedicated to the subject.[6]

Linda Hutcheon describes adaptations as 'deliberate, announced, and extended revisitations of prior works'.[7] 'My method', she continues, 'has been to identify a text-based issue that extends across a variety of media, find ways to study it comparatively, and then tease out the theoretical implications from multiple textual examples.'[8] Julie Sanders, in her general treatment of the phenomenon, *Adaptation and Appropriation*, describes how 'an adaptation signals a relationship with an informing source text or original' while 'the appropriated text or texts are not always as clearly signaled or acknowledged'.[9] Both Hutcheon and Sanders make reference to Shakespeare, primarily to film versions of his plays. Sanders, in a chapter devoted entirely to Shakespearean appropriations, sees Shakespeare's works as providing 'the essence of literary archetypes: their availability for rewriting means that they are texts constantly in flux, constantly metamorphosing in the process of adaptation and retelling. They persistently enact and re-enact their activity of storytelling, and Shakespeare has provided some of the most familiar stories of Western culture.'[10] Shakespeare appears frequently, if briefly, in Hutcheon's account of adaptation but she too, like Sanders, refers primarily to page, stage and screen adaptations, with a few quick references to opera, dance and musical theatre. Ballet is included by Hutcheon in a laundry list of media that 'show a story', which 'involves a direct aural and usually visual performance experienced in real time'.[11]

For the most part, opera and ballet are not even minor players in adaptation studies, which is one of several biases that has shaped the field. On the one hand Hutcheon suggests that adaptation treats a broad range of phenomena. In a complaint quite familiar to adaptation studies Hutcheon insists, 'Adaptation has run amok. That's why we can't understand its appeal and even its nature if we only consider novels and films.'[12] And yet although she gestures towards a widening of media types, Hutcheon's own model is not only 'text-based', as she puts it, but one that sets aside the specificity of individual media forms for the sake of an almost exclusive emphasis on narrative. She argues for a move away 'from particular individual media to the broader context of the three major ways we engage with stories (telling, showing, and interacting with them) [that] allows a series of different concerns to come to the fore'.[13] Sanders too emphasizes storytelling, so much so that she rather erroneously attributes 'some of the most familiar stories of Western culture' to Shakespeare, who, it is well known, was himself primarily an adapter of the narratives of others. And naturally, while there is great interest in the metamorphoses of narratives travelling through space, time and culture, what about non-narrative media or non-narrative elements within narrative media?

In a review essay on the equally robust tradition of writing on Shakespearean adaptation, Jennifer Clement makes a similar argument. 'The term "adaptation"', she argues, 'itself has proved useful for describing a range of inter-textual practices and processes. Yet in early modern studies, the field remains largely limited to two areas: Shakespeare and film.'[14] Few, if any, significant references to ballet or opera appear in such criticism, as becomes clear in a sample of representative sources. Christy Desmet and Robert Sawyer's collection *Shakespeare and Appropriation* and Pascale Aebischer, Ed Esche and Nigel Wheale's *Remaking Shakespeare: Performance Across Media, Genres and Cultures* concentrate on film, theatre and the larger cultural ramifications of Shakespeare's iconic status.[15] Diana Henderson's *Collaborations with the Past: Reshaping Shakespeare Across Time and Media* focuses on 'four exemplary instances in which his plays were reconceived within distinctively modern narrative forms (novels, film, video) and in the radically altered modern theater'.[16] Margaret Jane Kidnie's *Shakespeare and the Problem of Adaptation* consciously targets theatrical adaptations only, while Maurizio Calbi's *Spectral Shakespeares: Media Adaptations in the Twenty-First Century* focuses primarily on theatre, film and social media.[17] Where are opera and ballet in these conversations about adaptation and media? To read the entire run of the journal *Adaptation* is to find as few references to ballet and opera as is also true of the entire run of *Borrowers and Lenders*, which spares little room for Shakespeare and any kind of opera or dance.

Of course it would be far from true to suggest that dance history has lavished its attention on Shakespeare. Classics of dance history like Cyril Beaumont's *Complete Book of Ballets* (1937) or Lincoln Kirstein's *Four Centuries of Ballet: Fifty Masterworks* (1970) contain barely a scattering of references to Shakespeare, which is similarly true of Jennifer Homans's recent and quite well received *Apollo's Angels: A History of Ballet* (2010). Shakespeare is equally scarce in a range of scholarly journals, such as *Dance Chronicle*, *Dance Research* and *Dance Research Journal* in which he is more often to be found either in a catalogue of canonical figures a particular choreographer may have studied (thus serving as evidence of learnedness or worldliness), or as a vague analogue for profound creativity or genius. Far more likely are surface generalizations about the nature of Shakespeare and dance to be found in reviews of individual performances, which are of necessity characterized by brevity and frequently result in overblown moments of rhetoric, rather than analysis.[18]

Perhaps what is most fascinating about attention to the operatic and choreographic Shakespeare is a fundamental split between finding what Macaulay calls a 'natural fit' and what I initially experienced as a radical disjunction. Gary Schmidgall's *Shakespeare and Opera* finds a 'synonymy between operatic and Shakespearean', by which Schmidgall most often seems to mean that Shakespeare and opera are grandiose, iconic and iconoclastic all at once in character, language and dramatic strategies.[19] His study thus pursues similitudes and analogies between aspects of opera and aspects of the Shakespearean stage before targeting specific operatic productions. And yet a contemporaneous special forum called 'Shakespeare in Opera and Dance' introduces itself by noting that although Shakespeare's plays have 'served as the inspiration for some important operas and ballets ... There are, however, problems about turning the poetry of Shakespeare into the lyrics of opera.'[20] Even more damning, perhaps, is Winton Dean's pronouncement that although 'There have been so many operas founded on Shakespeare's plays – I know of nearly 200 … the average artistic level is not high. With the exception of a few masterpieces, which can be counted on the fingers of one hand, and a scarcely larger group, mostly based on the comedies, that are good for an occasional airing, you are never likely to hear them in performance. Any interest they possess is historical, and it concerns the history of opera rather than of Shakespeare.'[21] Adrian Streete, in an overview called 'Shakespeare and Opera', written for *The Edinburgh Companion to Shakespeare and the Arts*, similarly states that 'the vast majority of operas based on Shakespeare are not, nor are they likely to become, part of the repertoire of most opera houses'.[22] Daniel Albright largely concurs in *Musicking Shakespeare*, a study attentive to how particular operas are inspired by a clash of theatres in Shakespeare who characteristically 'juxtaposes two kinds of theater within a single play'.[23] And yet Albright finds 'the candidates for such analysis are surprisingly few, given the larger number of operas that make use of Shakespearean plot lines. Most of them, however, were prepared by librettists and composers who seem to have had little interest in Shakespeare beyond the stories he tells.'[24] The specificity of Shakespeare, for Albright, lies in 'unsettled and warring stage models', which opera duplicates.[25] 'Every opera', he argues, 'is a transgression against itself. Music always ends by both reinforcing and contradicting the verbal text that it tries to set; for music is far more rich in interrelations, far more semantically replete than spoken drama.'[26] Thus Albright valorizes tension between composition and text; the operatic work that results succeeds not because of congruence but because of contradiction.

Nonetheless, for theatre and dance critic Clive Barnes, narrative congruence is the reason for such successful translations of Shakespeare to the choreographic stage. 'This is why Shakespeare is so popular', Barnes argues, 'the difficulty of ballet is to be specific in narrative … As a result, choreographers have tried to find themes that are readily recognizable – emblematically recognizable – by the mass audience, and there are not too many kinds of themes that everyone knows.'[27] Language, on the other hand, is not merely a diminished medium, as Albright would have it. It is dispensable in both dance and opera. Barnes argues, 'there is a certain advantage to Shakespeare in translation ... It was Brecht who first really understood that when you translate a play, you can do much more with it than if you have the solid, all too solid, solid text.'[28] Robin Wharton also reflects this same sense that the solidity of stories makes Shakespeare Shakespeare. 'Turning to Shakespeare, of course', she argues 'permits a choreographer to take advantage of an audience's presumed familiarity with the plot to introduce a previously unavailable level of narrative complexity.'[29]

This purported familiarity with Shakespearean narrative paradoxically allows for a different kind of story to arise once the particularity of Shakespearean language falls away. Marjorie Garber in her treatment of *Romeo and Juliet* as 'the normative love story of our time', a story of young love, similarly argues for the efficacy of stripping Shakespeare of language. She argues, 'one way of "universalizing" the love story in the play would have been through its translation into ballet, since without the specificity of words, and with the presumptive requirement that the dancers be young, lithe, and visually beautiful, the particulars of the plot would almost directly yield to the embodied ideology of young love'.[30] (See Rebeca Helfer in this volume for more on Garber's reading of *Romeo and Juliet*.) Or, as Barnes had already put it, '*Romeo and Juliet* is a natural for ballet. The story is well enough known for people not to have to worry about the details.'[31] Certainly, some try to find the genesis of Shakespeare's choreographic legacy in the plays themselves or in the conventions of Renaissance theatre, as when Rodney Stenning Edgecombe tries to locate the 'proto-balletic aspects of the Tudor stage' in *Romeo and Juliet*[32] or looks for continuities in thought about space and geometry that stretch from Euclid to Shakespeare's

A Midsummer Night's Dream to twentieth-century choreographer Frederick Ashton's *The Dream*.[33] But for the most part, story dominates, creating continuity and a sense of stable identity across transformation and adaptation.

The rich and complex story of the operatic *Romeo and Juliet* remains beyond my scope in this essay, yet even a quick glance at the tradition suggests very much a story of narrative re-situation and source selection, as works from Georg Benda's 1776 *Romeo und Julie* to Heinrich Sutermeister's 1940 *Romeo und Julia* to Arthur Laurents, Leonard Bernstein, Stephen Sondheim and Jerome Robbins's 1957 *West Side Story* and beyond stick close to core narrative conventions even as they revise the tale or offer it alternative temporal and geographic coordinates. Narrative elements combine and recombine, but composers seem to seek ever-truer musical equivalencies for theme, character and story or, we might say, the sound of the real *Romeo and Juliet*. The story of the choreographic *Romeo and Juliet* similarly begins with story. The eighteenth-century ballet-master Jean-Georges Noverre, often called the father of modern ballet, was responsible for the evolution of ballet from purely technical displays of prowess (often in the midst of operatic performances) or allegorical pageants toward the stand-alone *ballet d'action*, which were based on dramatic narratives often drawn from plays and which valued the representation of characters and emotive expression through movement and acting. As Edgecombe puts it, under the sway of Noverre 'ballet embraced its identity as a non-verbal but dramatic art'.[34] Noverre, who was highly influenced by the great Shakespearean actor David Garrick's dramaturgy, envisioned a highly theatrical mode of ballet: 'In a ballet there must be a good deal of spectacle and of action to replace speech, much passion and feeling to take the place of discourse, and, even so, the passion must be strongly expressed in order to create great effects.'[35] Susan Leigh Foster argues that under the sway of Noverre, 'the new dance demanded a substantial investment from dancers in learning the arts of pantomime and facial expression. The new choreography emphasized the dancer's ability to play a character convincingly as much or more than the deft execution of a complicated jumping pattern or the sensitive inflection of a phrase.'[36] And indeed Edward Nye argues that at this moment of dance history, the rise of the *ballet d'action* coincides with what would now seem like a lexical oddity, in that the emerging term choreography refers to 'the dramaturgical structure of a work not a system of notation'.[37] Noverre was not only the Shakespeare of Ballet, as David Garrick called him, but he 'produced *Antoine et Cléopâtre*, and *Les Amours d'Henri IV*', which Camille Cole Howard suggests, echoing Lincoln Kirstein, are 'the first recorded ballets based on Shakespeare plays'.[38]

Most scholars suggest that ballets based on *Romeo and Juliet* begin with Vincenzo Galeotti's *Romeo og Giulietta*, performed by the Royal Danish Ballet to great acclaim in 1811, although Howard cites several possible sources for Galeotti's ballet, including a 1793 opera by Daniel Steibelt. 'In 1785', she adds, 'an Italian ballet master, Luzzi, staged *Giulietta e Romeo* in Venice.'[39] But the real consolidation of *Romeo and Juliet* as the Shakespearean story ballet *par excellence* came later with the collaboration between composer Sergei Prokofiev and choreographer Leonid Lavrovsky for a ballet based on a scenario by playwright Adrian Piotrovsky and artistic director of the Leningrad State Academic Theatre of Opera and Ballet, Sergey Radlov. A number of features intensify the narrative focus of the work. Prokofiev's score follows closely the action laid out in Piotrovsky's scenario, with musical scenes equivalent to scenes of action. Prokofiev was, like so many, impacted significantly by the innovations of Wagner, including the use of leitmotifs, or repeated musical themes associated with particular characters, moods or situations, a subject Karen Bennett analyses in great detail to account for not only the way 'most of the characters are identified by at least one portrait theme' but also the way that 'there is a clear division between those that develop musically and those that do not (which of course offers another comparison with literature)'.[40] In addition to the powerful scenario and the heavy deployment of leitmotifs, a powerful through-composition kept the action front and centre. As Howard puts it, 'The ballet had a film-like continuity of action – no episodes or danced divertissements distracted from the main theme of the star-crossed lovers.'[41] The production was itself famously star-crossed and suffered a number of setbacks that have never been fully explained, as Bennett, and so many others, have pointed out.[42] Although Radlov approached Prokofiev in 1934, a series of reversals, delays and revisions held up the première until 11 January 1940. The production first toured outside the Soviet Union in 1956, where it met with mixed responses. Political difficulties resulting from a repressive Soviet regime resulted in many complex and anxious revisions, which means that only recently was Prokofiev's original version restored by Simon Morrison in conversation with the Prokofiev family and performed in 2008 by the Mark Morris Dance Group.[43]

Although the Bolshoi's touring production failed to strike a chord with audiences, the music and scenario had an undeniable impact and remain the primary choice for choreographic iterations of *Romeo and Juliet*. Frederick Ashton choreographed a less-frequently performed *Romeo and Juliet* for Royal Danish Ballet in 1955, a production recently restaged by Danish director Peter Schaufuss. According to Lyndsey Winship, 'Ashton bequeathed Schaufuss the rights to this *Romeo* in his will and it predates the Kenneth MacMillan version usually seen in Britain. While set to the same storming Prokofiev score, in terms of scale it's much more modest.'[44] John Cranko's 1962 *Romeo and Juliet* for Stuttgart Ballet was an immediate hit and seems to have significantly influenced the *Romeo and Juliet* Kenneth MacMillan choreographed for the Royal Ballet in 1965, which has now significantly outstripped Cranko's version in popularity.[45] Indeed, at the time of this writing, at least four different DVDs of Royal Ballet productions (and an additional one from Teatro alla Scala) of MacMillan's *Romeo and Juliet* are currently available, which offers the work greater exposure than many masterpieces of twentieth-century choreography, which were either never released or are no longer in production.[46]

One might say, then, that MacMillan represents a particular distillation of the balletic tradition with respect to *Romeo and Juliet*, one that offers a control against which other experiments might be compared. In fact, we might call this an iconic iteration of *Romeo and Juliet*. MacMillan not only deploys Prokofiev's score, but the première of his *Romeo and Juliet* featured the iconic pairing of Nureyev and Fonteyn, as did a 1966 film of this production. From the very beginning of that film, MacMillan offers a ballet-world fantasy of the feel of Verona as we meet the people of the city before the action truly begins. Virtuous women twirl with brooms through a central square as a series of courtesans flirt with anyone they can. These courtesans wear character shoes – not ballet slippers – and never appear *en pointe*. Although they seem ready to partner with nearly anyone, they will never be the ethereal beauties of ballet. A workman hauls what appears to be a (plaster) pig carcass or side of beef across the back of the stage as Romeo and his friends sample from huge jugs of wine. Viewers might be reminded both of the rustic scenes of story ballets and of Franco Zeffirelli's contemporary efforts, *Taming of the Shrew* (1967) and *Romeo and Juliet* (1968), which similarly attempt to create the feel of some fantasized Renaissance civic space where even the small parts suggest whole, if not central, lives. Some information is conveyed by acting or mime, as when the wife or girlfriend of someone wounded in the opening brawl between the Capulets and Montagues gesticulates wildly of her loss to the Prince. The ballet, in other words, sets up the expectation that we are in a world full of characters, each with a story ready to be told.

To meet Juliet is to begin to see the alignment of a particular characterization of Shakespeare's naïve heroine with the angelic allure of ballet. In her bedroom, she dances with spritely and delicate steps referred to as *petite batterie*, her small kicks and jumps and turns contrasting with the lumbering Nurse in a costume as voluminous as Juliet's is ethereal. Finally, we see the ballerina *en pointe* – no sweeper of streets or walker of the streets is she. Juliet teases the Nurse, dangling a stuffed animal just out of reach as her parents enter and attempt to introduce her to Paris. Fonteyn's Juliet is skittish and playful. While she performs a bit for him and then partners, she seeks to return to her fun. Even later at the Capulet ball, she partners Paris as if it were a game and as if she does not understand her parents' matrimonial ambitions. Her coy and girlish formality melts away as soon as she meets Romeo, becomes responsive and even begins to improvise. The balcony scene is, not surprisingly, exquisite. Juliet descends from above and clearly wants to dance but also wants to flee. She runs off as he leaps about the stage lyrically and heroically, showing off for his new love. As they partner, they become more and more intimate. Romeo lifts her into what is called a fish dive, her legs crossed and held back as her back arches and he supports her weight against his body. It is precisely this sequence Romeo will try to re-enact in the tomb with the seemingly lifeless body of Juliet. The longing for union finds its perfect equivalent in the partnering of dancers. After Romeo's death and Juliet awakens, she poisons herself, hauls her body across the slab of the tomb and reaches down to his body as if she might have the strength to haul him into motion. MacMillan thus seems to codify what we already think we know about the sweet Juliet, her boyish Romeo and their tragic end. The chemistry between Fonteyn and Nureyev is undeniable: all they seem to need are the right steps to fit their story, which MacMillan eagerly provides.[47]

Although MacMillan was by no means the last word in *Romeo and Juliet*, few could resist the lure of this narrative. Neumeier, who also choreographed his own *A Midsummer Night's Dream*, mounted a *Romeo and Juliet* for Hamburg Ballet in 1971 in the wake of and in response to these mid-century masterpieces. 'The complexity of Shakespeare's text,' he said in an interview, 'demands something not quite as easy as the things we've seen.'[48] The dominance of Prokofiev's score means that most productions, from

Jean-Christophe Maillot's 1996 *Romeo and Juliet* to Michael Pink's 2008 *Romeo and Juliet* for the Milwaukee Ballet to Alexei Ratmansky's celebrated 2011 production for National Ballet of Canada to Stanton Welch's for Houston Ballet, which premièred in 2015, continue to fall under the spell of story especially as embedded in Prokofiev's powerful score. Even celebrated ballets considered radically revisionary, such as Angelin Preljocaj's 1990 *Romeo and Juliet* for the Lyons Opera Ballet, retains the core narrative elements of a tale of forbidden love as it sets the story in an oppressive society, where a wall with guard towers dominates the scene, as opposed to a walled Renaissance villa. The Capulet and Montague feud is not the story of rival families but is, rather, the story of lovers divided by a society composed of an overclass and underclass. As Anna Kisselgoff describes the ballet in her *New York Times* review: 'When the familiar music from the balcony scene begins in this production for the Lyons Opera Ballet, the balcony turns out to be a catwalk near a watchtower, patrolled by a guard with a flashlight and, later, a German shepherd. The choreographer's ingeniously twisted image here, which goes against conventional associations, brilliantly sums up his radical reinterpretation: Romeo and Juliet live in a police state.' Preljocaj was not the first to render *Romeo and Juliet* a political allegory. Maurice Béjart's 1967 *Roméo et Juliette*, choreographed to Berlioz's score, reflected its Vietnam-era creation in focusing on oppositional group dynamics. Rennie Harris's 2000 *Rome and Jewels*, an evening-length hip-hop *Romeo and Juliet*, departs radically with respect to choreographic idiom and yet clings to the telling of story as its primary motivation, even as it reformats that narrative with contemporary social circumstances in mind. Mats Ek's *Juliet and Romeo*, set to a selection of works by Tchaikovsky and premiered by the Royal Swedish Ballet in 2013, features a similarly brutal and brutalizing world emblematized by a series of movable walls dividing the stage. Ek promises a new vision of *Romeo and Juliet* distilled in the inverted title, which signals that 'it is time to reverse the title of the world's greatest love story and to consider the plot from a fresh angle'.[49] It is 'Juliet's perspective' and 'her actions and emotions' that drive the choreography, and yet to watch the production is to be struck by a familiar narrative. As for the inversion of the title, one wonders to what extent Juliet has actually been downplayed in the history of staging. One also wonders what it is about this production that focuses significantly more attention on Juliet than any other production, which also suggests that inversion is not a form of innovation.

Such re-situations, invigorating as they may be, neither abandon narrative nor do they necessarily advance conversations embedded within Shakespeare's text, as Kisselgoff's commentary on Preljocaj indicates: 'For all its clever updating and imagination, Mr. Preljocaj's treatment is decidedly un-Shakespearean. The flaw is not that the poetry of the text can rarely be identified with a score that has been cut and rearranged. It is, rather, that the play's symmetry has been destroyed and, with it, a degree of dramatic tension. There are no parents or even rival gangs, as in "West Side Story." For Mr. Preljocaj, the Capulets are the oppressive ruling class, the Montagues the underclass. The customary balance is upset, making for a simpler study in power.'[50]

In as much as *Romeo and Juliet* represents a kind of story we cannot seem to stop retelling, it should be no surprise that the narrative holds on in an artistic medium dominated by centuries of story ballets based on dramatic action and characterization. And yet twentieth- and twenty-first-century dance would not be what it is had it not both expanded the idea of what could constitute choreographic language and revised the very idea of what a narrative could be. With respect to *Romeo and Juliet*, experimentation with what form that ballet might take begins at least as early as Antony Tudor's 1943 one-act *Romeo and Juliet*. Not satisfied with a mere rehashing of the story, Tudor mounted an abstract and emotionally concentrated work. As Howard puts it, 'Tudor's distillation of the play was effected, at least in part, by compression. The production never swept through the action of the five-act play. Rather, Tudor sped up its heartbeat and compressed the entire ballet into a single act.'[51] Tudor deployed his own style of classically derived movement, gesture and pointe work and focused on interior, psychological dramas, as he did in his original scenarios for his more widely popular ballets like *Jardin aux Lilas*. However, his greatest and perhaps most enabling departure was the abandonment of the Prokofiev score,.preferring, instead, an arrangement of selections from Delius, including from his adaptation *A Village Romeo and Juliet*.

More recently, choreographers have spiralled ever further away from narrative. Two productions, in particular, stand out with respect to this effort to move beyond story. Mauro Bigonzetti, an increasingly sought-after Italian choreographer, created in 2006 a *Romeo and Juliet* in collaboration with artist and set-and-costume-designer Fabrizio Plessi, set to Prokofiev's score and performed by his *Campagnia Aterbaletto*. Edward Clug, the Romanian-born artistic director of the Slovenian company Ballet Maribor, created *Radio and Juliet*, set to the music of Radiohead, in 2005, which has been performed frequently since its debut, including at Jacob's Pillow Dance Festival in the Berkshires in 2009. In interviews about their versions of *Romeo and Juliet*, Clug and Bigonzetti both express an exhaustion with the familiar story of Juliet and her Romeo. Clug insists, 'Everyone knows the story so well. I found no reason to tell it again.'[52] Similarly Bigonzetti notes, 'We didn't want to tell the Romeo and Juliet story.'[53]

So what were these choreographers after? We might begin with Bigonzetti since, in spite of the desire to distance himself from the active re-telling of a story, he retains the powerful narrative architecture of Prokofiev's score. But Bigonzetti's interests in *Romeo and Juliet* seem to lie in velocity and violence. 'I think *Romeo and Juliet* is one of the most violent works ever written', Bigonzetti insists.[54] That violence accounts for the odd scenario of this ballet, a kind of post-industrial wasteland, both shiny and grim, in which live occupants garbed in tattered street or sport clothing.

At different moments, dancers perform with a motorcycle helmet on one foot, a potentially gimmicky gesture but one that encourages a conversation about capacity and capability as a consequence of the marring or disabling of the sublime body of the dancer. Bigonzetti alters other core features of the balletic *Romeo and Juliet*. Early in Prokofiev's score, in a scene called, 'The City Awakens', the audience is introduced to a bustling city. In MacMillan and most other versions, this becomes the opportunity to introduce the feel of the Renaissance as townspeople go about their business. And yet when Bigonzetti deploys this music, a wholly different world emerges. Any contact between the dancers could break into conflict. Conflict is not an interruption of the civic, as it is in Shakespeare's text, but rather conflict is the civic. Moreover, everyone is Romeo and Juliet, with no necessary distinction between the various couples that emerge on the stage. The iconic status of two singular lovers is consistently dwarfed by the surroundings, as in a signature *pas de deux* in which two dancers relate to one another in and around a massive industrial fan.

Clearly Bigonzetti was mindful of contemporary urban life, a life in which mechanical conveniences menace youthful flesh. And yet his focus on violence and velocity in civic space finds ample resonance with Shakespeare's text. While some, like Lord Capulet, wish to rush events to their inevitable conclusions, others are wary of speed. Parting from Romeo the morning after their first encounter, Juliet says,

> I have no joy of this contract tonight;
> It is too rash, too unadvised, too sudden,
> Too like the lightning which doth cease to be
> Ere one can say 'it lightens'.
>
> (2.2.117–20)

And yet eager for news of Romeo from the Nurse, Juliet claims, 'Love's heralds should be thoughts, / Which ten times faster glides than the sun's beams' (2.5.4–5). It is only a few scenes before the sun rages again in Juliet's famous 'Gallop apace, you fiery-footed steeds' soliloquy (3.2.1), as Juliet impatiently anticipates her next meeting with her love. The blinding heat of the sun marks the intensity of love, its vicious rapidity and also the violence of a city at war with itself. It is no idle moment when Benvolio notices 'The day is hot' (3.1.2) at the opening of the scene in which Tybalt kills Mercutio and Romeo kills Tybalt. Heat distils the claustrophobia of civic violence, just as the sun indexes the damaging velocity of the play. No wonder Shakespeare altered his source, moving the steamy events of the play from Christmas to summer. Poor Friar Laurence hopes he can reach Romeo with a messenger before it is too late and, near the end, he even calls out 'Saint Francis be my speed' (5.3.121) in the futile hope that velocity might be of aid. Speed is a kind of poison, which Romeo seeks when he asks the apothecary for a swift substance with a 'soon-speeding gear' (5.1.60) or praises him, moments before his death, 'O true apothecary, / Thy drugs are quick' (5.3.119–20). Like theatre, dance forces us to think about time, about what Scott Maisano thinks of as the eternal 'now' of performance. And perhaps even more vividly than theatre, dance forces us to experience radically divergent velocities, from the whip-like movements of frenzied bodies to the stretched time of a languorous *pas de deux*.

Clug even more radically departs from the conventional architecture of the story ballet in *Radio and Juliet* by setting his ballet to music not composed for the purpose, in this case popular lyrics from Radiohead. Clug innovates in a number of other respects. His ballet introduces two film sequences, which both introduce new material and reiterate live movement. The ballet pairs one Juliet with six male dancers, each a potential Romeo. Velocity and violence mark Bigonzetti's *Romeo and Juliet*, but it is fluidity, depersonalization and interchangeability that mark *Radio and Juliet*.

If in Kenneth MacMillan's vision, meeting Juliet means being introduced to a set of received ideas about Juliet – her youthfulness, vigour, and even impetuousness – through the idiom of classical ballet, we meet a very different Juliet in Clug's choreography. *Radio and Juliet* opens with a film clip that Clug edited himself in collaboration with a film-maker. We see a woman, let us say Juliet, in a bare apartment, on a stripped bed on the floor. The camera gradually considers parts of Juliet's body and flashes forward to action yet to be seen in the ballet. There is a dream-like quality here, but it is not the gauzy romantic dream ruined by star-crossed circumstance. It is as if what we see is the dream of Juliet: is it before or after the disaster? How Juliet feels we cannot say. Romeo is absent. Nearly all the trappings are in abeyance. We see a woman alone, isolated from the enclosing context of tragic romance. Juliet is dressed in a corset-like outfit, suggesting discipline and structure but also restriction. Her movement is based on classical technique, to be sure, but it is both mechanical and virtuosic; little energy is spared for anything that creates a sense of characterization. Radiohead offers up a computer-generated voice: 'happier, fitter, more productive, no paranoia, care for all animals'. Soulful alienation characterizes both the music and the movement. Bale characterizes Radiohead's music as 'deeply emotional and depersonalizing', which is precisely the feeling we get from Clug's choreography, a choreography that inhabits the *Romeo and Juliet* myth to limn the contours of love, which we might describe as a machine of deep beauty and depersonalization. To a certain extent, Clug also captures something about what happens when a story becomes a myth, a process that is beautiful but results in abstraction. In some ways, this is the reverse process of several centuries of evolution of *Romeo and Juliet* toward an ever more personal, rather than civic, tragedy between two lovers who just want to be left alone by their family, friends and the whole world. 'Romeo, doff thy name', Juliet insists as she imagines a world beyond obligations signalled by names, 'And for thy name, which is no part of thee, / Take all myself' (2.2.47–9). Later Juliet imagines her love beyond the watchful eye of Verona when she summons him to 'Leap to these arms, untalked of and unseen' (3.2.7).

What, indeed, is her noted apostrophe to Night if not an invocation of privacy?

In spite of Clug's up-ending of story, recognizable moments appear – a fight scene, perhaps a party scene and certainly a wedding scene. The latter is of particular interest since it emphasizes not only depersonalization but also radical interchangeability. In Clug's marriage, Juliet stands downstage with her back to the audience. She steps forward moving methodically towards a figure upstage who seems to officiate the ceremony. At her first step, a Romeo figure joins her. As she takes another step, that Romeo figure is replaced by another again and again until she reaches the marriage itself. The myth of romantic love we attach to *Romeo and Juliet* is by necessity radically depersonalizing, which explains how widely it circulates. The intense focus on two lovers, so often the central feature of the Romeo and Juliet myth, suggests particularity and personality – in other words profound characterization and emotional expression. But to be capable of such broad distribution, a myth requires the sacrifice of some measure of particularity, which becomes clear in the revelatory conjunction of Clug's choreography and Radiohead's lyrics. The former, like Bigonzetti, privileges intensity of velocity, but for Clug that force is privileged over intensity of affect. The affectively laden lyrics of Radiohead are powerfully delivered, but at times with diminished affect and at times by nonhuman speakers. Broad circulation requires interchangeability, as if anyone can enter the story at any moment. Of course, the one constant in Clug's choreography is Juliet. She is the stable and often stationary focus of Clug's film, which lingers on Juliet's celluloid body amidst the ephemeral experiences on the stage. Juliet even seems to survive the tragic end of the story, which is where *Radio and Juliet* begins. Certainly, Juliet seems always to be the centre of gravity in choreographic productions of *Romeo and Juliet*, and in this Clug's distinctive vision swears fealty to tradition, to both Juliet's ascendancy and to centuries of ballerina-centred dance.

As vivid as these lovers have seemed to so many in the past four centuries, Shakespeare's own text again gives us reason to wonder if Clug's interest in depersonalization and interchangeability might in fact be essential to this great love story. Early on, still depressed over his rejection by Rosaline, Romeo insists, 'Tut, I have lost myself. I am not here. / This is not Romeo, he's some otherwhere' (1.1.195–6). These lines find an uncanny resonance with 'How to Disappear Completely', a Radiohead song Clug deploys in *Radio and Juliet*: 'That there, that's not me ... I'm not here. This isn't happening.'[55] In the play, Juliet replaces Rosaline and Paris is to replace Romeo. The dead Tybalt might have been the dead Romeo. Even Juliet's father identifies his daughter as part of a multitude from which Paris might choose at the Capulet ball:

> Hear all, all see,
> And like her most whose merit most shall be;
> Which, on more view, of many mine being one,
> May stand in number, though in reckoning none.
> (1.2.29–32)

Paris might find Juliet the singular beauty of the ball or she might be one of many. We all might be Romeos and Juliets, both Clug and Bigonzetti seem to suggest. When Juliet longs to immortalize her love, to 'Take him and cut him out in little stars' (3.2.22), she creates a constellation, which, for all its starry eternity, is an exemplar of interchangeability. Such is the nature of constellations, which are singular but imitable. Each time a pattern materializes before us – when an actor or dancer assumes a role – a tension between the iconic nature of the role and its ephemeral realization arises. Perhaps this is easier to observe when one is forced to look past language in the broad sweep of choreographic Shakespeares and to look past narrative and character in the more adventurous stagings of *Romeo and Juliet*.

Of course, not all respond well to deviations from narrative. On the blog Gramilano, Graham Spicer writes of Bigonzetti:

'Maybe it was unnecessary to call the ballet *Romeo and Juliet* at all, there are no parents, no friars, no daggers or bottles of poison. Why not simply present the evening as aspects of young love on the music of Sergei Prokofiev?'[56] Similarly, Brian Seifert's review of *Radio and Juliet* found the work to be intensely plot driven, which he imagines a virtue: 'Mr. Clug's reduction retains the basic outline of Shakespeare's play. His deviations are invariably diminishments.'[57] Deviation need not involve diminishment, which the long and varied legacy of Shakespearean metamorphoses proves and which brings us back to our original questions – 'What's Shakespeare?' and 'What's *Romeo and Juliet*?' For Spicer and Seifert *Romeo and Juliet* is a set of characters, an inevitable plot and a series of themes, especially young or adolescent love. Certainly, the history of iterations across the arts confirms such notions. But is this the promised end? And of course to acquiesce to theme allows us to set aside scepticism about the popularity of *Romeo and Juliet*. One of many rejoinders might be Anna Kisselgoff's, which she makes in her review of Preljocaj: 'But I don't agree with those French critics who feel that the evergreen story of doomed love has special appeal for choreographers in our troubled times. The reason for any "Romeo and Juliet", including this one, is pure box office.'[58] *Romeo and Juliet* may always sell and on all sorts of stages – but to reduce it to its simplest coordinates of plot, character and theme, is to sell it far too cheap and to miss that in addition to a compelling story, vibrant characters and a myth of tragic love, we have also been given instructions for dancing.

7

New Directions: The Names of the Rose: *Romeo and Juliet* in Italy

Shaul Bassi

Bringing Romeo and Juliet back to their native Italy invites a set of questions that illuminate the larger issue of how Shakespeare travels in space and time, across languages, cultures and different media. What did the Italian setting and plot mean for Shakespeare? How does a different cultural, linguistic, and religious context affect the reception and reconfiguration of a play? How does Shakespeare influence his sources? How does a Shakespearean myth become commodified, fetishized, trivialized? How do actors become interpreters of Shakespeare through their national identity, body, gender, age, speech, gestural vocabulary and so on? How does the city of Verona deal with its world-famous myth? This chapter takes the form of a return trip, from Italy to Shakespeare and back, an exploration of representative episodes in the Italian genealogy and afterlife of *Romeo and Juliet*. The first leg of the journey starts in the Middle Ages and traces the various sources that provided Shakespeare with the basic plot and characters of the play. The second leg involves a far more complicated and fuzzy itinerary, charting the various routes followed by *Romeo and Juliet* in Italy, involving on-going mutual interaction with the sources, with changing internal and external perceptions of the country, and with its primary location, the city of Verona.

Juliet's hands

'An analysis of the way the play treats its sources', writes Catherine Belsey, 'is as close as we can get to seeing Shakespeare at work.'[1] It may not be inappropriate to compare Shakespeare's approach to his literary sources, his ability to turn sophisticated texts geared at an elite readership into dramatic plays favoured by a much larger and socially mixed audience, to the contemporary Hollywood director or screen-writer who picks a novel read by thousands and turns it into a motion picture seen by millions. And as the novel sometimes reflects the glory of its more successful adaptation, returning to the market with the picture of the actors on the cover, in Italy Shakespeare's sources were later rediscovered thanks to the international reputation of *Romeo and Juliet* and thus came to re-assert their influence on the play's later reception.

Identifying these sources is not an easy task in itself, because every character, situation, theme and motif has one or more precedents in literature, all the way back to the classics, as the monumental work by Geoffrey Bullough, *Narrative and Dramatic Sources of Shakespeare* testifies.[2] We follow the majority of scholars in narrowing down our attention to the more recent texts, where the situation is moved to the specific moment of medieval Italy. In Masuccio Salernitano's *Il Novellino* (1476) Story 33 is summarized in this way:

> Mariotto from Siena, in love with Ganozza, flees to Alexandria after becoming a murderer. Ganozza pretends to be dead and,

> having been taken out of her tomb, goes in search of her lover. Mariotto, having heard of Ganozza's death, seeks his own death by returning to Siena. He is recognised, captured, his head cut off. Not finding Mariotto in Alexandria, Ganozza returns to Siena where she learns her lover has been beheaded. She dies of grief embracing his body.[3]

This synopsis presents a gruesome plot developed over a very extended temporal and geographical scope and corresponding to a slower narrative pace. Two later and better-known versions present the story as an already widely circulating narrative, with direct reference to its oral transmission and popularity at a time when 'civil conversation' was an important value in Renaissance aristocratic society.[4] It is in Luigi Da Porto's 'Hystoria novellamente ritrovata di due nobili amanti' (1524), that the action moves to Verona, during a specific period of the early fourteenth century, and that the rival families acquire names derived from Dante: 'Vieni a veder Montecchi e Cappelletti' ('Come and see the Montecchi and Cappelletti'), *Purgatory* (VI, 106). We also owe to Da Porto the names Romeo and Giulietta (imagine the lines in 2.2.2–3 reading 'But soft, what light through yonder window breaks? / It is the east, and Ganozza is the sun'). The same plot is expanded by Matteo Bandello in 'La sfortunata morte di dui infelicissimi amanti', the ninth of 214 novellas published in 1554, which was also one of six cautionary tales translated into French by Pierre Boaistuau in his *Histoires tragiques* (Paris, 1559). This 'Histoire troisième de deux Amants' became in turn the source of two English versions, one in verse by Arthur Brooke, 'The Tragicall Historye of Romeus and Juliet' (1562, reprinted 1582, 1587)[5] and one in prose, William Painter's *Palace of Pleasure* (1567). The critical consensus is that Shakespeare was familiar with both texts, but made specific use of Brooke. Nicole Prunster reminds us that all these texts were part of a larger cultural system and network of influences: 'Verona, as it is represented in these three novellas [Da Porto, Bandello, Boaistuau], appears as a synecdoche for the broader political situation against which Dante rails so vehemently in the *Purgatorio*.'[6] She argues that the new setting may also signify the 'wish to elevate the love of Romeo and Juliet to the ranks of Dante's love for Beatrice',[7] and that these specific references 'help to explain the common confusion between historical fact and fiction where the Romeo and Juliet tale is concerned', a 'misconception' that accounts for the visits of tourists to the balcony and grave of Juliet in Verona,[8] a phenomenon we shall analyse later.

Having reconstructed this complex family tree, let us now zoom in on a specific episode to see Shakespeare at work. If in Masuccio Salernitano's short tale there is no detail of the first meeting between the two young lovers, in Da Porto a carnival party organized by the Cappelletti offers Romeo the occasion to sneak into Giulietta's house. As the last dance is about to begin, the girl finds herself seated next to a man with a very unpleasant physical feature, 'Marcuccio the Cross-Eyed, whose hands were habitually very cold, in July no less than in January':

> Thus when Romeo Montecchi – for this was the young man's name – arrived on the woman's left and, as is done in this dance, took her fair hand in his, the maid said to him almost immediately, perhaps eager to hear him speak: 'Blessed be your arrival here at my side, because you at least will keep my left hand warm while Marcuccio freezes my right one.' Romeo, somewhat emboldened, continued: 'If I warm your hand with mine, you set my heart on fire with your beautiful eyes.' After a fleeting smile the woman spoke further to him, taking care not to be seen with him or heard speaking to him: 'I swear to you Romeo, on my faith, that no woman present appears as beautiful to my eyes as you do.' To which the youth replied, 'Whatever I may be, should it not displease your beauty, I shall be its faithful servant.'[9]

In Bandello's longer novella Marcuccio is portrayed as a very agreeable and witty courtier, still irredeemably damaged by his icy hands. When Romeo takes Giulietta's hand,

> she turned slightly towards him, perhaps eager to hear him speak, and said with a happy expression and trembling voice: 'Blessed be your arrival at my side!'; and thus saying, she squeezed his hand lovingly. The astute youth, who was nobody's fool, answered her thus while gently squeezing her hand: 'My lady, what does this blessing of yours mean?'; and looking at her beseechingly, he hung on her answer, sighing. Laughing sweetly, she then answered: 'Do not be amazed, kind young sir, if I bless your coming here, for Messer Marcuccio has for some time been freezing me all over with the chill of his cold hand and you mercifully warm me with your soft hand.' To this Romeo immediately added: 'My lady, it means a great deal to me that I am able to do you some service, and I yearn for nothing else in the world other than to be able to serve you. Hence I shall consider myself blessed whenever you deign to command me as you would your humblest servant. I can truly say that if my hand warms you, with the fire of your beautiful eyes you make me burn all over, ensuring that if you deny me help so that I can withstand such a fire, it will not be long before you see me burn up and turn to ashes.'[10]

Compared to Da Porto, Bandello indulges more in the lovers' body language and makes the girl even more clever, forthright and uninhibited. The religious trope of blessing is expanded, becoming almost hyperbolic in Romeo's devotional rhetoric. In Boaistuau, who as it was common in this period translates Bandello far from literally, the previously inoffensive Marcucio (now spelt with one 'c') becomes 'as bold amongst virgins as a lion is amongst lambs' and seizes Juliette's hand, provoking Rhomeo's reaction.

> Rhomeo, who was on Julliette's [sic] left, seeing that Marcucio was holding her right hand, took Julliette's other hand so as not to fail in his duty and, clasping it tightly for a while, felt so overwhelmed by this new favour that he was dumbstruck, incapable of replying. But Julliette, who

> realised from the change in his colour that this shortcoming was due to uncontrollable love, turned towards him eager to hear him speak. In a voice trembling with both virginal shyness and modesty she said to him: 'Blessed be the moment of your arrival at my side'; then, though intending to go on, love so sealed her lips that she was unable to finish what she had started out to say.[11]

From source to source, a far bolder and pushier Marcucio corresponds a more modest and reticent Juliette, more in line with Counter-Reformation morals, and the sparkling exchange between the new lovers is replaced by a tight-lipped, emotional situation of impasse. With Arthur Brooke we have the crucial transition to poetry, Marcucio becomes Mercutio, and Romeo and Juliet remain dumbstruck. In a poignant alternation they both desire to speak, but are muted by their overwhelming feelings. Brooke's Juliet is almost paralysed with shyness and when she finally summons the courage to speak, she explains to Romeo smilingly: 'Marvel no whit, my heart's delight, my only knight and fere, / Mercutio's icy hand had all-to frozen mine, / And of thy goodness thou again hast warmed it with thine.' Romeo takes the metaphor and unfolds it:

> But if my touched hand have warmed yours some deal,
> Assure yourself the heat is cold, which in your hand you feel,
> Compared to such quick sparks and glowing furious glead,
> As from your beauty's pleasant eyne, Love causéd to proceed;
> Which have so set on fire each feeling part of mine,
> That lo, my mind doth melt away, my outward parts do pine.
> And but you help, all whole, to ashes shall I turn;
> Wherefore, alas, have ruth on him, whom you do force to burn. (ll. 301–8)

As we finally come to Shakespeare, the hands have remained a central trope, but everything else has changed.

ROMEO
If I profane with my unworthiest hand
This holy shrine, the gentle sin is this:
My lips, two blushing pilgrims, ready stand
To smooth that rough touch with a tender kiss.

JULIET
Good pilgrim, you do wrong your hand too much,
Which mannerly devotion shows in this,
For saints have hands that pilgrims' hands do touch,
And palm to palm is holy palmers' kiss.

ROMEO
Have not saints lips and holy palmers too?

JULIET
Ay, pilgrim, lips that they must use in prayer.

ROMEO
O then, dear saint, let lips do what hands do –
They pray; grant thou, lest faith turn to despair.

JULIET
Saints do not move, though grant for prayers' sake.

ROMEO
Then move not while my prayer's effect I take.
[Kisses her.]
Thus from my lips by thine my sin is purged.
(1.5.92–106)

We can appreciate Shakespeare's editorial choices as he adapts the lengthy narrative and description to the needs of a dramatic dialogue, registering all the characters, themes and motifs, editing out certain elements and displacing or amplifying others. The most evident change is the removal of the rival from the scene. A character named Mercutio remains elsewhere in the tragedy, and Paris is the chosen intended of Capulet, but the emphasis now is no longer on Romeo getting the upper hand (pun intended) in the triangle, but on the pure, reciprocal love at first sight of Romeo and Juliet, who also come across as much closer to the talkative couple of Da Porto and Bandello than to the bashful and timorous youth of Boaistuau and Brooke. The shyness of Juliet is transferred to Romeo's 'blushing lips'. Shakespeare picks up on the trope of religion introduced by the 'blessing', and turns it into the extended metaphor of pilgrimage, putting its spiritual content into creative tension with the sensual and corporeal element of the lips.[12] The literary convention of the lovers' pilgrimage acquires special meaning, as Italy was historically the most important religious destination after Jerusalem, with Rome as capital of Christendom and Venice as the main port to the Holy Land.

Since the title of the first quarto (1597) defines the tragedy as *conceited*, it has been hypothesized that *Romeo and Juliet* may have been originally written for a private and educated audience.[13] At the formal level, not only does Shakespeare take the prose of the Italian tales and Brooke's verse and turn them into a dramatic form, but he also enriches it with frequent lyrical insertions. Specifically, the dialogue between Romeo and Juliet has the fourteen-line structure of a sonnet, a famous Italian import, a form in which Shakespeare excelled and that in his times had already been a well-honed and almost exhausted form in England. In *Romeo and Juliet* Shakespeare manages to parody the great Italian model of Petrarch (or rather his countless imitators), when he makes Romeo a caricature of the languishing, forlorn lover, and is simultaneously able to revive its form in this dramatic exchange.[14] The sonnet here gives voice not to the solipsistic meditation of the poet worshipping a typically idealized and silent woman at a safe remove, but to two sharp-witted and flirtatious young people with a pronounced sense of the erotic charge of language. Their final kiss is the dramatic action that both crowns and overcomes the poetic essence of the sonnet.[15] (For more critical discussion of sonnets in the play, see Rebeca Helfer's 'The State of the Art' in this volume.)

Alongside these narrative and literary elements, it is important to remember that Shakespeare also took other anthropological and political materials from Italy. François Laroque has demonstrated how *Romeo and Juliet* is one of the Italian plays where Shakespeare borrows 'carnivalesque elements with masques, torches, fifes and drums, cross-dressing as well as more subversive aspects such as those concerned with sexuality and satire' and his theatrical practices interact with that of *commedia dell'arte*.[16] These comic elements do not function only as jocose counterpoints to the tragic action of *Romeo and Juliet* or *Othello*, but are themselves ambivalent. Carnivalesque situations challenge the social order, staging the mockery and defiance of patriarchal authority and, in the eyes of the English, they were also potential occasions for outbreaks of civic violence or even full-scale rebellions. In the popular imagination of Protestant countries, Italy is still often associated with festive occasions and with the Catholic taste for ceremonies and pomp, in an ambivalent attitude of attraction and repulsion. The dangerous contiguity between feast and riot, order and chaos, also points to the political overtones of *Romeo and Juliet*, where the relationship between the private and the public sphere, whose distinction was not fully articulated in the early modern era, is another prominent theme. The civic issues that underlie the society of Capulets and Montagues correspond to larger political questions fiercely debated in Shakespeare's time and place.[17] The role of civil unrest, the relationship between the spiritual and the secular power, the Catholic doctrine and its opponents, the obedience of children toward parental authority, the different, overlapping jurisdictions (secular law, canon law, individual deliberation) that could enter in some sort of friction regarding marriage: in all of these areas, Italy was a mirror and a political laboratory, one where Niccolò Machiavelli was teaching Europe to consider the state not as an idealized realm of benevolent rule, but as a practical battleground where facing the naked truth was a prerequisite for any efficacious action. Friar Laurence, for instance, is deeply aware of the political dimension of Romeo and Juliet's romance: 'In one respect I'll thy assistant be, / For this alliance may so happy prove, / To turn your households' rancour to pure love' (2.3.86–8). In this he proves, as it were, a good reader of Machiavelli, who denounced the dangers of factionalism for any political community: 'in a strong principality such factions will never be allowed, since they are profitable only in peacetime, allowing the subjects to be more easily manipulated by such means; but when war comes, such arrangements reveal their fallacious nature' (*The Prince*, Chapter 20).[18] It is a telling semantic inversion that the liaison between Romeo and Juliet is defined as an 'alliance' while that of the two rival families is associated with 'love'. And yet the Friar's scheme to reunite the two after Romeo's banishment is so complicated and haphazard that he finally seems to prove right also Machiavelli's judgement that the church is one of the main factors of political division in Italy, being too weak to extend its temporal power to the whole country and yet too powerful to allow any external power to guarantee the necessary unity (*Discourses on Livy*, I, 12).[19]

Juliet's feet

With the second leg of the trip, the religious pilgrimage to medieval Italy gradually transitioned into the secular Grand Tour to Romantic Italy and eventually into the modern-day experience of the *Lonely Planet* tourist. In a history of multiple displacements and dislocations, Shakespeare turned Italian tales and themes into successful plays for the stage and Italians struck back by taking his plays and adapting them into a variety of forms and media, before they were convinced to applaud the dramatic form Shakespeare had given them. Italians began to be interested in Shakespeare in the late eighteenth century. His indifference to the Aristotelian unities made him a champion of innovation for Romantic Italian intellectuals fighting against the constraints of neoclassical literature, but they considered him more a theoretical paragon than an author to imitate or stage. Initially Shakespeare came to Italy by way of France and the earliest recorded performance of *Romeo and Juliet* is a *Tragedia Veronese* staged in Venice in 1785 and based on Ducis's French version. But while one had to wait until the second half of the nineteenth century to have complete translations and successful stagings of the plays in Italian, the stories of Romeo and Juliet came to be a very popular subject in painting, music and dance, particularly in *melodramma* (opera). It appears that the European vogue of Shakespeare's *Romeo and Juliet*, which produced significant musical versions in France and Germany as well, made Italians re-discover their home-grown plot, but also inclined them towards the local variants. Italian composers produced several *Giulietta e Romeos* or *Romeo e Giuliettas* that were only loosely based on the Shakespearean text and drew extensively from the Italian sources. A telling example is Vincenzo Bellini's *I Capuleti e i Montecchi* (1830), preceded by no less than five musical versions. The libretto by Felice Romani was a rewrite of an earlier text prepared for a different composer, itself inspired by Luigi Scevola's play *Giulietta e Romeo* (1818). As the title suggests, the emphasis is placed less on the two protagonists than on the feud between families, cast as representatives of the Guelph (pro-Pope) and Ghibelline (pro-Emperor) political factions that had characterized medieval Italy. The extreme emotions and grand dramatic situations associated with the genre of opera and its musical means were particularly suitable to the final scene, where Romeo drinks poison at the tomb of Giulietta, who had taken a sleeping potion counterfeiting death, and sings his farewell aria. When Giulietta wakes up and learns from Romeo about his suicidal act, she falls dead upon his body in the very moment when the two families appear on the scene. A politically fragmented and colonized Italy (the country would not achieve unification until 1861) may explain both the interest for ancient internecine rivalries and the reclamation of the Italian sources of the play, with comparatively little attention to the Shakespearean text and a generalized hostility to the genre of tragedy, a genre that had always been more congenial to the stages of powerful nations (France, Spain, England) than to the small theatres of Italian city states. This view is corroborated by the coeval effort to demonstrate that Romeo and Juliet had been real historical characters and their story based in fact. The claim was made in a book published in 1831 by a political exile, when Verona and the whole of Northern Italy were under Austrian rule. As Paola Pugliatti shows, the pleasures and values of the civil conversation that had framed the tales by Da Porto and Bandello gave way to the priority of factuality and originality and to 'the vindication of local identity and the pride of one's own traditions and history'.[20]

A similar phenomenon can be observed in painting, where the decline of mythology and religion as favourite pictorial themes corresponded to the rise of historical themes and of real-life characters with whom one could empathize. It is in this context that Francesco Hayez was commissioned to paint the large canvas *Romeo and Juliet's Last Kiss* (1823), which enjoyed a phenomenal success. That Shakespeare was not Hayez's main source is demonstrated by his companion piece, *The Marriage of Romeo and Juliet* (1830), depicting an episode from Da Porto's novella that does not appear in Shakespeare.[21] Hayez's experiment may have been influenced by Shakespearean illustrations made in France and Germany, showing once more the hybridization of Shakespeare and his sources matched by the artistic struggle between old and new styles. The painter wanted to authenticate the backdrop of the scene (the long subtitle ends with the note 'the architecture is reminiscent of the times in wich [sic] the ill-fated lovers lived'), and he echoed contemporary Italian commentators in their praise for Shakespeare's historical truthfulness and psychological insight. Hayez's realism was acclaimed by many but also heavily criticized: a German art historian scolded him for painting a 'muscular' Juliet that looked like one of the Bacchae and a Romeo 'with the shoulders of a porter'.[22] The controversy may have contributed to the countless prints and miniatures imitating the subject and to the four different versions later realized by Hayez himself. *Romeo and Juliet's Last Farewell* of 1833 shows the two lovers in the same embraced posture, but their lips are now parted and Juliet's foot, which in a touch of domestic realism that had shocked the neoclassical decor was enfolded in a slipper, is now more modestly covered by the flowing nightgown.

These musical and pictorial expressions (to which one should add various choreographies; see chapter by Joseph Campana in this volume) belonged to the vast artistic and cultural movement of Romanticism, a term whose invention is credited to the French writer Madame de Staël and her novel *Corinne ou l'Italie*. In the novel the titular heroine Corinne travels to Italy and attends a performance of *Romeo and Juliet*:

> Romeo and Juliet is an Italian subject. The scene takes place in Verona. People there still point out the lovers' tomb. Shakespeare wrote the play with the full power of the southern imagination, an imagination which is triumphant in happiness and yet goes so easily from that happiness to despair, and from despair to death ... Shakespeare, better than any other foreign writer, understood Italy's national character, the fertile mind which invents a thousand different ways of expressing the same feeling, and the oriental eloquence which uses the images from the whole of nature to depict what takes place in the heart ... In this work, there is the sap of life, a brilliance of language which is characteristic of the country and its inhabitants. The play of *Romeo and Juliet*, translated into Italian, seems to return to its native tongue.[23]

In Madame de Staël's emphasis on intense emotions, on the force of nature, on the faculty of imagination, and on a national character, *Romeo and Juliet* becomes a catalyst for all the elements associated with Romanticism. The notion of a 'return to its mother tongue' attributes a newly recognized anthropological quality to Shakespeare's play, precisely at a time, the early nineteenth century, in which our modern theories and stereotypes of race and ethnicity are formed. (See Naomi Conn Liebler's 'Critical Backstory' for more on the North–South dynamics shaping the play's nineteenth-century reception.) It is important to notice at this point that whenever *Romeo and Juliet* is set in Italy, even when adapted to a different age, perceptions of Italy become part of the show. The 'Alfa Romeo *Romeo and Juliet*' (after the car that Michael Bogdanov brought on stage in his 1986 Royal Shakespeare Company production) is an oft-quoted example of how a stereotypical Italy is made a sort of additional character of the play.

Joseph Luzzi has demonstrated both the ways in which numerous travellers brought to Italy a number of concerns that created an imaginary country whose influence continues to this day and the ways in which Italian writers constructed a sense of national identity hinged on the relationship with the past, whether that of classical antiquity or that of the Middle Ages and the Renaissance: 'the particular anachronism that Italy offered in the Romantic age suggests our abiding desire to return to cultural homelands that never existed'.[24] Corinne represents the ambivalent attitude to Italy, a critique and self-critique of modernity.

Italy itself internalized these notions, and when *Romeo and Juliet* finally became famous in dramatic forms (by Shakespeare or other authors), the intrinsic Italianness of the play was always highlighted. A special example is provided by the diva Eleonora Duse (1858–1924), the major Italian actress of all time (her own name is still synonymous with 'great actress'). From anecdotes disseminated during her lifetime (and probably cultivated by Duse herself) to more recent biographies, there is a peculiar, epiphanic moment connected to her interpretation of the young lover in Verona. Her legendary status is still linked to her debut as Juliet when she was fourteen (ironically in a non-Shakespearean version). The harsh conditions and the physical and psychological exploitation that she and many child actors probably suffered was far less touching than the drama of a young Italian actress destined to international fame, impersonating the young Italian character in the city where it all began.[25] The various anecdotes were given canonical form by Duse's lover Gabriele D'Annunzio in his novel *The Flame of Life*:

> We entered Verona one evening in the month of May through the gate of the Palio, anxiety suffocated me. I held the copy-book, where I had copied out the part of Juliet with my own hand, tightly against my heart, and constantly repeated to myself the words of my first entrance: 'How now! Who calls? I am here. What is your will?' A strange coincidence had excited my imagination: I was fourteen years old on that very day, – the age of Juliet! The gossip of the Nurse buzzed in my ears; little by little my destiny seemed to be getting mixed up with the destiny of the Veronese maiden. At the corner of every street I thought I saw a crowd coming towards me and accompanying a coffin covered with white roses. As soon as I saw the Arche degli Scaligeri, closed with iron nails, I cried out to my mother, 'Here is the tomb of Juliet.' And I began to weep bitterly with a desperate desire of love and death … One Sunday in May, in the immense arena in the ancient amphitheatre under the open sky, I have been Juliet before a popular multitude that had breathed in the legend of love and death. No quiver from the most vibrating audiences, no applause, no triumph has ever meant the same to me as the fulness and the intoxication of that great hour.[26]

Duse is here transfigured into the woman who literally abandons herself to the role, fusing with it in a unique symbiosis among national identity, character acting and place. Madame de Staël's notion that Shakespeare had captured some anthropological truth about his Italian characters was borne out by the often repeated fact that Italian actors were naturally made to embody them. And here gender plays a crucial role, because the adolescent Duse literally *becomes* Juliet, thanks to the perceived feminine capacity for sentimental identification. In the case of male actors it remained more conventional to praise their dramatic talent rather than their fusion with the character, as when Ernesto Rossi impersonated Romeo with great acclaim until he was forty-six-years old.

The Italian appropriation of *Romeo and Juliet* reached its international peak in 1968 with Franco Zeffirelli's award-winning film – one that paid a stunning visual tribute to the art and culture of Renaissance Italy and concurrently celebrated the decade of sexual liberation and intergenerational conflict of its age[27] (see Ian Munro's 'Performance History' in this volume). Yet we concentrate on a different twentieth-century example which offers an anti-sentimental, anti-naturalistic, anti-narrative adaptation challenging the mythology and stereotypes of *Romeo and Juliet*. The symbiosis between the Shakespearean text and its sources finds in the avant-garde actor and director Carmelo Bene's postmodern version at once its apotheosis and its ultimate deconstruction. In 1976, when he brought his *Romeo e Giulietta* on stage, the tragedy had long become a canonical work and a national icon. Bene managed to push the national tradition to its extreme in his interpolation of Shakespeare's text with Da Porto's tale and Bellini's music, but he was also innovative in his radical strategy of 'amputation and subtraction' of the text informed by post-structuralist theory. He intended to curtail, if not effectively block, the psychological and emotional dimension of the play by deliberately deconstructing the very concept of character. He transformed the role of Mercuzio[28] by keeping him in agony, but alive, even after he has been killed on stage. This gesture aimed at occluding identification with character and at preventing the catharsis associated with the death of tragic heroes, the two standard elements of classical tragedy. The dissociation of actor and voice, or the frequent gender switches of certain characters were also part of Bene's technique of enstrangement.[29] When Romeo dies at the end, the last words of Juliet are: 'Tonight ... again' and those of

Mercuzio: 'He is dead! He was a strange guy after all ... He must have taken his part too seriously without telling me or maybe he let himself go with improvised poetry or with drinking or with consumption or with nothing or ... maybe ... with me (*music*).'[30] More pastiche than parody, Bene's metatheatrical playtext exploded all sentimental clichés and emphasized the artificiality and literariness of *Romeo and Juliet* as a constantly rewritten palimpsest.

Juliet's bones

Ultimately the most extraordinary Italian adaptation of Shakespeare, the most surprising contamination of the text and its sources, is the city of Verona itself. A literary myth can overflow the boundaries of the aesthetic and spill into other domains such as onomastics, tourism, industry and advertising. Verona is an important urban centre in one of the richest regions of Italy and Europe, and when the Englishman Richard Lassels described it in his *Voyage of Italy* (1670), he recommended a visit to 'The famous tomb of the Signori della Scala, who once were Masters here, and from whom Joseph and Julius Scaliger pretend to have come.'[31] Little could he suspect that one day, thanks to Shakespeare, the tomb of Escalus would be far less famous than another sepulchre, as recorded in 1817 by Lord Byron: 'I have been over Verona. The amphitheatre is wonderful – beats even Greece. Of the truth of Juliet's story, they seem tenacious to a degree, insisting on the fact – giving a date (1303) and showing a tomb. It is a plain, open, and partly decayed sarcophagus, with withered leaves in it, in a wild and desolate conventual garden, once a cemetery, now ruined to the very graves.'[32] Today Romeo and Juliet are a landmark and trademark of Verona and the tomb is still a popular destination, but the real attraction is Juliet's house, with its famous balcony, visited by a million people every year. The paradox is that the place that promises the illusion of the closest contact with the reality of Romeo and Juliet is also the most self-consciously fictional. In 1935 the Hollywood producer Irving Thalberg sent a troupe to Verona to research the city's libraries and photograph several locations for George Cukor's film *Romeo and Juliet* (1936).[33] After ruling out the possibility of shooting in Italy due to the political uncertainties of Europe, 'an imaginary Verona was built on MGM's largest back lot',[34] less a realistic version of the city than an idealized setting that would eclectically combine several styles and motifs to fit the dramatic action of the play. The balcony, in particular, was modelled after the exterior pulpit of the Cathedral of Prato, decorated by Donatello in the fifteenth century. The international success of the movie rekindled curiosity for the sites linked to the story, unmarked for a long time, and Antonio Avena, director of the city museums, opened the house as a tourist site. The first floor was redesigned on the model of Hayez's *The Last Kiss* and although the English Shakespeare and the American Hollywood epitomized Fascist Italy's sworn enemies, 'The literary prestige of the Romeo and Juliet play was harnessed by the regime as a manifestation of Verona's great cultural tradition and evidence of its Italian genius.'[35] The additional irony is that the balcony is in fact a tomb, a medieval sarcophagus that was previously held at the museum of Castelvecchio. Ramie Targoff has suggested that the play expresses a new sense of marital intimacy that continues after death into the grave.[36] Today, Juliet's Tomb is the site where many couples come from all over the world to crown their dream of love and get married in the place where Romeo and Juliet saw their hopes shattered. Clearly the bond of love that kept the two lovers together until the very end is stronger than any bad omen related to their violent death.

Juliet's breast

When Paola Marini, director of Verona city museums, describes in the official guide to the site the 'ritual-like experience of one's pilgrimage to this special site in fair Verona',[37] she acknowledges that the pilgrim lovers have given way to the pilgrim tourist, the traveller who seeks 'the security of pure cliché'.[38] It may be helpful here to introduce the distinction between pop and kitsch, two categories that guide the way consumer culture processes Romeo and Juliet's mythology, transforming the story into a variety of commodities that can be acquired inexpensively and are supposed to provide quick and easy access to the world of Shakespeare. Over the dead body of Juliet, Romeo's father celebrates the uniqueness of art as an antidote to mortality: 'For I will raise her statue in pure gold, / That whiles Verona by that name is known, / There shall no figure at such rate be set / As that of true and faithful Juliet' (5.3.299–302). Popular culture (a category to which Shakespeare belonged to some extent) tries to make art more accessible; kitsch attempts to completely annul the distance, a mechanism that can be seen at work in *Juliet's Statue*, a sculpture realized in 1972 and placed in the museum's courtyard. A tradition that cannot be older than that suggests that touching Juliet's right breast brings good luck in love, making that body part 'worn shiny by contact with so many hands'[39] and forcing the city to commission a replica of the statue to remedy the wear and tear. A whole wall behind the statue is covered with constantly removed sticky love notes and love padlocks, an effect of a 'padlock craze' started in 2004 by the blockbuster novel *Three Meters Above Heaven* by cult author Federico Moccia.[40] Kitsch provides instant gratification and the impression of having had access to the love of Romeo and Juliet without any need to read or see the play. One may agree with Paola Marini's tongue-in-cheek remark that '[b]ecause of their immaterial quality, the values at stake here can hardly be threatened by mass tourism',[41] but it may also be instructive to seek popular adaptations of Romeo and Juliet that do not trivialize their legend. And it may be counter-intuitive to find that in a soccer stadium. In fact many Italians still remember a banner unrolled by Neapolitan fans at Verona stadium, as a retort to the local hooligans' racist slogans inciting Mount Vesuvius to turn Naples into a new Pompeii: 'Juliet was a whore.' One may be rightly irritated by the vulgarity and misogyny of the banner (one that unwittingly echoes the characteristic split image of woman in Italian culture, saint or whore), but paradoxically this was a speech act that took Shakespeare and Juliet very seriously, acknowledging their centrality for the cultural identity of Verona. I would take this as a partial but successful adaptation of the play into popular culture, one that jars with the far more benign, tame and ultimately ineffectual expressions of kitsch in Verona and elsewhere.

Pop and kitsch probably intermingle in another famous phenomenon. Inside the museum there is a room called Juliet's Desk where you can choose whether to contact your heroine by ordinary mail or by email. Corresponding with Juliet is made possible by the *Juliet Club*, a group 'in charge of a very unique task: replying to the thousands of letters that are addressed to "Juliet" from everywhere in the world. A team of experienced volunteers read all the letters and answer back, in all different languages.' Volunteers are actively sought, with a preference for 'candidates with backgrounds in foreign languages, psychology, sociology, literature and journalism' who must be fluent in written English; 'Particularly welcome are skills like psychology, creativity and empathy, meaning the ability to transmit messages of love and hope on behalf of Juliet.'[42] Conceived in the 1930s by Ettore Solimani, after he collected the first letters that people left at the feet of Juliet's tomb where he worked as a keeper, the group acquired its present form in 1991, when Giulio Tamassia enlisted university students to help with the translation and replies. The club was made famous by Lise and Ceil Friedman's book *Letters to Juliet* (2006)[43] and the film by the same title (2010).[44] If *Romeo and Juliet* is about adolescent love challenging social and political obstacles, and if the book pays tribute to the writers' ability to discern and respond to genuine desires and troubles, in the American film the parallel romance between two elderly widowers who had fallen in love in their youth and two younger people who try to reunite the old couple celebrates passion without impediment, rivalry and strife. With the scene rapidly shifting from Verona to the stereotypical Tuscan countryside beloved by foreign visitors, the old and new lovers are happily (re)united in no time, and everybody else is happy too. Paul Kottman has argued[45] that *Romeo and Juliet* foreshadows a distinctly modern sense of individualism. The movie envisions a society of liquid love where individualism is becoming more and more an unhindered satisfaction without any social obligation or cost.[46] All the elements of Shakespearean comedy, where the happy ending is predicated on the overcoming of several obstacles, are absent in this contemporary comedy. The political laboratory of early modern Italy has given way to the postcard country where under the Tuscan sun love and pleasure (always accompanied by delicious catering) can be consumed à la carte with no hindrance.

When asked about the meaning of the title of his medieval murder mystery *The Name of the Rose,* the defining novel of Italian postmodernism, Umberto Eco explained that the multiplicity of meanings attached to that symbolic flower could usefully confound the readers.[47] Curiously, among the many literary and cultural examples he listed, from the War of the Roses to Gertrude Stein's 'a rose is a rose',[48] he did not mention the famous lines by Juliet 'What's in a name? That which we call a rose / By any other word would smell as sweet' (2.2.43–4). Like the medieval sentence 'stat rosa pristina nomine, nomina nuda tenemus' that had inspired Eco's title, Juliet's words express the tension between signifier and signified that was one of the dominant themes of the debates about post-structuralism and postmodernism in the 1970s and 1980s. (See Liebler and Helfer in this volume.) In

Juliet's house the timeless love of Romeo and Juliet is represented in a truly postmodern way, in a seamless juxtaposition of artifacts from different epochs. In contemporary Italy, Romeo and Juliet constitute a complex web of signs, a multimedia myth where the reading or staging of Shakespeare's play is not the only or even the most central event. We have seen early narratives of the two lovers metamorphosing in Shakespeare's *Romeo and Juliet* and the play itself mutating into multiple versions in multiple media, from highbrow theatrical adaptations to tacky souvenirs. Arguably, some of the signs of Romeo and Juliet have become floating signifiers, loosely connected to their original sources, but taking a life of their own in the consumer culture of merchandise. The 'timeless' love of Romeo and Juliet seems to say something also about who we are here and now.

8

Teaching Resources: Critical and Pedagogical Approaches

M. Barbara Mello

Romeo and Juliet is often the first Shakespeare play that students encounter, and for good reason: this perennially popular drama of doomed young love seems forever young itself, accessible across the divides of space and time, language and culture, bridging the very generation gap that the play so movingly portrays. This chapter offers a selection of approaches to teaching *Romeo and Juliet*, a play whose poetic language and dramatic actions fuse love, aggression and wit on civic and domestic stages. Shakespeare's tragedy has undergone continual renewal on stage, in film, ballet and opera, and in commerce and tourism, and the play's proteanism makes it a particularly fruitful object of study in today's classrooms. The resources gathered in the annotated bibliography below, including scholarly editions, critical and pedagogical works, performance histories, media sources and major websites, invite an array of interpretative approaches and classroom practices.

Scholarly editions

Scholarly editions of *Romeo and Juliet* support exploration of foundational critical questions about author, text and context for courses on Shakespeare or early English dramatic works.[1] Both undergraduate and graduate students will benefit from engaging with the scholarly record concerning Shakespeare's personal and professional life as well as important contexts provided in most scholarly editions. These editions also offer extensive footnotes and glosses of words whose meaning has changed or are no longer in use today and provide useful notes and information on the original texts – quartos and folios – on which modern editions are based. For *Romeo and Juliet*, this information is vital, given that there are five extant quarto editions of Shakespeare's *Romeo and Juliet*. Q2 (1599) is the most authoritative source, since Q3 (1609) and Q4 (1622) and the 1623 First Folio versions of this play seem to be derived from it. Q1 (1597) has almost 700 fewer lines than Q2.[2] Students may enjoy learning about some of these variations and debating the value and meaning of certain cuts or additions. For example, the play's famous Prologue is found in Q1 and Q2 but not in the Folio version. Students might compare and evaluate the different theatrical advantages and interpretative consequences of these two different ways of opening the play.

In the 1980 second Arden edition of *Romeo and Juliet,* editor Brian Gibbons provides a thorough discussion of the editorial similarities and differences between Q1 and Q2. This edition also includes extracts of Shakespeare's source material, Arthur Brooke's *Tragicall Historye of Romeus and Juliet*, 1562.[3] For the 2012 third Arden series of this play, René Weis offers a detailed account of editorial practices concerning the differing quartos and folios. In addition to exploring a range of subjects, from rhetoric to romantic love, Weis also considers adaptations of Shakespeare's tragedy on stage and film as well as in ballet and opera.[4]

The Bedford *Romeo and Juliet*, edited by Dympna Callaghan, provides extensive excerpts from other texts of the period, which introduce students to important historical and cultural contexts. Callaghan's introduction sets this play within its own literary and theatrical moment and explains how Shakespeare's dramatic work speaks to the rhetorical and lyrical styles flourishing in the 1590s. Although *Romeo and Juliet* is often credited with forming modern notions of love, Callaghan show us how the play stages its own cultural moment's ideas of love such as 'love at first sight'.[5] Callaghan bridges early modern notions of love with postmodern ideals, addressing early modern ideas of homoeroticism, compulsory heterosexuality, and the domestic, public and religious spaces that housed familial and communal life.[6]

James Loehlin's edition, *Romeo and Juliet: Shakespeare in Production*, directs students' attention to the performance history of Shakespeare's play. Loehlin provides an overview of important productions and the various actors who brought these famous roles to life. His consideration of actors and acting companies invites students to ponder the many choices actors, directors and designers must make to re-create the play. For the Oxford edition of *Romeo and Juliet*, editor Jill Levenson provides a comprehensive discussion of the performance history of *Romeo and Juliet* in addition to analysis of important themes.

Major one-volume editions of Shakespeare include David Bevington's *The Complete Works of Shakespeare*, now in its seventh edition. Bevington's introductory essays to the plays enable students to understand major themes and issues as well as English history and culture. *The Oxford Shakespeare: The Complete Works*, second edition, edited by Stanley Wells, provides useful illustrations and introductory materials. *The Norton Shakespeare*, third edition, with Stephen Greenblatt as general editor, uses the Oxford edition of Shakespeare's plays and provides extensive contextual and critical analysis by prominent historicist scholars; the third edition features an enhanced digital edition that includes an extensive documents section. *The Riverside Shakespeare,* second edition, under the general editorship of G. Blakemore Evans and J. J. M. Tobin, includes a comprehensive overview of Shakespeare and his culture by Harry Levin and a survey of critical discourses by Heather Dubrow. These collections support courses that explore several of Shakespeare's plays or examine Shakespeare's development as a playwright; ancillary materials, such as maps and portraits, offer a variety of ways for teachers and students to engage with this playwright and his culture.

Critical and pedagogical approaches

One of the many pleasures in studying *Romeo and Juliet* is the play's rhetorical and poetic virtuosity. Catherine Belsey's *Romeo and Juliet: Language and Writing* is particularly useful in the classroom.[7] Belsey explores the play's use of language around the theme of love and death, while guiding the reader through the action of the play, its characters and early modern culture and stagecraft. Gillian Woods' *Romeo and Juliet: A Reader's Guide to Essential Criticism* is a comprehensive account of literary and theatrical responses to the play.[8] Marjorie Garber's *Shakespeare After All* insightfully considers Shakespeare's uses of the sonnet form to create the palpable tension between star-crossed love and civil strife played out on stage. In *Shakespeare and the Arts of Language*, Russ McDonald examines the instability of language in *Romeo and Juliet* and provides an overview of English rhetorical culture; his thoughtful analysis of Shakespeare's world and professional life focuses on Shakespeare's development and mastery of language.

New Historicism and Cultural Materialism scholarship of the 1990s, exemplified in the work by scholars such as Stephen Greenblatt, Catherine Gallagher, Jean Howard and Alan Sinfield, can help students explore *Romeo and Juliet* from various social and political perspectives, which can be complemented by feminist and post-colonial interpretations of the play. In 'The Ideology of Romantic Love', for example, Dympna Callaghan shows how a feminist materialist methodology puts pressure on ideals of romantic love in *Romeo and Juliet*. She explains that in England during the 1590s, when this play was first performed, the institution of marriage was undergoing many changes. Protestant, specifically Puritan, reformers were forcefully attempting to align marriage laws and customs with the emerging ideals of capitalism. This move enforced heterosexuality and encouraged ideas of romantic love in order to place women under patriarchal control. Jonathan Gil Harris also offers a compelling deployment of cultural materialism in 'Mechanical Turks, mammet tricks and messianic time'. Turning our attention to Capulet's description of his rebellious daughter as a 'mammet' (3.5.185), Harris explains that this term can refer to the name Mohammed or to a mechanical puppet; Harris argues that the term mechanizes Juliet as she struggles to assert her own agency. Fairies always fascinate: in *Troublesome Things: A History of Fairies and Fairy Stories*, Diane Purkiss argues that Shakespeare's plays began the process of draining the power out of these dangerous beings and transforming them into the pretty creatures of today.[9]

The scholarly analysis of law, order and custom in the early modern period helps students understand both the play's world and the way in which the play's cultural moment has informed our own. Early modern ideas of domesticity and hospitality, for example, are arguably still practised today. In 'Making Room, Affording Hospitality: Environments of Entertainment in *Romeo and Juliet*', Julia Lupton takes us into the Capulets' household to examine Renaissance hospitality as a form of home theatre.[10] In *A Feminist Perspective on Renaissance Drama*, Alison Findlay also focuses on the domestic sphere to consider parental power structures and betrothal rituals. Findlay argues that Juliet's choice to forego parental approval and marry Romeo is a move to claim power that disrupts the parental structures in this domestic sphere.[11] Lupton's and Findlay's work on domesticity encourages students to reflect on early modern conventions and rituals that continue to be played out in our own cultural moment.

Performance studies, another fruitful approach to teaching Shakespeare's play, emphasizes early modern stage practices in dialogue with subsequent performance history. In the classroom, this teaching method can use recorded performances of the play (see the annotated bibliography, below) or invite students to act out specific scenes as a means of engaging critically and creatively with Shakespeare. James Loehlin uses this pedagogical approach in his edition of *Romeo and Juliet*. Milla Cozart Riggio, in *Teaching Shakespeare through Performance,* also offers invaluable strategies for incorporating performance into the classroom in order to involve students immersed in today's film and television culture.[12] In Riggio's collection, Jill L. Levenson's '*Romeo and Juliet* on the Stage' offers instructions for composing a performance study guide that allows students to develop close reading and critical thinking skills through a variety of perspectives, depending upon the demands of the character's role and stage practices of the play. In the same volume, Cary M. Mazer's 'Playing the Action' promotes acting strategies such as using active verbs to sketch out a character's objectives and stage movement. Lynda E. Boose and Richard Burt's *Shakespeare, The Movie: Popularizing the Plays on Film, TV, and Video* includes Robert Hapgood's study of Franco Zeffirelli's popular film of the play and Laurie E. Osborne's analysis of animated versions of *Romeo and Juliet.* Both essays show how these films use early modern English culture to illuminate their own cultural moment. Samuel Crowl's *Shakespeare and Film: A Norton Guide* provides an overview of film-making and its terminology; Crowl's analysis of cinematic and televised versions of the play considers the use of the camera positions and editing processes in constructing and communicating meaning.

Shakespeare's *Romeo and Juliet* reveals, resists, exposes and explores a vast array of cultural meanings that speak to a range of historical moments and a diversity of cultures. The annotated bibliography that follows provides selected works that can be used to investigate the many worlds of *Romeo and Juliet*.

Annotated bibliography

Scholarly editions

Bevington, David, ed. *The Complete Works of Shakespeare*, 6th edn. New York: Longman, 2008.

Callaghan, Dympna, ed. *Romeo and Juliet: Texts and Contexts*. Boston, MA: Bedford/St Martin's, 2003.

Daniel, P. A., ed. *Romeo and Juliet: Parallel Texts of the First Two Quartos*. Published for the New Shakspere Society, London: N. Trübner & Co., 1874.

Evans, G. Blakemore, Herschel Baker and J. J. M. Tobin, eds. *The Riverside Shakespeare*, 2nd edn. Boston: Houghton Mifflin, 1997.

Gibbons, Brian, ed. *Romeo and Juliet*, Arden 2nd series. London: Methuen, 1980.

Greenblatt, Stephen, Walter Cohen, Jean E. Howard and Katharine Eisaman Maus, eds. *The Norton Shakespeare*, 2nd edn. New York: W. W. Norton & Co., 2008.

Greenblatt, Stephen, Walter Cohen, Jean E. Howard, Katharine Eisaman Maus, Gordon McMullan and Suzanne Gossett, eds. *The Norton Shakespeare*, 3rd edn. New York: W. W. Norton & Co., 2016.

Levenson, Jill L., ed. *The Oxford Shakespeare: Romeo and Juliet*. Oxford: Oxford University Press, 2000.

Loehlin, James N., ed. *Romeo and Juliet: Shakespeare in Production*. Cambridge: Cambridge University Press, 2002.

Weis, René, ed. *Romeo and Juliet*, Arden 3rd series. London: Bloomsbury, 2012.

Wells, Stanley and Gary Taylor, John Jowett and William Montgomery, eds. *William Shakespeare: The Complete Works*, 2nd edn. Oxford: Clarendon Press, 2005.

Critical works

Bloom, Harold. *Shakespeare: The Invention of the Human*. New York: The Berkley Publishing Group, 1998.
Bloom's critically acclaimed text is an ambitious and comprehensive critical assessment of the Shakespearean canon and his unapologetic bardolatry is, at times, infectious and exhilarating. Bloom's general premise is that Shakespeare's multi-layered, self-reflecting characters create the notion of human introspection and self-discovery. Bloom's analysis of *Romeo and Juliet* as a celebration of romantic love outlines important historical and critical engagements with this play.

Booth, Stephen. 'Shakespeare's Language and the Language of Shakespeare's Time'. *Shakespeare Survey* 50 (1997): 1–15.
In this essay, Booth brings his formidable skills in explicating Shakespeare's poetic genius in the sonnets to Shakespeare's dramatic works. This is an invaluable study for scholars of all levels to deepen our understanding of and appreciation for Shakespeare's poetic devices in his plays.

Dobson, Michael. *The Making of the National Poet: Shakespeare, Adaptation and Authorship, 1660–1769*. Oxford: Oxford University Press, 1992.
Dobson's study of the construction of Shakespeare as England's national writer engages performances and works from Thomas Betterton's seventeenth-century stage adaptations to Stanley Fish's twenty-first century scholarship on Shakespeare's works. This could be a useful text for classroom discussion on the institutionalizing of Shakespeare's writings.

Gender studies

Goldberg, Jonathan. '*Romeo and Juliet's* Open Rs'. In *New Casebooks: Romeo and Juliet*, edited by R. S. White, 194–212. Houndmills and New York: Palgrave Macmillan, 2001.
Goldberg provocatively intervenes in received ideas about the play's lovers as the model of ideal heterosexuality. Goldberg's claim that Romeo's easy substitution of Juliet for Rosaline exposes the lack of

female agency and presence in this play should provoke compelling classroom discussions.

Paster, Gail Kern. *The Body Embarrassed: Drama and the Disciplines of Shame in Early Modern England*. Ithaca, NY: Cornell University Press, 1993.
Paster examines the ambivalent ways in which the female body was understood, disciplined and shamed into social compliance in the early modern period. The final chapter, 'Quarreling with the Dug, or I am Glad You Did Not Nurse Him', considers the normative practice of wet nurses functioning as surrogate mothers in early modern England.

Smith, Bruce R. *Shakespeare and Masculinity*. Oxford: Oxford University Press, 2000.
Smith examines Shakespeare's use of early modern humour theory and Galenic medicine to construct masculinity in his plays. For example, in Act 1, Scene 1 of *Romeo and Juliet*, Samson and Gregory's punning on the word 'choler' refers to a hangman's noose and the humour that provokes aggression as they look forward to a possible fight with Montague's men. Smith's work can stimulate understanding of early modern ideas of gender and science in the classroom.

Performance studies and performance history

Brown, John Russell. *Studying Shakespeare in Performance*. New York: Palgrave Macmillan, 2011.
Brown distinguishes play texts from other forms of literature. He begins with critical approaches to Shakespeare's plays, moves to a consideration of stage practices, and finally looks at specific performances such as Zeffirelli's *Romeo and Juliet*.

Hodgdon, Barbara and W. B. Worthen, eds. *A Companion to Shakespeare and Performance*. Malden, MA: Blackwell, 2008.
Essays on *Romeo and Juliet* in this volume include Simon Palfrey and Tiffany Stern on parts and cues and Wendy Wall on performing desire.

Porter, Joseph Ashby, ed. *Critical Essays on Shakespeare's* Romeo and Juliet. New York: G. K. Hall & Co., 1997.
This compact volume includes seminal essays by Catherine Belsey and Jonathan Goldberg, as well as Gayle Whittier's 'The Sonnet's Body and the Body Sonnetized in *Romeo and Juliet*'.

Wall, Alison. 'The Feud and Shakespeare's *Romeo and Juliet*: A Reconsideration', *Sydney Studies in English* 5 (1979): 84–95.
Wall provocatively argues for an additional and alternative cultural context for Shakespeare's play: the historic feud between two important early modern English families, the houses of Thynne and Marvin.

Watson, Robert N. and Stephen Dickey. 'Wherefore Art Thou Tereu? Juliet and the Legacy of Rape'. *Renaissance Quarterly* 58 (2005): 127–56.
Watson and Dickey's brilliant and controversial essay points to the many allusions to rape in *Romeo and Juliet*. This challenging study can lead to thoughtful class discussions of Juliet's vulnerability as a girl, daughter and wife and to the history of concepts of sexual violence and sexual consent.

White, R. S., ed. *New Casebooks: Romeo and Juliet*. Houndmills and New York: Palgrave, 2001.
This helpful volume includes Catherine Belsey's 'The Name of the Rose in *Romeo and Juliet*',[13] Julia Kristeva's '*Romeo and Juliet*: Love-Hatred in the Couple'[14] and Barbara Hodgdon's 'Baz Luhrmann's William Shakespeare's *Romeo + Juliet*'.

Pedagogical works

Conaway, Charles. 'Teaching *Romeo and Juliet* in and against Modern Popular Culture'. *This Rough Magic* 2 (December 2011): 25–52. Available online: http://www.thisroughmagic.org/ (accessed 6 June 2015).
Conaway offers compelling strategies to engage undergraduate and graduate students with this play by examining past and current youth popular culture.

Hunt, Maurice, ed. *Approaches to Teaching Shakespeare's* Romeo and Juliet. New York: Modern Language Association, 2000.
Scholars such as Arthur F. Kinney, Sara Munson Deats and Dorothea Kehler use their own experience in teaching this play to outline various strategies for contemporary classrooms.

McDonald, Russ. *The Bedford Companion to Shakespeare: An Introduction with Documents*, 2nd edn. Boston and New York: Bedford/St Martin's Press, 2001.
McDonald developed this text for teachers of Shakespeare's works, providing both critical discourses and important contextual material. McDonald's imaginative reconstruction of the first performance of *Romeo and Juliet* is both fun and informative.

O'Brien, Peggy and Jeanne Addison Roberts, Michael Tolaydo and Nancy Goodwin, eds. *Shakespeare Set Free: Teaching* Romeo and Juliet, Macbeth *and* A Midsummer Night's Dream. New York: Washington Square Press, 1993.
The Shakespeare Set Free series is formulated to satisfy current Common Core Standards in the United States.[15] Some of the exercises can be adapted to provide university students with fun and useful ways into Shakespeare's *Romeo and Juliet,* such as creating masks to explore early modern cultural meanings.

Works cited for teaching resources

Belsey, Catherine. *Romeo and Juliet: Language & Writing*. Arden Shakespeare. London: Bloomsbury, 2014.

Boose, Lynda E. and Richard Burt, eds. *Shakespeare, The Movie: Popularizing the plays on film, TV, and video*. London: Routledge, 1997.

Callaghan, Dympna. 'The Ideology of Romantic Love: The Case of *Romeo and Juliet*'. In *The Weyward Sisters: Shakespeare and Feminist Politics*, edited by Dympna Callaghan, Lorraine Helms and Jyotsna Singh, 59–101. Oxford and Cambridge, MA: Blackwell, 1994,

Crowl, Samuel. *Shakespeare and Film: A Norton Guide*. New York: W. W. Norton & Co., 2008.

Findlay, Alison. *A Feminist Perspective on Renaissance Drama.* Oxford: Blackwell, 1999.

Garber, Marjorie. *Shakespeare After All.* New York: Anchor Books, 2004.

Harris, Jonathan Gil. 'Mechanical Turks, Mammet Tricks and Messianic Time'. *Postmedieval: A Journal of Medieval Cultural Studies* 1, no 2 (2010): 80–7.

Kottman, Paul. 'Defying the Stars: Tragic Love as the Struggle for Freedom in *Romeo and Juliet*'. *Shakespeare Quarterly* 63 (2012): 1–38.

Lupton, Julia Reinhard, 'Making Room, Affording Hospitality: Environments of Entertainment in *Romeo and Juliet*'. *The Journal of Medieval and Early Modern Studies* 43 (2013): 145–72.

McDonald, Russ. *Shakespeare and the Arts of Language*. Oxford: Oxford University Press, 2001.

Wall, Alison. 'The Feud and Shakespeare's *Romeo and Juliet*: A Reconsideration'. *Sydney Studies* 5 (1979): 84–95.

Media resources

The following is a list of performances available on DVD.

Stage

Romeo & Juliet (1978), [DVD]. Dir. Alvin Rakoff. Principal cast: John Gielgud, Michael Hordern, Alan Rickman, Patrick Ryecart, Rebecca Saire and Celia Johnson. UK: BBC Worldwide.

This production is part of the BBC Television series *The Complete Dramatic Works of William Shakespeare,* broadcast from 1978–85. Though produced for television, the plays are taped in a venue similar to stage productions. The production of *Romeo and Juliet* offers compelling performances by Shakespearean actors Sir John Gielgud as Chorus, Sir Michael Hordern as Capulet, Celia Johnson as the Nurse and Alan Rickman as a snarling Tybalt.

Romeo & Juliet (1993), [DVD]. Dir. Norman Campbell. Principal cast: Antoni Cimolino, Megan Follows, Colm Feore and Barbara Bryne. Canada: Canadian Broadcasting Corporation.
This Stratford Festival production of *Romeo and Juliet* was filmed on the stage of the Festival's theatre in Stratford, Ontario, Canada; the setting was fascist Italy. (The 1992 stage production was directed by Richard Monette.) Antoni Cimolino is Romeo, Megan Follows is Juliet and Barbara Bryne is the Nurse. Colm Feore's performance as Mercutio is delightful, especially in the Queen Mab speech.

Romeo & Juliet (2010), [DVD]. Dir. Dominic Dromgoole. Principal cast: Adetomiwa Edun, Ellie Kendrick. UK: Opus Arte.
This production of *Romeo and Juliet* was filmed live in 2009 on the stage of Shakespeare's Globe Theatre, London. This theatre is a reconstruction of the original Globe Theatre built in 1599 by the Lord Chamberlain's Men, Shakespeare's company.

Film

William Shakespeare's Romeo and Juliet (1936), [Film]. Dir. George Cukor. Principal cast: John Barrymore, Leslie Howard and Norma Shearer. USA: Warner Home Video [DVD].
Cukor's film gives us a glimpse into nineteenth-century performances of this play. The film also offers performances by legendary actors of stage and film.

Romeo and Juliet (1968) [Film]. Dir. Franco Zeffirelli. Principal cast: Olivia Hussey, Leonard Whiting, Michael York. Screenplay by Franco Brusati and Masolino D'Amico. UK: Paramount Home Entertainment [DVD].
Filmed in 1968, Zeffirelli celebrates the 1960s youth culture and sexual revolution within a lovely Italian Renaissance setting. The actors seem to embrace rebellion in their compelling performances, which remain popular today.

William Shakespeare's Romeo + Juliet (1997), [Film]. Dir. Baz Luhrmann. Principal cast: Leonardo DiCaprio, Claire Danes. UK: Fox [DVD].

Luhrmann's production, shot in Mexico and set in southern California, integrates popular media into Shakespeare's play, and uses today's culture of gang violence to focus the hostility between the Montagues and the Capulets. DiCaprio and Danes, as the tragic lovers, add to the currency of this production.

West Side Story, (1961), [Film]. Dirs Jerome Robbins and Robert Wise. Principal cast: George Chakiris and Natalie Wood. UK: Twentieth Century Fox [DVD].
This is a film adaptation of the 1950s Broadway musical of the same name developed from Shakespeare's *Romeo and Juliet*. The libretto is by Arthur Laurents, with music by Leonard Bernstein and lyrics by Stephen Sondheim. The choreography is by Jerome Robbins. As in the Broadway musical, the film revises Shakespeare's plot with a racially charged valence. The tragic lovers belong to different ethnic groups who wage war against each other with violence, dance and music on the streets of New York.

Cultural adaptations

The following are available DVDs of the films that Ian Munro discusses in this volume.

Amar te deule (2002), [DVD]. Dir. Fernando Sariñana. Principal cast: Luis Fernando Peña and Martha Higareda. USA: Lions Gate.
Bollywood Queen (2002), [DVD]. Dir. Jeremy Wooding. Principal cast: Preeya Kalidas, James McAvoy, Ray Panthaki and Ciarán McMenamin. UK: Warner.
Brooklyn Babylon, (2001), [DVD]. Dir. Marc Levin., 2001. Principal cast: Tariq Trotter and Karen Starc. USA: Lions Gate.
Goliyon Ki Rasleela Ram-Leela (2013), [DVD]. Dir. Sanjay Leela Bhansali. Principal cast: Deepika Padukone and Ranveer Singh. UK: Eros International.
Romeo and Juliet Get Married (2005), [DVD]. Dir. Bruno Barreto. Principal cast: Luana Piovani and Luiz Gustavo. USA: Vanguard Cinema.
Romeo and Juliet in Yiddish (2010), [DVD]. Dir. Eve Annenberg. Principal cast: Eve Annenberg, Lazer Weiss and Melissa Weisz. USA: Nancy Fishman Film Releasing.

West Bank Story (2005), [DVD]. Dir. Ari Sandel, in 'A Collection of 2006 Academy Award Nominated Short Films'. USA: Magnolia Home Entertainment.

Ballet and opera

The following DVDs are available of productions that Joseph Campana discusses in this volume.

Prokofiev's *Romeo and Juliet* (1966), [DVD]. Dir. Paul Czinner. Chor. Kenneth MacMillan. Principal cast: Margot Fonteyn and Rudolf Nureyev, The Royal Ballet. UK: Pulp Video.

Prokofiev's *Romeo and Juliet* (1992), [DVD]. Dir. Alexandre Tarta. Chor. Angelin Preljocaj. Principal cast: Pascale Doye and Nicholas Dufloux, Lyon Opera Ballet. UK: Arthaus Musik.

Tchaikovsky's *Juliet & Romeo* (2013), [DVD]. Dir. Thomas Grimm, Chor. Mats Ek. Principal cast: Anthony Lomuljo, Alexander Polianichko and Mariko Kida, Royal Swedish Ballet USA: C Major Entertainment.

Online resources

Educational

The Folger Shakespeare Library Online. http://www.folger.edu (accessed 7 June 2015).

This research institution offers many online resources, including Folger Digital Texts and an extensive 'Teach and Learn' section with lesson plans and short articles about Shakespeare's life, times, print history and theatres.

Royal Shakespeare Company. http://www.rsc.org.uk/education/resources/bank/ (accessed 7 June 2015).

The Royal Shakespeare Company is known for its innovative performances of Shakespeare's plays. Its online website offers teacher resources on each play that include a breakdown of the play, notes and videos of key scenes.

Shakespeare's Globe Theatre. http://2013.playingshakespeare.org (accessed 7 June 2015).
Globe Education is a resource for England's secondary school system, but the site's tools can be adapted to serve any educational level. For the section on *Romeo and Juliet*, the actors blogged about the rehearsal process as they worked on developing their characters. Actors' notes consider blocking and lighting as well as character development.

Scholarly

The Bodleian Library First Folio facsimile. http://firstfolio.bodleian.ox.ac.uk/ (accessed 7 June 2015).

Internet Shakespeare Editions. Facsimiles of the folios and many quartos.

http://internetshakespeare.uvic.ca/Library/facsimile/ (accessed 7 June 2015).

This Rough Magic. Co-founded in 2009 by Michael Boecherer and Bente Videbaek. A peer-reviewed, academic, online journal dedicated to the teaching of Medieval and Renaissance literature. http://www.thisroughmagic.org/about.html (accessed 7 June 2015).

Shakespeare Birthplace Trust Research Materials. http://www.shakespeare.org.uk (accessed 7 June 2015).

The Shakespeare Quarto Archive. http://www.quartos.org (accessed 7 June 2015).

Shakespeare's Staging: Shakespeare's Performance and his Globe Theatre. http://shakespeare.berkeley.edu/ (accessed 7 June 2015).

NOTES

Introduction

1 Unless otherwise noted, in this volume citations from *Romeo and Juliet* are taken from the Arden Third Series edition of the play, edited by René Weis (London: Bloomsbury, 2012).

2 Philosopher of literature Tzachi Zamir describes love in the play as 'a penetration of [the world] through heightened perception', in *Double Vision: Moral Philosophy and Shakespearean Drama* (Princeton: Princeton University Press, 2012), 122. Caroline Spurgeon identified the play's interest in light as part of its thematic texture and atmospheric effects in *Shakespeare's Imagery and What It Tells Us* (Cambridge: Cambridge University Press, 1935), 310–16.

3 Stage direction from the second quarto (Q2) and First Folio (F); Weis, *Romeo and Juliet*, Arden 3 (London: Bloomsbury, 2012), 250.

4 Walter Pater, 'Aesthetic Poetry', in *Appreciations, With an Essay on Style* (London: Macmillan, 1889), 202. The essay originated with Pater's 1868 review in the *Westminster Review* of William Morris's *The Earthly Paradise*; that review is available online at: http://morrisedition.lib.uiowa.edu/eptalessupplecritPater2.html (accessed 6 June 2015).

5 In this volume, see Naomi Conn Liebler and Robert N. Watson on oxymoron.

6 On *Romeo and Juliet* in tourism, see Shaul Bassi in this volume. On *Romeo and Juliet* in pornography, see Richard Burt's *Unspeakable ShaXXXspeares: Revised Edition: Queer Theory and American Kiddie Culture* (New York and London: St Martin's Press and Macmillan Press, 1999).

7 Weis, 'Introduction', *Romeo and Juliet*, Arden 3, 33–9.

8 This volume, Shaul Bassi, 'Names of the Rose', 177–98.

9 For a comparison of the two plays, see Cynthia Rodriguez-Badendyck, 'The Neglected Alternative: Shakespeare's *Romeo and Juliet* and Lope de Vega's *Castelvines y Monteses*', in *Parallel Lives: Spanish and English National Drama, 1580–1680*, eds Louise and Peter Fothergill-Payne (Cranbury, NJ: Associated Universities Presses, 1991), 91–107.

10 In *Shakespeare and World Cinema,* Mark Thornton Burnett devotes full chapters to only two plays, *Romeo and Juliet* and *Macbeth* (Cambridge: Cambridge University Press, 2013), 195–231.

11 Weis, Introduction to *Romeo and Juliet*, Arden 3, 2.

12 Janice Valls-Russell shows how Ovidian myths are dramaturgical resource for the play: 'the lovers' drive for union and fulfilment is conditioned by a spatial environment whose vertical and horizontal perspectives it simultaneously remodels'. See 'Erotic Perspectives: When Pyramus and Thisbe Meet Hero and Leander in *Romeo and Juliet*', in *Shakespeare's Erotic Mythology and Ovidian Renaissance Culture*, ed. Agnès Lafont (Farnham: Ashgate, 2013), 78.

13 Ruth Nevo, 'Tragic Form in *Romeo and Juliet*', *Studies in English Literature, 1500–1900* 9, no. 2 (1969): 243.

14 This volume, Liebler, 'Critical Backstory', 31.

15 Harold F. Brooks, ed., *A Midsummer Night's Dream* (London: Bloomsbury, 1979).

16 On the importance of the pharmaceutical trope to *Romeo and Juliet*, see Naomi Conn Liebler, *Shakespeare's Festive Tragedy* (London: Routledge, 1996), 148–53.

17 On falconry in the play, see Carolyn E. Brown, 'Juliet's Taming of Romeo', *Studies in English Literature, 1500–1900* 36, no. 2 (1996): 333–55; and Sean Benson, '"If I do prove her haggard": Shakespeare's Application of Hawking Tropes to Marriage', *Studies in Philology* 103 (2006): 186–207.

18 Robert N. Watson and Stephen Dickey, 'Wherefore Art Thou Tereu? Juliet and the Legacy of Rape', in *William Shakespeare's Romeo and Juliet*, ed. Harold Bloom, new edition (New York: Bloom's Literary Criticism, 2009), 112.

19 Tzachi Zamir, *Double Vision*, 119.

20 This volume, Liebler, 26.

21 Paul A. Kottman, 'Defying the Stars: Tragic Love as the Struggle for Freedom in *Romeo and Juliet*', *Shakespeare Quarterly* 63, no. 1 (2012): 20.

22 Nevo, 'Tragic Form in *Romeo and Juliet*', 241.

23 Kottman, 'Defying the Stars'.

24 This volume, Watson, 114.

25 Paul A. Kottman, 'Why think about Shakespearean tragedy today?' in *The Cambridge Companion to Shakespearean Tragedy*, ed. Claire McEachern (Cambridge: Cambridge University Press, 2013), 245.

26 Kottman, 'Defying the Stars', 6.

27 This volume, Watson, 106.

28 Hugh Grady, *Shakespeare and Impure Aesthetics* (Cambridge: Cambridge University Press, 2009), 223; cited by Helfer in 'The State of the Art' in this volume, 93.

29 Grady, *Impure Aesthetics*, 203.

30 Goldberg argues that 'the idealization of the lovers ... serves an ideological function', namely the mystification of heterosexuality as both normative and outside the social, see '*Romeo and Juliet*'s Open Rs', in *Critical Essays on Romeo and Juliet*, ed. Joseph A. Porter (New York: G. K. Hall and Co., 1997), 83. Callaghan exposes romantic love in the play as 'a classic instance of false consciousness' (cited in this volume by Helfer, 88).

31 See Rebeca Helfer's summaries in this volume of historicist essays by Targoff, Levenson, Fitter, Lucking, Groves, Sohmer, Palmer and others.

Chapter 1

1 I thank my extraordinary graduate assistant, Angel Garcia-Ivanov, for her indispensable help with the research informing this essay; thanks also to Jonathan Greenberg, my colleague at Montclair State University, for astute counsel and sharp critical reading.

2 Richard Levin, *New Readings vs. Old Plays: Recent Trends in the Reinterpretation of English Renaissance Drama* (Chicago and London: University of Chicago Press, 1979), 1.

3 Samuel Johnson, 'Preface to *The Plays of William Shakespeare*', in *Samuel Johnson: Selected Poetry and Prose*, eds Frank Brady and W. K. Wimsatt (Berkeley: University of California Press, 1977), 326–7.

4 Francis Meres, *Palladis Tamia: Wits Treasury Being the Second part of Wits Common wealth* (London: Cuthbert Burbie, 1598), 47v–48r.

5 Katherine Duncan-Jones, 'Francis Meres, Playgoer', *Notes and Queries* 56 (2009): 579.

6 Samuel Pepys, *Diary* II, 1 March 1662. Available online: http://www.pepysdiary.com/diary/1662/03/01/ (accessed 4 June 2015).

7 Gerard Langbaine, *An Account of the English Dramatick Poets* (1691), quoted in *William Shakespeare: The Critical Heritage, Volume 1 (1623–1692)*, ed. Brian Vickers (London and New York: Routledge, 1974), 422.

8 David Garrick, 'Advertisement', *Romeo and Juliet by Shakespear. With Alterations, and an additional Scene by D. Garrick as it is performed at the Theatre-Royal in Drury-Lane* (London: J. and R. Tonson and S. Draper, 1753), A3. There is a facsimile of Garrick's *Romeo and Juliet* available online: http://sceti.library.upenn.edu/sceti/printedbooksNew/index.cfm?TextID=rj_garrick&PagePosition=5 (accessed 4 June 2015).

9 Arthur Murphy, 'Free Remarks on the Tragedy of Romeo and Juliet', *The Student* (20 October 1750). Reported in *William Shakespeare: The Critical Heritage, Volume 3 (1733–1752)*, ed. Brian Vickers (London and New York: Routledge, 1975), 374.

10 Ibid., 374–5.

11 'Account of the Novel and Play of *Romeo and Juliet*' from *The Universal Museum* 3 (1764), 509–10, quoted in *William Shakespeare: The Critical Heritage, Volume 4 (1753–1765)*, ed. Brian Vickers (London and New York: Routledge, 1976), 539.

12 Boaistuau's *Histoires tragiques* (Paris, 1559) contains six cautionary tales translated from Matteo Bandello's *Novelle*; the third story, 'Histoire troisieme de deux Amants, dont l'un

mourut de venin, l'autre de tristesse', is generally regarded as one of the sources for Shakespeare's play.

13 Thomas Bowdler, ed., *The Family Shakspeare, in Ten Volumes, in Which Nothing Is Added to the Original Text: But Those Words And Expressions Are Omitted Which Cannot With Propriety Be Read Aloud In a Family*, 4th edition (London: Longman, 1825).

14 William Hazlitt, *Characters of Shakespear's Plays* (London: C. H. Reynell, 1817), 145–6.

15 Ibid., 146.

16 S. T. Coleridge, 'Seventh Lecture' in *Seven Lectures on Shakespeare and Milton*, ed. J. Payne Collier (London: Chapman and Hall, 1856), 57–8. There is an online facsimile at https://archive.org/details/acv8819.0001.001.umich.edu (accessed 10 June 2015). Cf. the remark apocryphally attributed to Shakespeare, reported by Dryden, and derided by Johnson, that 'he was obliged to kill Mercutio in the third act, lest he should have been killed by him. Yet [Dryden] thinks him no such formidable person, but that he might have lived through the play, and died in his bed, without danger to a poet': quoted in *A New Variorum Edition of Shakespeare*, vol. 1, ed. H. H. Furness (Philadelphia: J. B. Lippincott & Co., 1913), 299.

17 Coleridge, 'Seventh Lecture', 58–9.

18 Ibid., 59.

19 Ibid., 64–5.

20 Henry Mercer Graves, *An Essay on the Genius of Shakespeare, with Critical Remarks on the characters of Romeo, Hamlet, Juliet and Ophelia, Together with some observations on the Writings of Sir Walter Scott* (London: Ibotson and Palmer, 1826), 9. There is an online facsimile available: http://babel.hathitrust.org/cgi/pt?id=loc.ark:/13960/t3wt00t6m;view=1up;seq=5 (accessed 4 June 2015).

21 Ibid., 18.

22 Edward Dowden, *Shakspere: A Critical Study of his Mind and Art* (London: Henry S. King, 1875). In this essay we use the page numbers from the first edition, but there is an online facsimile of the third edition available: https://archive.org/

stream/shaksperecritica00dowd#page/n5/mode/2up (accessed 4 June 2015).

23 A. C. Bradley, *Shakespearean Tragedy: Lectures on* Hamlet, Othello, King Lear *and* Macbeth (London: Macmillan and Co., 1904). Available online: http://www.gutenberg.org/files/16966/16966-h/16966-h.htm (accessed 4 June 2015).

24 Dowden, *Shakspere*, 100.

25 Ibid., 109.

26 Ibid., 123.

27 René Girard, 'The Passionate Oxymoron in Shakespeare's *Romeo and Juliet*' (2005), in *Mimesis and Theory: Essays on Literature and Criticism, 1953–2005*, ed. Robert Doran (Stanford: Stanford University Press, 2008), 180.

28 Ibid., 286.

29 Ibid., 287.

30 Herbert Weisinger, *Tragedy and the Paradox of the Fortunate Fall* (East Lansing: Michigan State College Press, 1953).

31 Irving Ribner, *Patterns in Shakespearian Tragedy* (London: Methuen, 1960), 28–9.

32 Ibid., 33–4.

33 Paul N. Siegel, 'Christianity and the Religion of Love in *Romeo and Juliet*', *Shakespeare Quarterly* 12 (1961): 372.

34 Victor Turner, *The Ritual Process: Structure and Anti-Structure* (Ithaca, NY: Cornell University Press, 1969), 95–6.

35 Northrop Frye, *Northrop Frye on Shakespeare* (Markham, Ontario: Fitzhenry and Whiteside, 1986).

36 Ibid., 26–7.

37 Ibid., 24.

38 Ibid., 29.

39 Ibid., 32.

40 Ribner, *Patterns*, 34.

41 Ibid., 35.

42 W. H. Auden, '*Romeo and Juliet*' (1946) in *Lectures on*

Shakespeare, reconstructed and ed. Arthur Kirsch (Princeton: Princeton University Press, 2000), 45.

43 Ibid., 47–8.

44 Ibid., 48.

45 Norman Rabkin, 'Eros and Death' in *Shakespeare and the Common Understanding* (New York: Free Press, 1967), 151.

46 Ibid., 179.

47 Ibid., 180.

48 Ibid., 181. Walter Pater also identified this speech as an epithalamium, in the 1889 edition of *Appreciations*, as quoted in *Selected Writings of Walter Pater*, ed. Harold Bloom (New York: Columbia University Press, 1974), 194.

49 Ibid., 184.

50 Elizabeth Simpson Inchbald, 'Selected Remarks from The British Theatre' (1808) in *Women Critics 1660–1820: An Anthology*, ed. the Folger Collective on Early Women Critics (Bloomington and Indianapolis: Indiana University Press, 1995), 247–8. Inchbald notes that Garrick and, before him James Howard, altered Shakespeare's play by preserving the protagonists' lives, and that, 'when Sir William Davenant was manager of the theatre, he had the original and the altered play alternately performed for several nights together; thus consulting the different tastes of the auditors for joy and sorrow', 248.

51 See Georgianna Ziegler, *Shakespeare's Unruly Women* (Washington, DC: Folger Shakespeare Library, 1997), 47.

52 Constance O'Brien, 'Shakspere Talks With Uncritical People', *The Monthly Packet*, 1879–91, reported in *Women Reading Shakespeare: 1660–1900*, eds Ann Thompson and Sasha Roberts (Manchester and New York: Manchester University Press, 1997), 143.

53 Ibid.

54 Ibid., 144.

55 Madeline Leigh-Noel, 'Juliet' in *Shakespeare's Garden of Girls* (1885), reported in Thompson and Roberts, *Women Reading Shakespeare: 1660–1900*, eds Ann Thompson and Sasha Roberts (Manchester and New York: Manchester University Press,

1997), 176. Leigh-Noel was working from Garrick's edition of the play, altered (as noted above) in a number of points from the play we recognize today; hence the odd representations of plot and character, such as the assumptions about the ages of Juliet's parents and whether there had been other children.

56 Ibid., 178.

57 Ibid.

58 Agnes Mure Mackenzie, *The Women in Shakespeare's Plays: A Critical Study from the Dramatic and the Psychological Points of View and in Relation to the Development of Shakespeare's Art* (London: W. Heinemann Ltd, 1924), vii.

59 Ibid., xii.

60 Ibid.

61 Ibid., 2.

62 Ibid., 67–8.

63 Ibid., 69.

64 Carolyn Ruth Swift Lenz, Gayle Greene and Carol Thomas Neely, eds, *The Woman's Part: Feminist Criticism of Shakespeare* (Urbana and Champaign, IL: University of Illinois Press, 1980), 11.

65 Coppélia Kahn, 'Coming of Age in Verona' in *The Women's Part: Feminist Criticism of Shakespeare*, eds Carolyn Ruth Swift Lenz, Gayle Greene, Carol Thomas Neely (Urbana and Champaign, IL: University of Illinois Press, 1980), 171.

66 Ibid., 172–3.

67 Ibid., 185.

68 Ibid., 192, note 16.

69 Susan Snyder, *The Comic Matrix of Shakespeare's Tragedies:* Romeo and Juliet, Hamlet, Othello, *and* King Lear (Princeton: University of Princeton Press, 1979), 57.

70 Ibid., 65.

71 Ibid., 66.

72 Ibid., 68.

73 Marjorie Garber, *Coming of Age in Shakespeare* (London and New York: Methuen, 1981), vi.

74 Ibid., 116.

75 Ibid., 119.

76 Ibid., 120.

77 Irene G. Dash, *Wooing, Wedding, and Power: Women in Shakespeare's Plays* (New York: Columbia University Press, 1981), 71.

78 Ibid., 100.

79 Julia Kristeva, '*Romeo and Juliet*: Love-Hatred in the Couple' (1987) in *Shakespearean Tragedy*, ed. John Drakakis (London and New York: Longman, 1992), 297.

80 Ibid., 297–8.

81 Ibid., 299.

82 Ibid., 298.

83 Ibid., 303.

84 Ibid., 308.

85 Jacques Derrida, 'This Strange Institution Called Literature: An Interview with Jacques Derrida' (1989), trans. Geoffrey Bennington and Rachel Bowlby, in *Acts of Literature*, ed. Derek Attridge (New York and London: Routledge, 1992), 39.

86 Ibid., 65–6.

87 Jacques Derrida, 'Aphorism Countertime' (1986), trans. Nicholas Royle, in *Acts of Literature*, ed. Derek Attridge (New York and London: Routledge, 1992), 416.

88 Ibid.

89 Ibid., 417–18.

90 Ibid., 419.

91 Ibid., 422.

92 Ibid., 430.

Chapter 2

1 Jill L. Levenson, ed., *The Oxford Shakespeare: Romeo and Juliet* (Oxford: Oxford University Press, 2008). See also the excellent

James N. Loehlin, ed., *Shakespeare in Production: Romeo and Juliet* (Cambridge: Cambridge University Press, 2002).

2 See online site: http://www.oktheater.org/ (accessed 4 June 2015).

3 Charles Isherwood, 'Just the Gist of a Star-Cross'd Tale', *The New York Times*, 21 December 2009.

4 On the degree to which this production nevertheless reinforces an iconic, scriptural and literary understanding of Shakespeare, see William B. Worthen, '"What light through yonder window speaks?": The Nature Theater of Oklahoma *Romeo and Juliet* and the Cult(ure) of Shakespeare', in *Shakespeare and the Urgency of Now: Criticism and Theory in the 21st Century*, eds Cary Pietro and Hugh Grady (New York: Palgrave Macmillan, 2013).

5 On Q1 as an acting version of the play (a highly contested theory), see especially Lukas Erne, *Shakespeare as Literary Dramatist* (Cambridge: Cambridge University Press, 2003), ch. 8, *passim*.

6 René Weis, ed., *Romeo and Juliet*, Arden 3rd Series (London: Bloomsbury, 2012), 417.

7 See Robert Weimann, 'Thresholds to Memory and Commodity in Shakespeare's Endings', *Representations* 53 (Winter 1996): 1–20.

8 As Levenson has noted, between 1597 and 1599 there is a flurry of allusions to *Romeo and Juliet* in a variety of plays and other works – evidence, perhaps, of its sudden popularity (Levenson, *Oxford: Romeo and Juliet*, 97–8).

9 Paul A. Kottman, 'Defying the Stars: Tragic Love as the Struggle for Freedom in *Romeo and Juliet*', *Shakespeare Quarterly* 63, no. 1 (2012): 1–38, 4.

10 There were two earlier productions: William Davenant's in 1662, which Samuel Pepys hated, and a tragicomic version of the play adapted by James Howard shortly thereafter, in which Romeo and Juliet survive. See Levenson, *Oxford: Romeo and Juliet*, 70–1 and Weis, *Romeo and Juliet*, Arden 3, 57–8 for more discussion.

11 Thomas Otway, *The History and Fall of Caius Marius. A*

Tragedy. As it is Acted at the Duke's Theatre. (London: Tho. Flesher, 1680), sig. D1v. See Weis and especially Levenson for more on the significance of Otway's play in the performance history of *Romeo and Juliet*.

12 See especially John Wallace, 'Otway's *Caius Marius* and the Exclusion Crisis', *Modern Philology* 85 (May 1988): 363–72; and Jessica Munns, '"The Dark Disorders of a Divided State": Otway and Shakespeare's *Romeo and Juliet*', *Comparative Drama* 19 (1985–6): 347–62.

13 Levenson, *Oxford: Romeo and Juliet*, 73–4.

14 Munns, 'The Dark Disorders', 354.

15 Weis, *Romeo and Juliet*, Arden 3, 61.

16 Ibid.

17 Quoted in George Branam, 'The Genesis of David Garrick's *Romeo and Juliet*', *Shakespeare Quarterly* 35 (1984): 170–9, 176. For Garrick's play, see also Weis, *Romeo and Juliet*, Arden 3, 60–6 and Levenson, *Oxford: Romeo and Juliet*, 75–80.

18 *Shakespeare's Romeo and Juliet, A Tragedy; Adapted to the Stage by David Garrick; Revised by J. P. Kemble; and Published as it is Acted at The Theatre Royal in Covent Garden* (London, 1811), 75.

19 Quoted in Branam, 'The Genesis', 177.

20 Quoted in G. Blakemore Evans, ed., *Romeo and Juliet* (Cambridge: Cambridge University Press, 2003), 41.

21 Weis, *Romeo and Juliet*, Arden 3, 66–7, 69, 75. For more of these musical productions, see Daniel Albright, *Musicking Shakespeare* (Rochester: University of Rochester Press, 2007).

22 Levenson, *Oxford: Romeo and Juliet*, 80.

23 Loehlin, *Shakespeare in Production*, 15.

24 *West Side Story* (1961), [Film] Dirs Jerome Robbins and Robert Wise, USA: The Mirisch Corporation.

25 See, for example, Catherine Belsey, 'The Name of the Rose in *Romeo and Juliet*', *The Yearbook of English Studies* 23 (1993): 126–52; and Alexander Leggatt, *Shakespeare's Tragedies: Violation and Identity* (Cambridge: Cambridge University Press, 2005).

26 *Romeo + Juliet* (1996), [Film]. Dir. Baz Luhrmann, USA: Twentieth Century Fox.

27 Levenson, *Oxford: Romeo and Juliet*, 80–4, and Weis, *Romeo and Juliet*, Arden 3, 67–9.

28 Weis, *Romeo and Juliet*, Arden 3, 71–4, and Levenson, *Oxford: Romeo and Juliet*, 84–7.

29 Levenson, *Oxford: Romeo and Juliet*, 85.

30 Quoted in Levenson, *Oxford: Romeo and Juliet*, 85.

31 Peter Holding, *Romeo and Juliet: Text and Performance* (London: Macmillan Education Ltd, 1992), 47.

32 Loehlin, *Shakespeare in Production,* 60.

33 Also see Weis's discussion of the Shakespeare's Globe 2004 Old Pronunciation *Romeo and Juliet* (Weis, *Romeo and Juliet*, Arden 3, 91–4), a production which both radicalizes the play by defamiliarizing its language and proceeds under a specifically iconodulic impulse of restoring the play to its original, correct phonology.

34 Shakespeare on the Saskatchewan. Available online: http://www.shakespeareonthesaskatchewan.com/about_us (accessed 4 June 2015)

35 Aleksandar Sasa Dundjerovic, *The Theatricality of Robert Lepage* (Montreal and Kingston: McGill-Queen's University Press, 2007), 50.

36 Alexa Huang, *Chinese Shakespeares: Two Centuries of Cultural Exchange* (New York: Columbia University Press, 2009), 14.

37 Levenson, *Oxford: Romeo and Juliet*, 89.

38 More recently, lesbian productions of the play have started to be produced; see, for example, Curio Theatre Company's 2013 production in Philadelphia, with Rachel Gluck and Isa St Clair in the two lead roles.

39 Weis, *Romeo and Juliet*, Arden 3, 85–6.

40 See Aimara da Cunha Resende, 'Introduction: Brazilian Appropriations of Shakespeare', in *Foreign Accents: Brazilian Readings of Shakespeare*, eds Aimara da Cunha Resende and Thomas LaBorie Burns (Newark: University of Delaware Press, 2002), 25. See also Resende, 'Text, Context, and Audience: Two

Versions of *Romeo and Juliet* in Brazilian Popular Culture', in *Latin American Shakespeares*, eds Bernice W. Kliman and Rick J. Santos (Madison: Farleigh Dickinson University Press, 2005).

41 Resende, 'Introduction', 24.

42 For more on this production, see Resende, 'Text, Context, and Audience', and Candace Slater, '*Romeo and Juliet* in the Brazilian Backlands', *Journal of Folklore Research* 20 (May 1983): 35–53.

43 Loehlin, *Shakespeare in Production*, 66.

44 For more on these issues, see especially Margaret Jane Kidnie, *Shakespeare and the Problem of Adaptation* (New York: Routledge, 2009) and W. B. Worthen, *Shakespeare and the Force of Modern Performance* (Cambridge: Cambridge University Press, 2003).

45 See Claire Lee, '"Romeo and Juliet" in China', *The Wall Street Journal*, 7 November 2013.

46 Daryl H. Miller, 'Two culture-cross'd lovers', *The Los Angeles Times,* 10 March 2005.

47 *Indian Romeo and Juliet* (1912), [Film]. Dir. Laurence Trimble. USA: Vitagraph Company of America.

48 *Brooklyn Babylon* (2001), [Film]. Dir. Marc Levin. USA, France: Bac Films, Canal+, StudioCanal.

49 *Romeo and Juliet in Yiddish* (2010), [Film]. Dir. Eve Annenberg. USA: Vilna City Films, Oscar Productions, Stratford Upon the Dnieper Productions.

50 *Bollywood Queen* (2002), [Film]. Dir. Jeremy Wooding. UK: Dream Fish Productions, Enterprise Films, Great British Films.

51 *Amar te duele* (2002), [Film]. Dir. Fernando Sariñana, Mexico: Altavista Films, Videocine.

52 *Gucha* (*Distant Trumpet*), (2006), [Film]. Dir. Dusan Milic. Serbia, Bulgaria, Austria, Germany: Pallas Film, Film Deluxe International, Dakar Film.

53 *Romeo Juliet* (2009), [DVD]. Script and dir. Andibachtiar Yusuf. Indonesia: Bogalakon Pictures; *O Casamento de Romeu e Julieta* (2005), [Film] Dir. Bruno Barreto, Brazil: BMG Models, Filmes do Equador, Geração Conteúdo.

54 *Goliyon Ki Raasleela Ram-Leela* (2013), [Film]. Script and dir. Sanjay Leela Bhansali. India: Eros International, SLB Films (Pvt) Ltd; *Issaq* (2013), [Film]. Dir. Manish Tiwary. India: Dhaval Gada Productions, Manish Tiwary Films, Paramhans Creations & Movies n More; V. Lakshmi, 'Hansika, Ravi are the villains in *Romeo Juliet*', *The Times of India*, 2 June 2014; Ankur Pathak, 'Romil Juggal: Ekta Kapoor's gay romantic film is back on track', *The Times of India*, 8 July 2014.

55 Wikipedia has an extremely useful inventory of *Romeo and Juliet* films; available online: http://en.wikipedia.org/wiki/Romeo_and_Juliet_%28films%29 (accessed 4 June 2015). See also, Mark Thornton Burnett, *Shakespeare and World Cinema* (Cambridge: Cambridge University Press, 2013).

56 *In Fair Palestine: A Story of Romeo and Juliet* (2008), [Film]. Dir. Yazan Nahas. Palestine: Ramallah Friends Schools; *West Bank Story* (2005), [Film]. Dir. Ari Sandel. USA: Independent.

57 Dan Fesperman, 'Arab–Israeli "Romeo" rings with reality', *The Baltimore Sun*, 15 June 1994.

58 Freddie Rokem, 'Postcard from the Peace Process: Some thoughts on a Palestinian–Israeli co-production of *Romeo and Juliet*', *Palestine-Israel Journal* 2, no. 1 (1995): 1–4.

59 Ibid., 3.

60 Ibid., 4.

61 See online: http://www.rsc.org.uk/whats-on/_archived/romeo-and-juliet-in-baghdad/ (accessed 4 June 2015).

62 Daood's statement is from the programme notes, quoted in Ben Monks, '*Romeo and Juliet in Baghdad* at Riverside Studios', *Exeunt Magazine*, available online: http://exeuntmagazine.com/reviews/romeo-and-juliet-in-baghdad/ (accessed 4 June 2015). For more on the folktale, see Deborah Shaw, 'It's Shakespeare, but not as you know it: World Theatre Day (27 March), World Shakespeare Festival (23 April)', *The Times Educational Supplement*, 16 March 2012. See also Tim Arango 'Montague and Capulet as Shiite and Sunni', *The New York Times*, 28 April 2012.

63 Quoted in Monks, '*Romeo and Juliet in Baghdad*'.

64 Quoted in Jason Burg, 'Romeo and Juliet in Baghdad', http://

jasonaburg.wordpress.com/reviews/romeo-and-juliet-in-baghdad/ (accessed 4 June 2015); quoted in Katherine Steele Brokaw, '*Romeo and Juliet in Baghdad* (review)', *Shakespeare Bulletin* 31 (June 2013): 267–72, 271.

65 Shaw quoted in Rebecca McLaughlin-Duane, 'Romeo and Juliet gets a Middle Eastern twist', *The National*, 2 April 2012; for Rasool, see, for example, Brokaw, '*Romeo and Juliet in Baghdad* (review)', 269 and Richard Spencer, '"Romeo and Juliet in Baghdad" comes to London', *The Telegraph*, 4 April 2012.

66 Moreas Madani, 'Shakespeare in post-war Iraq', *The Arab Review*, available online: http://www.thearabreview.org/theatre-romeo-and-juliet-in-baghdad-review/ (accessed 4 June 2015); Margaret Litvin, 'NYT Reviews "R&J in Baghdad" in Baghdad', *Send Down the Basket*, 30 April 2012, available online: http://margaretlitvin.com/2012/04/30/nyt-reviews-rj-in-baghdad-in-baghdad/ (accessed 4 June 2015).

67 Brokaw, '*Romeo and Juliet in Baghdad* (review)', 271.

68 See online link: http://bp-or-not-bp.org/news/romeo-and-juliet/ (accessed 4 June 2015) for more details, including a video of the interruption.

69 Otway, *The History and Fall of Caius Marius*, sig. A3.

70 Ibid., sigs. A3–A3v.

71 Ibid., sig. A3v.

72 Ibid., sig. K2.

Chapter 3

1 Marjorie Garber, *Shakespeare and Modern Culture* (New York: Pantheon, 2008), 34.

2 Ibid., 51, 53.

3 Ibid., 53.

4 Wall, Wendy. 'Editors in Love?: Performing Desire in *Romeo and Juliet*', in *A Companion to Shakespeare and Performance*, eds Barbara Hodgdon and W. B. Worthen (Oxford: Blackwell, 2005), 197–211.

5 Ibid., 198.

6 Ibid., 204.

7 Jonathan Goldberg, '"What? in a names that which we call a Rose": The Desired Texts of *Romeo and Juliet*' (University of Minnesota Press, 2003), [originally published in *Crisis in Editing: Texts of the English Renaissance*, ed. Randall McLeod (New York: AMS Press, 1994), 37–64].

8 Ibid., 254.

9 Ibid.

10 Barbara Hodgdon, 'Absent Bodies, Present Voices: Performance Work and the Close of Romeo and Juliet's Golden Story', in *Romeo and Juliet: Critical Essays*, ed. John F. Andrews (New York: Garland, 1993), 243–65 [reprinted from *Theatre Journal*, 41, no. 3 (1989): 341–59].

11 Ibid., 245.

12 Ibid., 255.

13 Ibid., 256, 258.

14 Worthen, '"What light through yonder window speaks?": The Nature Theater of Oklahoma *Romeo and Juliet* and the Cult(ure) of Shakespeare', in *Shakespeare and the Urgency of Now: Criticism and Theory in the 21st Century*, eds. Cary DiPietro and Hugh Grady (New York: Palgrave Macmillan, 2013), 148–71.

15 Ibid., 149.

16 Ibid., 151–2.

17 Ibid., 154.

18 Mark Thornton Burnett, *Shakespeare and World Cinema* (Cambridge: Cambridge University Press, 2012).

19 Ibid., 196.

20 Ibid., 226–7.

21 Lynette Hunter and Peter Lichtenfels, *Negotiating Shakespeare's Language in* Romeo and Juliet*: Reading Strategies from Criticism, Editing and the Theatre* (Farnham and Burlington: Ashgate, 2009).

22 Ibid., 2.

23 Ibid., 4, 2.

24 Laurie Maguire, *Shakespeare's Names* (Oxford: Oxford University Press, 2007).

25 Ibid., 55.

26 Ibid., 56.

27 William N. West, 'Mercutio's Bad Language', in *Rematerializing Shakespeare: Authority and Representation on the Early Modern English Stage*, eds Bryan Reynolds and William N. West (New York: Palgrave Macmillan, 2005), 115, 117.

28 Ibid., 119.

29 Ibid., 127.

30 Madhavi Menon, *Wanton Words: Rhetoric and Sexuality in English Renaissance Drama* (Toronto: University of Toronto Press, 2004).

31 Ibid., 78.

32 Ibid.

33 Kiernan Ryan, *Shakespeare*, 2nd edition (London and New York: Prentice Hall, 1995), 75–86, 77.

34 Ibid., 79.

35 Ibid., 82–3.

36 David Schalkwyk, *Speech and Performance in Shakespeare's Sonnets and Plays* (Cambridge: Cambridge University Press, 2002). See also, Diana Henderson's *Passion Made Public: Elizabethan Lyric, Gender, and Performance* (Champaign: University of Illinois Press, 1995), which begins with a discussion of *Romeo and Juliet* that establishes the larger stakes of her argument about 'the nexus of associations among gender, performance, and lyric operative within Elizabethan poetic drama', 3–4.

37 Schalkwyk, *Speech and Performance*, 64–5.

38 Ibid., 65.

39 Catherine Belsey, 'The Name of the Rose in *Romeo and Juliet*', in *Critical Essays on Shakespeare's* Romeo and Juliet', ed. Joseph A. Porter (New York: Simon & Schuster, 1997), 64–81 [originally published in *Yearbook of English Studies* 23 (1993): 126–42]. See also Belsey's recent volume in the Arden Student

Skills Series, *Romeo and Juliet: Language and Writing* (London: Bloomsbury, 2014).

40 Belsey, 'The Name of the Rose', 79.

41 Lloyd Davis, '"Death-Marked Love": Desire and Presence in *Romeo and Juliet*', in *Shakespeare Survey 49: Romeo and Juliet and its Afterlife*, ed. Stanley Wells (Cambridge: Cambridge University Press, 1996), 57–67, 62, 57, 67.

42 Ibid., 67.

43 Dympna Callaghan, 'The Ideology of Romantic Love: The Case of *Romeo and Juliet*', in *The Weyward Sisters: Shakespeare and Feminist Politics*, eds Dympna C. Callaghan, Lorraine Helms and Jyotsna Singh (Oxford: Blackwell, 1994), 59–101, 60.

44 Ibid., 71, 60.

45 Jonathan Goldberg, '*Romeo and Juliet*'s Open Rs', in *Critical Essays on Shakespeare's* Romeo and Juliet, ed. Joseph A. Porter (New York: Simon & Shuster, 1997), 82–96 [originally published in Jonathan Goldberg, ed., *Queering the Renaissance* (Durham, NC: Duke University Press, 1994), 218–35].

46 Ibid., 90.

47 Ibid., 83.

48 Ibid., 94.

49 Robert Appelbaum, '"Standing to the Wall": The Pressures of Masculinity in *Romeo and Juliet*', *Shakespeare Quarterly* 48, no. 3 (1997): 251–72, 253.

50 Ibid., 271.

51 Ibid., 271–2.

52 Paul A. Kottman, 'Defying the Stars': Tragic Love as the Struggle for Freedom in *Romeo and Juliet*', *Shakespeare Quarterly* 63, no. 1 (2012): 1–38.

53 Ibid., 1.

54 Ibid., 2.

55 Ibid., 6–7.

56 Jill L. Levenson, '"*Alla stoccado* carries it away": Codes of Violence in *Romeo and Juliet*', in *Shakespeare's* Romeo and

Juliet: *Texts, Contexts, and Interpretation*, ed. Jay L. Halio (Newark: University of Delaware Press, 1995), 83–96.

57 Ibid., 83.

58 Ibid., 84, 94.

59 Ibid., 85.

60 Ibid., 85–6.

61 Chris Fitter, *Radical Shakespeare: Politics and Stagecraft in the Early Career* (New York: Routledge, 2012).

62 Ibid., 145.

63 Ibid.

64 Robert N. Watson and Stephen Dickey, 'Wherefore Art Thou Tereu? Juliet and the Legacy of Rape' in *Bloom's Modern Critical Reinterpretations: William Shakespeare's* Romeo and Juliet, ed. Harold Bloom (New York: Bloom's Literary Criticism, 2009), 92–120 [originally published, *Renaissance Quarterly* 58, no. 1 (2005): 127–56].

65 Ibid., 91.

66 Ibid., 108.

67 Ibid., 110–11.

68 William M. McKim, 'Romeo's "Death-markt" Imagination and its Tragic Consequences' in *William Shakespeare's* Romeo and Juliet, ed. Harold Bloom (New York: Bloom's Literary Criticism, 2009), 79–90 [originally published, *Kentucky Philological Review* 20 (2005): 38–45].

69 Ibid., 80.

70 Ibid., 87.

71 Ramie Targoff, 'Mortal Love: Shakespeare's *Romeo and Juliet* and the Practice of Joint Burial', *Representations* 120, no. 1 (2012): 17–38.

72 Ibid., 17.

73 Ibid., 35.

74 Hugh Grady, *Shakespeare and Impure Aesthetics* (Cambridge: Cambridge University Press, 2009), 195.

75 Ibid., 194.

76 Ibid., 223.

77 Naomi Conn Liebler, '"There is no world without Verona Walls": The City in *Romeo and Juliet*', in *A Companion to Shakespeare's Works, Volume I: The Tragedies*, eds Richard Dutton and Jean E. Howard (Malden, MA: Blackwell, 2003), 303–18. See also, Liebler's important discussion of genre in relation to 'sacrifice' in *Romeo and Juliet*, in *Shakespeare's Festive Tragedy: The Ritual Foundations of Genre* (New York: Routledge, 1995), 148–55.

78 Liebler, 'The City in *Romeo and Juliet*', 305.

79 Ibid., 315.

80 Paul A. Kottman, *A Politics of the Scene* (Stanford: Stanford University Press, 2008), 183.

81 Ibid., 182–3.

82 Ibid., 184.

83 Julia Reinhard Lupton, 'Making Room, Affording Hospitality: Environments of Entertainment in *Romeo and Juliet*', *Journal of Medieval and Early Modern Studies* 43, no. 1 (2013): 145–72.

84 Ibid., 167.

85 Ibid.

86 David Lucking, 'Unkind Hours and Timeless Ends: Uncomfortable Time in *Romeo and Juliet*', in *The Shakespearean Name: Essays on* Romeo and Juliet, The Tempest *and Other Plays* (Bern: Peter Lang, 2007), 67–86.

87 Ibid., p. 69.

88 Steve Sohmer, 'Shakespeare's Time-Riddles in *Romeo and Juliet* Solved', *English Literary Renaissance* 35, no. 3 (2005): 407–28.

89 Ibid., 408.

90 Ibid., 415, 414.

91 Ibid., 428.

92 Philippa Berry, 'Between Idolatry and Astrology: Modes of Temporal Repetition in *Romeo and Juliet*', in *A Feminist Companion to Shakespeare*, ed. Dympna Callaghan (Malden, MA: Blackwell, 2000), 358–72.

93 Ibid., 359.

94 Ibid.

95 Beatrice Groves, *Texts and Traditions: Religion in Shakespeare, 1592–1604* (Oxford: Clarendon Press, 2007), 61.

96 Ibid., 63.

97 Ibid., 88.

98 Tanya Pollard, '"A Thing Like Death": Sleeping Potions and Poisons in *Romeo and Juliet* and *Antony and Cleopatra*' in *William Shakespeare's* Romeo and Juliet, ed. Harold Bloom (New York: Bloom's Literary Criticism, 2009), 29–54 [originally published in *Renaissance Drama* 32 (2003): 95–121].

99 Karen Raber, 'Vermin and Parasites: Shakespeare's Animal Architectures', in *Ecocritical Shakespeare*, eds Lynne Bruckner and Dan Brayton (Farnham: Ashgate, 2011): 13–32.

100 Ibid., 19.

101 Ibid., 20.

102 Ibid., 21.

103 Matthew Spellberg, 'Feeling Dreams in *Romeo and Juliet*', *English Literary Renaissance* 4, no. 31 (2013): 62–85.

104 Ibid., 63.

105 Ibid., 63.

106 Ibid., 73.

107 Ibid., 83–4.

108 Daryl W. Palmer, 'Motion and Mercutio in *Romeo and Juliet*' in *William Shakespeare's* Romeo and Juliet, ed. Harold Bloom (New York: Bloom's Literary Criticism, 2009), 185–98 [originally published, *Philosophy and Literature* 30, no. 2 (2006): 540–54].

109 Ibid., 186, 189.

110 Ibid., 189.

111 Ibid., 193, 196.

112 Lina Perkins Wilder, *Shakespeare's Memory Theatre: Recollection, Properties and Character* (Cambridge: Cambridge University Press, 2010), 59–60.

113 Ibid., 60.

114 Ibid., 60–1.

115 Ibid., 81.

116 Grady, *Impure Aesthetics*, 225.

117 Ibid., 228.

118 Ibid., 233, 236–7.

Chapter 4

1 J. A. Bryant, Jr, ed., *Romeo and Juliet*, general ed. Sylvan Barnet (New York and London: New American Library/New English Library, 1963–4).

2 Jay Halio (ed.), *Romeo and Juliet: Parallel Texts of Quarto 1 (1597) and Quarto 2 (1599)* (Newark, DE: University of Delaware Press, 2008).

3 Colley Cibber, 1748, skipped the speech entirely, as did Thomas Otway's 1677 adaptation – *The History and Fall of Gaius Marius* – which held the stage for over sixty years.

4 George Cukor's 1936 version skipped the speech too, as did *West Side Story*.

5 Lynette Hunter and Peter Lichtenfels, *Negotiating Shakespeare's Language in Romeo and Juliet: Reading Strategies from Criticism, Editing and the Theatre* (Farnham: Ashgate, 2009), 41; see similarly, Edward L. Rocklin, *Romeo and Juliet: a guide to the text and the play in performance*, The Shakespeare Handbooks (New York: Palgrave Macmillan, 2010), 48: 'the reaction of Capulet can be revealing. His silence, for example, can indicate ambivalence about this death, either because Tybalt's propensity for fighting has made him difficult to control or because [Tybalt] had been cuckolding Capulet himself.'

6 Among the major early editors, this troubled Theobald enough that he tried a double-switch and proposed Lady Montague as the speaker – a choice sustained in the Warburton and Pope edition (1747) – while Rowe, oddly, proposed Lady Capulet.

7 Arthur Brooke, 'Romeus and Juliet' (1562), ed. J. J. Munro (London and New York: Chatto & Windus/Duffield and Company, 1908), line 1043.

8 William Painter, *The Palace of Pleasure*, ed. Joseph Jacobs (New York: Dover Publications, 1966), 3:96

9 D. Kay Johnston and Margaret Maurer, 'Teaching and Risk: Doing and Undoing Shakespeare', in *For All Time?: Critical Issues in Teaching Shakespeare*, eds Paul Skrebels and Sieta van der Hoeven (South Australia: Wakefield Press, 2002), 108, questions this speech heading, and I am grateful to the wonderfully perceptive Prof. Maurer for bringing it to my attention during an institute for high-school teachers at the Folger Shakespeare Library. I commented briefly on this issue in a footnote in Claire McEachern, ed., *The Cambridge Companion to Shakespearean Tragedy* (Cambridge: Cambridge University Press, 2002), and a bit more extensively in the second edition of that book (Cambridge: Cambridge University Press, 2013), 179–80.

10 Shakespeare might have seen an opportunity in Brooke's 'The Capulets disdain the presence of their foe, / Yet they suppress their stirred ire, the cause I do not know' (lines 183–4), and in Painter's uncertain and gnomic comment that they tolerated Romeo 'either for the honour of the company, or else for respect of his Age' (Painter, *Palace of Pleasure*, 3:84).

11 In this production – part of the international Shakespeare festival associated with the 2012 London Olympics – Juliet's Sunni father intends her marriage to a Shiite Romeo to heal Iraq's factional strife.

12 Harry Levin, 'Form and Formality in *Romeo and Juliet*', *Shakespeare Quarterly* 11 (1960): 6–8.

13 Painter, *Palace of Pleasure*, 3:124.

14 Hugh Grady, *Shakespeare and Impure Aesthetics* (Cambridge: Cambridge University Press, 2009), 223.

15 Snow argues this division eloquently, but does not see the binary relenting at the end of the play. However, Hugh Grady, *Impure Aesthetics,* 210, observes that 'the traditional gender relations are first put on display, then subtly undermined, and finally dissolved in explicit claims of mutuality and equality'.

16 In 'Wherefore Art Thou Tereu?: Juliet and the Legacy of Rape' in *William Shakespeare's* Romeo and Juliet, ed. Harold Bloom (New York: Bloom's Literary Criticism, 2009), Stephen

Dickey and Robert N. Watson argue that the play extensively and allusively challenges 'the fantasy that there is [no third alternative] between the benign melting-together of angelic lovers' and the horrors of rape.

17 For the observation that 'forth' hints at 'fourth' here, and that 'parents' recalls 'pair', I am indebted to a presentation (at the Folger Library's Teaching Shakespeare Institute) by Stephen Booth, the greatest microscopic reader of Shakespeare's transient subliminal effects.

18 The Python script counted the number of phrases between one and five words in length that were immediately repeated, without intervening words. Since the syndrome being sought was doubling, only two repetitions were allowed; if a word or phrase was repeated more than twice, the entire phrase was discarded. The text used was the Project Gutenberg *Complete Works of Shakespeare*, with headers, footers and copyright notices removed. Only dialogue was counted; other text such as *dramatis personae* listings, stage directions, speech prefixes and act and scene headings were ignored. Most punctuation was removed, but apostrophes (single quotation marks) were left so as to differentiate between, for example, 'won't' and 'wont', and the text was converted to lowercase. We then converted the text to words (defined as any sequence of characters separated by spaces). No stop words were used, and no attempt was made to normalize spelling, since the Project Gutenberg edition uses modern spellings. Prose lines were treated by their natural margin breaks, on the grounds that this would still show a proportion of doublings, and would avoid skewing the results away from plays heavy on prose. All of these choices could doubtless be refined, but I believe they are adequate to demonstrate the main points, given the overall strength of the outcomes.

19 These trials excluded 'shall', 'thou', 'thee', 'thine', 'thy', 'hast' and ''tis', as well as the standard NLTK (Natural Language Toolkit) list of the 127 most common words in modern English; see Steven Bird, Edward Loper and Ewan Klein, *Natural Language Processing with Python* (Sebastopol, California: O'Reilly Media, 2009). We searched for antonyms using the NLTK interface with the WordNet corpus produced by Princeton University, which tags words with semantic data, including their antonyms. Those

lists are based on modern rather than Elizabethan usage, but enough similarities remain to produce a meaningful estimate of Shakespeare's use of oppositional forms.

20 Ann Pasternak Slater, 'Petrarchanism Come True in *Romeo and Juliet*' in *Images of Shakespeare*, eds. Werner Habicht, D. J. Palmer and Roger Pringle (Cranbury, NJ: Associated University Presses, 1988), 131–2, offers a perceptive survey of these instances.

21 Samuel Johnson, from *The Plays of William Shakespeare, in Eight Volumes* (London, 1765) in *Shakespeare: The Critical Heritage*, vol. 5, ed. Brian Vickers (London: Routledge, 1979), 152–4.

22 Jill L. Levenson, 'Introduction', in *The Oxford Shakespeare: Romeo and Juliet* (Oxford: Oxford University Press, 2008), 46.

23 Frank Kermode, *Riverside Shakespeare* (Boston: Houghton Mifflin Company, 1974), 1057. Thomas Moisan, 'Rhetoric and the Rehearsal of Death: The "Lamentations" Scene in *Romeo and Juliet*', *Shakespeare Quarterly* 34 (1983): 389–404, argues that the rhetorical formulae are deployed partly to control anxieties about mortality.

24 Some of Romeo's other doublings in Q2 do seem to be simply erroneous, however: the meter-spoiling 'I will beleeve, / Shall I beleeve' (5.3.102), the coherent 'Depart againe' four lines before an incoherent 'Depart againe' (5.3.108, 112) and the implausibly doubled 'O true Appothecarie! / Thy drugs are quicke. Thus with a kisse I die' that occurs first between those two and repeats a dozen lines later. But those all occur on a single page of Q2, suggesting a local malfunction rather than an epidemic that would explain away the doublings I have been emphasizing.

25 Taylor Swift, 'Love Story' from *Fearless* (Big Machine Records, 2008). Complete lyrics available online: http://taylorswift.com/releases#/release/2822 (accessed 20 July 2015).

26 Available online: https://www.youtube.com/watch?v=8xg3vE8Ie_E (accessed 4 June 2015).

Chapter 5

1 The epigraph is taken from Konstantin Stanislavski, *My Life in Art*, trans. Jean Benedetti (London and New York; Routledge, 2008), 163, where it is offered as an example of the aphorisms he coined with his fellow impresario Nemirovich-Danchenko.

2 John Dryden, 'Defence of the EPILOGUE. Or, An Essay on the *Dramatique Poetry* of the last Age', in *The Conquest OF GRANADA BY THE SPANIARDS: In Two Parts. Acted at the Theatre-Royall.* (London: Henry Herringman, 1672), 172.

3 I have argued that Mercutio's punning, Cratylan language threatens to collapse both the binary logic of opposition that governs Verona, where the name is everything, and the possibility of transcending it that Romeo and Juliet seek, where a rose by any other name smells as sweet, in 'Mercutio's Bad Language', *Rematerializing Shakespeare: Authority and Representation on the Early Modern English Stage*, eds Bryan Reynolds and William N. West (New York: Palgrave Macmillan, 2005), 115–29; several other works on Mercutio are in the bibliography. In his *Guide to Shakespeare's Romeo and Juliet* (Chippenham: Connell Guides, 2012), 37–50, Simon Palfrey considers the threat that 'a wit so cold and brilliant' presents not just to *Romeo and Juliet* but to 'Shakespeare's own career as a sympathetic dramatist', 38.

4 Samuel Johnson and Samuel Taylor Coleridge, for instance, both take up Dryden's suggestion.

5 Samuel Taylor Coleridge in *Coleridge on Shakespeare: the text of the lectures of 1811–12*, ed. R. A. Foakes (London: Rouledge & Kegan Paul, 1979), 78.

6 Charles Lamb said of one of Coleridge's lectures, 'He promised a lecture on the Nurse in Romeo and Juliet, and he has given us instead one in the manner of the nurse.' See Thomas Sadler (ed.), *Diary, Reminiscences, and Correspondence of Henry Crabb Robinson* (New York and Cambridge: Hurd and Houghton/ The Riverside Press, 1877), 223. See the article by Liebler in this volume.

7 Caroline Spurgeon marvelously epitomizes the play's imagery as

'brilliance swiftly quenched', *Shakespeare's Imagery and What It Tells Us* (Cambridge: Cambridge University Press, 1935), 316.

8 On the prehistory of *Romeo and Juliet*, see Shaul Bassi's chapter in this volume. The play's afterlife is too vast and multifarious to be addressed in an endnote, but for Monadhil Daood's *Romeo and Juliet in Baghdad*, performed in the summer of 2012 in London, see Katherine Steele Brokaw's review, *Shakespeare Bulletin* 31, no. 2 (2013): 267–72, and Ian Munro's article in this volume. See also *Romeo and Juliet in Sarajevo* (Dir. John Zaritsky, National Film Board of Canada, 1994), a documentary film about Admira Ismić, a Bosnian Muslim, and Boško Brkić, a Bosnian Serb, a couple killed by snipers as they tried to escape besieged Sarajevo in 1993. A couple from different ethnic groups has been dubbed the 'Romeo and Juliet of Afghanistan' by *The New York Times* and the BBC, available online: http://www.nytimes.com/2014/03/10/world/asia/2-star-crossed-afghans-cling-to-love-even-at-risk-of-death.html (accessed 4 June 2015). *The New York Times* notes that neither of the young people in this case has heard of Shakespeare, thus naturalizing *Romeo and Juliet* as a type of true love.

9 The Prologue does not appear in the Folio. Is the folio format, usual for works of cultural weight like Bibles, theologies and classical texts, but still rare for works in English or of modern drama, perhaps monumental enough without it? One could speculate that quarto forms, which suggest the playhouse more than the library, use the Prologue to push back against the fluidity implied by performance. The Prologue becomes one voice among many, although it asserts the priority of organizing plot to refracting action; in a folio, perhaps the assertion in the Prologue's action of a totality risks becoming overwhelming.

10 Douglas Bruster and Robert Weimann, *Prologues to Shakespeare's Theatre: Performance and Liminality in Early Modern Drama* (London: Routledge, 2004), 112–14. Note the interplay of writing and performance in this passage. The sonnet is given new vitality in the play when Romeo and Juliet create one in their first words together, then overshoot the concluding couplet by four lines, apparently beginning another one before they are interrupted by the Nurse.

11 I am grateful to Robert Watson for suggesting this possible reading to me.

12 Simon Palfrey names something like the distinction I am making here, the difference between plot-oriented and part-oriented performance, after two kinds of document used by Elizabethan playing companies. The shared company 'plot' was posted backstage for all to see, and provided an overview of the order of scenes and which players were in each. 'Parts' were distributed to each of the players and recorded each player's lines and cues, with no particular regard for what else was going on. See *Shakespeare's Possible Worlds* (Cambridge: Cambridge University Press, 2014).

13 In the sense developed by Roberto Esposito, 'a protective response in the face of a risk', see *Immunitas: The Protection and Negation of Life* (Cambridge: Polity Press, 2011), 1. As Esposito's subsequent discussions clarify, immunization is represented as a 'homeopathic protection practice – which excludes by including and affirms by negating' (ibid., 8) '*reaction*' (ibid., 7) to an incursion at a border, a justification of incorporating some of the Other into the self in the name of preserving the self.

14 Ramie Targoff, 'The Capulet Tomb', *Posthumous Love: Eros and the Afterlife in Renaissance England* (Chicago: University of Chicago Press, 2014), 105–14, shows in detail how readily Romeo and Juliet link love and death.

15 Denis de Rougemont, *Love in the Western World* (Princeton: Princeton University Press, 1983), first published in French in 1939. In a different register, the psychoanalytic tradition concurs in seeing love and death as powerfully entwined drives; e.g. Freud's *Beyond the Pleasure Principle*.

16 Kottman, 'Defying the Stars: Tragic Love as the Struggle for Freedom in *Romeo and Juliet*', *Shakespeare Quarterly* 63 (2012), 1–38, 28, reminds us that Juliet's explicit plan is to take the potion, wake up and elope to Mantua with Romeo. Hugh Grady offers a convincing overview of readings of *Romeo and Juliet* in the tradition of *Liebestod*, and a convincing rejection of it: 'Beautiful Death in *Romeo and Juliet*', in *Shakespeare and Impure Aesthetics* (Cambridge: Cambridge University Press, 2009), 196–204. In *The Connell Guide to Shakespeare's* Romeo and Juliet (Chippenham: Connell Guides, 2012), Simon Palfrey

embraces the *Liebestod* motif. Ramie Targoff's *Posthumous Love* powerfully revises it, arguing that while Romeo and Juliet immediately discern death in their love, they do so without the usual consolation of imagining a love after death. Their love is mortal, not transcendent. See *Posthumous Love: Eros and the Afterlife in Renaissance England* (Chicago: University of Chicago Press, 2014).

17 Julia Kristeva, *Tales of Love*, trans. Leon S. Roudiez (New York: Columbia University Press, 1987), 233.

18 Lucretius' definition, in William Ellery Leonard and Stanley Barney Smith, (eds), *De Rerum Natura*, (Madison: University of Wisconsin Press, 1942), 1.670–71 (repeated 1.792–93, 2.753–54, 3.519–20), quoted approvingly by Bacon and others: 'nam quod cumque suis mutatum finibus exit, / continuo hoc mors est illius quod fuit ante' (for whatever when changed passes outside its limits, at once this is the death of what it was before).

19 The importance of coincidence to the plot has been widely noted in criticism; see, for example, Ruth Nevo, 'Tragic Form in *Romeo and Juliet*', *Studies in English Literature* 9 (1969): 241–58, esp. 241–6. It has generally been decried; Hugh Grady reviews some notable critical condemnations in *Impure Aesthetics*, 204–5.

20 John D. Lyons, *The Phantom of Chance: From Fortune to Randomness in Seventeenth-Century French Literature* (Edinburgh: Edinburgh University Press, 2012), 6, but see also his discussion of Aristotle, 1–8.

21 W. K. C. Guthrie, *Aristotle: an encounter*, vol. 6 in *A History of Greek Philosophy* (Cambridge: Cambridge University Press, 1981), 238. My emphasis.

22 John Downes, *Roscius Anglicanus, or, An historical review of the stage from 1660 to 1706* (London, 1708), 22. The fact that these versions alternated suggests that something quite different is taking place with *Romeo and Juliet* than with, for instance, Nahum Tate's happy-ending *King Lear* replacing Shakespeare's. Tragedy is not what is rejected, but inevitability.

23 Romeo's generosity is noted by Targoff, 'The Capulet Tomb', 123–5.

24 Robert Watson, 'Why No One Hears Lord Capulet's Line', in this volume.

25 Thomas Nashe, *An Almond for a Parrat* (London, 1589?), A2r.

26 Shakespeare's son Hamnet died at the age of eleven in 1596, about the time scholars think *Romeo and Juliet* was written, and the number of years since the earthquake that the Nurse uses to recall Juliet's, and Susan's, age. Like Susan, Hamnet was survived by his (actual rather than virtual) twin, Judith. He also had an older sister named Susannah, and Susannah would have been the age of Juliet at the likely date of the play. See René Weis, ed., *Romeo and Juliet*, Arden 3rd Series (London: Bloomsbury, 2012), 36. Weis also cites Marjorie Garber, *Coming of Age in Shakespeare* (London and New York: Methuen 1981), 37, on Susan's 'alternative fate'.

27 See Watson, 'Why No One Hears', in this volume.

28 Here I differ significantly from Kottman, 'Defying the Stars', 6–13, which argues that *Romeo and Juliet* represents an innovation in the horizon within which freedom and individuality is asserted. In this play Shakespeare sets aside the duel, in which one's life is literally staked and the winner takes all, in favour of sexual love, in which recognition may be mutually achieved. Kottman's incisive reading nevertheless seems to me to remain fascinated by the encounter that is the duel, and stages love in much the same way: as an urgent, punctual, decisive event. To be sure, the play shares this sense of urgency. But it also multiplies decisive turning points; they are intense but precisely *not* decisive, or no more decisive than many other moments, no single tide which, taken at the flood, leads on to either inalienable fortune or binding miseries.

29 David Blixt's *The Master of Verona* (New York: St Martin's Press, 2007) and other novels in his *Star-Cross'd* series, and the film *Shakespeare in Love* (1998. Dir. John Madden. UK and USA: Miramax, Universal Pictures) are both examples of alternative histories (or exceptionally well-produced fan fictions) of *Romeo and Juliet*. Many more less-polished fan fictions circulate on the internet. I am grateful to Elizabeth Hunter for introducing me to this less-visible corpus.

30 Both tendencies seem part of Natasha Parry's performance

in Zeffirelli's 1968 film, noted by James N. Loehlin, ed., *Shakespeare in Production:* Romeo and Juliet (Cambridge: Cambridge University Press, 2002), 101, 173. See also *Romeo and Juliet* (1968) [Film]. Dir. Franco Zeffirelli, Italy: Paramount Pictures. The early marriage of Lady Capulet was masterfully caught in a 2014 staging of *Romeo and Juliet* at New Swan Shakespeare Festival, Irvine, California, in which she seemed closer in age to her daughter than to her husband, and more Tybalt's peer than Capulet's.

31 Lina Perkins Wilder, *Shakespeare's Memory Theatre: Recollection, Properties, and Character* (Cambridge: Cambridge University Press, 2010), 65 n.12, citing Tiffany Stern, *Rehearsal from Shakespeare to Sheridan* (Oxford: Oxford University Press, 2000), 89–90.

32 On actuality and virtualities in Aristotle, see Palfrey, *Possible Worlds*, 213–16, and more widely in early modern thought, 213–42.

33 Jorge Luis Borges, 'The Garden of Forking Paths', in *Labyrinths: Selected Stories and Other Writings*, trans. Donald A. Yates (New York: New Editions, 1964).

34 Lauren Berlant writes of the deceptive 'gift of alternativity' made by the promises of a better world in 'Cruel Optimism: on Marx, Loss and the Senses', *New Formations* 63 (2007/08): 33–51, 49. My sense of the alternatives in *Romeo and Juliet* is more optimistic or less cruel than those Berlant considers, because they represent alternatives that can actually be lived, and indeed are.

35 Demetrius, still under the effects of the love in idleness at the play's end – or has he just realized that he really does love Helena? – is one notable exception. The flickering, undecidable almost-transformation of Rosalind into the boy actor in the Epilogue of *As You Like It* is another.

36 Northrop Frye, 'The Argument of Comedy', *English Institute Essays, 1948* (New York, Columbia University Press, 1948), 58–73, and Harry Berger, Jr., *Second World and Green World: Studies in Renaissance Fiction-Making* (Berkeley: University of California Press 1990) remain the most suggestive formulations of this gesture.

37 Frye, 'Argument', 70.

38 Roland Barthes calls this the effect of the real in 'The Reality Effect', in *The Rustle of Language*, trans. Richard Howard (New York: Hill and Wang, 1986), 141–8.

39 I follow the ambiguous punctuation of Q1.

40 It is instructive to compare Hermia's dream of the snake in *A Midsummer Night's Dream*, which in contrast to the dreams in *Romeo and Juliet* is not actually but affectively – which is to say virtually – true.

41 In this volume Robert Watson offers a very different reading of Romeo's dream of death as intimating the possibility of a 'magical resurrection'. But I would insist on the magical quality; Romeo's dream simply negates death by standing it on its head as new life. The alternatives that the play shows are richer, more varied and not utopian.

Chapter 6

1 Theodore Bale, 'Brilliant "Romeo" caps season', *Boston Herald*, 9 May 2003 (accessed 25 August 2014).

2 See online site: http://sleepnomorenyc.com (accessed 5 June 2015). Also *Borrowers and Lenders: The Journal of Shakespeare and Appropriation*, 7, no. 2 (Fall 2012 / Winter 2013) for special cluster on *Sleep No More*.

3 For instance, librettist Meredith Oakes translates Miranda's heartfelt sympathy for Prospero, upon hearing of the circumstances of their banishment and exile, from: 'O, my heart bleeds / To think o' th' teen that I have turned you to, / Which is from my remembrance.' (William Shakespeare, *The Tempest*, eds Virginia Mason Vaughan and Alden T. Vaughan (London: Cengage, 1999), 1.2.63–5), to: 'Fearful story / I'm so sorry.' (Meredith Oakes, *The Tempest: An Opera in Three Acts* (London: Faber, 2004), 7.)

4 Alastair MacCauley, 'To Dance, Perchance to Dream', *New York Times*, 28 March 2014 (accessed 25 August 2014).

5 While the operatic *Romeo and Juliet* seems less likely to be

staged in radically different times and places, the various versions draw from different source texts and make narrative adjustments along the way, making for narrative variation without really varying from the dominance of narrative.

6 Two commonly-read overviews, Linda Hutcheon's *A Theory of Adaptation* and Julie Sanders's *Adaptation and Appropriation*, were both published in 2006. The journal *Adaptation* launched in 2008 whereas the journal *Borrowers and Lenders: The Journal of Shakespeare and Appropriation* launched in 2005 to consider Shakespeare's legacy in a wide range of cultural forms.

7 Linda Hutcheon, *A Theory of Adaptation*, 2nd edn (London: Rouledge, 2013), xvi.

8 Ibid, xiv.

9 Julie Sanders, *Appropriation and Adaptation* (London: Routledge, 2006), 27.

10 Ibid., 62.

11 Hutcheon, *Theory of Adaptation*, 13.

12 Ibid., xiii.

13 Ibid., xvi.

14 Jennifer Clement, 'Beyond Shakespeare: Early Modern Adaptation Studies and Its Potential', *Literature Compass* 10 (2013): 677.

15 Christy Desmet and Robert Sawyer, *Shakespeare and Appropriation* (London and New York: Routledge, 1999); Pascale Aebischer, Edward J. Esche and Nigel Wheale, *Remaking Shakespeare: Performance Across Media, Genres and Cultures* (London and New York: Palgrave Macmillan, 2003).

16 Diana Henderson, *Collaborations with the Past: Reshaping Shakespeare Across Time and Media* (Ithaca: Cornell University Press, 2006), 1.

17 Margaret Jane Kidnie, *Shakespeare and the Problem of Adaptation* (Abingdon and New York: Routledge, 2009); Maurizio Calbi, *Spectral Shakespeares: Media Adaptations in the Twenty-First Century* (London and New York: Palgrave Macmillan, 2013).

18 As, for instance, when Nancy Reynolds enthuses, in the opening

of a review of a 1987 *Romeo and Juliet* choreographed by Kent Stowell for the Pacific Northwest Ballet, 'The tale of Romeo and Juliet will never die as long as there are dance stages left in the world; in its full evening-length version, it has become virtually a classic of the twentieth-century', in 'Romeo Revisited', *Dance Chronicle* 18, no. 2 (1995): 261.

19 Gary Schmidgall, *Shakespeare and Opera* (Oxford: Oxford University Press, 1990), xii. For a related investigation of the 'operatic' Shakespeare, see also Lisa Hopkins, '"What did thy song bode, lady?": *Othello* as Operatic Text', *The Shakespeare Yearbook* 4 (1994): 61–70.

20 Clive Barnes, Edward Downes, Karoly Kope and Siegmund Levarie, 'Shakespeare in Opera and Ballet', in *Staging Shakespeare: Seminars on Production Problems*, ed. Glenn Loney (New York: Garland, 1990), 201.

21 Winton Dean, 'Shakespeare in the Opera House', *Shakespeare Survey* 18 (1965): 75.

22 Adrian Streete, 'Shakespeare and Opera', in *The Edinburgh Companion to Shakespeare and the Arts*, eds Mark Thomas Burnett, Adrian Streete and Ramona Wray (Edinburgh: Edinburgh University Press, 2011), 144.

23 Daniel Albright, *Musicking Shakespeare: A Conflict of Theaters* (Rochester: University of Rochester Press, 2007), 29.

24 Ibid., 28.

25 Ibid., 30.

26 Ibid., 33.

27 Barnes, 'Shakespeare in Opera', 211.

28 Ibid., 210.

29 Robin Wharton, '"There Are No Mothers-In-Law in Ballet": "Doing" Shakespeare in Dance', *Shakespeare Bulletin: A Journal Of Performance Criticism And Scholarship* 23, no. 3 (2005): 10.

30 Marjorie Garber, *Shakespeare and Modern Culture* (New York: Random House, 2008), 44.

31 Barnes, 'Shakespeare in Opera', 215.

32 Rodney Stenning Edgecombe, 'Trans-formal Translation: Plays into Ballets, with special reference to Kenneth MacMillan's

Romeo and Juliet', *Yearbook of English Studies* 36, no. 1 (2006): 70.

33 Rodney Stenning Edgecombe, 'Shakespeare, Ballet and Dance', in *The Edinburgh Companion to Shakespeare and the Arts*, eds Mark Thomas Burnett, Adrian Streete and Ramona Wray (Edinburgh: Edinburgh University Press, 2011), 200–18.

34 Edgecombe, 'Trans-formal', 67.

35 Quoted in Edgecombe, 'Trans-formal', 67–8.

36 Susan Leigh Foster, *Choreography and Narrative: Ballet's Staging of Story and Desire* (Bloomington: Indiana University Press, 1996), 76.

37 Edward Nye, '"Choreography" is Narrative: The Programmes of the Eighteenth-Century *Ballet d'Action*', *Dance Research: The Journal of the Society for Dance Research* 26, no. 1 (Summer 2008): 42.

38 Camille Cole Howard, *The Staging of Shakespeare's* Romeo and Juliet *as a Ballet* (San Francisco: Mellen Research University Press, 1992), xi.

39 Ibid., 16.

40 Karen Bennett, 'Star-cross'd Lovers: Shakespeare and Prokofiev's "pas de deux" in *Romeo and Juliet*', *Cambridge Quarterly* 32, no. 4 (2003): 316. Bennett includes an informative index with a chart comparing the narrative structure of Prokofiev's composition with the balletic structure of Rudolph Nureyev's 1995 production of *Romeo and Juliet* for the Paris Opera Ballet.

41 Howard, *The Staging*, 45.

42 Karen Bennett, 'Prokofiev's *Romeo and Juliet* and Socialist Realism: A Case Study in Intersemiotic Translation', in *Shakespeare and European Politics*, eds Dirk Delabastita, Josef de Vos, and Paul Franssen (Newark: University of Delaware Press, 2008), 319. See also Garber, *Shakespeare and Modern Culture*, 44–6, and Howard, *The Staging*, 49–58.

43 See the project website: http://lovelives.net (accessed 4 June 2015).

44 Lyndsey Winship, 'Sir Frederick Ashton's *Romeo and Juliet*', *Guardian*, 16 July 2011 (accessed 5 October 2014).

45 On Cranko's *Romeo and Juliet*, see Nancy Isenberg, 'Accommodating Shakespeare to Ballet: John Cranko's *Romeo and Juliet*', in *Shifting the Scene: Shakespeare in European Culture*, eds Ladina Bezzola Lambert and Balz Engler (Newark: University of Delaware Press, 2004), 129–39.

46 Those productions, including casts with Rudolf Nureyev and Margot Fonteyn (1965), Wayne Eagling and Alessandra Ferri (1984), Carlos Acosta and Tamara Rojo (2007), and Lauren Cutherbertson and Federico Bonelli (2012). A DVD of Teatro alla Scala's 2000 *Romeo and Juliet* with Angel Corella and Alessandra Ferri (2000) is now out of production, but brings the number of major recent versions of MacMillan's ballet to at least five.

47 Rudolf Nureyev, with whom Margot Fonteyn triumphed in the première of MacMillan's *Romeo and Juliet*, choreographed his own *Romeo and Juliet* in 1977, which was remounted numerous times including in 1980 at the La Scala Opera Ballet. Nureyev's former Juliet, Fonteyn, played the role of Lady Capulet for that production.

48 John Neumeier, interview by Joseph Campana, Houston Ballet Studios, 29 August 2014.

49 *Juliet and Romeo* ([2013] 2014), [DVD]. Chor. Mats Ek (Berlin: C Major Entertainment).

50 Anna Kisselgoff, 'Romeo and Juliet, Divorced From Romance', *New York Times*, 19 January 1992 (accessed 3 August 2014).

51 Howard, *The Staging*, 79.

52 Edward Clug, interview by Maura Keefe, Jacob's Pillow Dance Festival, 4 July 2009.

53 *Romeo and Juliet* ([2006] 2010), [DVD] Chor. Mauro Bigonzetti (Halle: Arthaus).

54 Ibid.

55 Radiohead, 'How to Disappear Completely' on *Kid A* (Parlophone Records, October 2000).

56 Graham Spicer, '*Aterballetto*'s *Romeo and Juliet* in Milan: contemporary dance at its highest level'; available online: http://www.gramilano.com/2012/05/aterballettos-romeo-and-juliet-in-milan-contemporary-dance-at-its-highest-level/ (accessed 26 October 2014).

57 Brian Seifert, 'Romeo Meets Radiohead in a Love Story of Twitches', *New York Times*, 24 October 2011 (accessed 22 September 2014).

58 Kisselgoff, 'Divorced from Romance'.

Chapter 7

1 Catherine Belsey, *Romeo and Juliet: Language and Writing* (London: Bloomsbury Publishing, 2014), 68.

2 Geoffrey Bullough, *Narrative and Dramatic Sources of Shakespeare* (New York: Columbia University Press, 1957).

3 Nicole Prunster, *Romeo and Juliet before Shakespeare: Four Early Stories of Star-Crossed Love* (Toronto: Victoria University, 2000), 19.

4 Paola Pugliatti, 'The True History of Romeo and Juliet: A Veronese Plot of the 1830s', in *Shakespeare and the Mediterranean: the Selected Proceedings of the International Shakespeare Association World Congress*, Valencia, 2001, eds Tom Clayton, Susan Brock and Vicente Fores (Newark: The University of Delaware Press, 2004), 393.

5 Arthur Brooke, *The Tragicall Historye of Romeus and Juliet*, (1562).

6 Prunster, *Romeo and Juliet before Shakespeare*, 11.

7 Ibid., 15.

8 Ibid., 11.

9 Ibid., 30 (modified).

10 Ibid., 55.

11 Ibid., 90.

12 Patricia Ann Kennan, 'Le forme e i motivi dell'amor cortese in *Romeo and Juliet*: fatti e antefatti' in Romeo and Juliet*: dal testo alla scena*, ed. Mariangela Tempera (Bologna; CLUEB, 1986), 118–19.

13 Giorgio Melchiori, 'Uno, due, mille Romeo and Juliet' in

Rileggere/Re-reading Romeo and Juliet, ed. A. Righetti (Verona: Verona University, 1999), 17.

14 Mario Praz, 'Petrarch in England', in *The Flaming Heart* (New York: Doubleday & Co., 1958), 276.

15 Gayle Whittier, 'The Sonnet's Body and the Body Sonnetized in "Romeo and Juliet"', *Shakespeare Quarterly* 40 (1989): 27–41.

16 François Laroque, 'Shakespeare's Italian Carnival: Venice and Verona Revisited', *Shakespeare and Renaissance literary theories: Anglo-Italian transactions*, ed. Michele Marrapodi (Farnham: Ashgate, 2011), 204.

17 Glenn Clark, 'The Civil Mutinies of *Romeo and Juliet*', *English Literary Renaissance* 41 (2011): 280–300.

18 Niccolò Machiavelli, *The Prince*, trans. and ed. Peter Bondanella (Oxford: Oxford University Press, 2008), 73.

19 Niccolò Machiavelli, *Discourses on Livy,* trans. Julia Conaway Bondanella and Peter Bondanella (Oxford: Oxford University Press, 2009), 55.

20 Pugliatti, 'The True History', 395.

21 Maria Grazia Messina, 'Da *Romeo e Giulietta* a *Otello*: melodramma shakespeariano nell'immaginario visivo del romanticismo italiano', *Memoria di Shakespeare* 6 (2008): 175–7.

22 Fernando Mazzocca, ed., [*Francesco*] *Hayez. Dal mito al bacio, catalogo della mostra* (Venice: Marsilio, 1998), 100.

23 Madame de Staël, *Corinne, or Italy*, trans. Sylvia Raphael (Oxford: Oxford University Press, 2009), 123–4.

24 Joseph Luzzi, *Romantic Europe and the Ghost of Italy* (New Haven and London: Yale University Press, 2008), 21.

25 Roberto Cuppone, '"Io fui Giulietta". La prima volta di Eleonora', in *Voci e Anime, Corpi e Scritture. Atti del convegno internazionale su Eleonora Duse*, eds Maria Ida Biggi and Paolo Puppa (Rome: Bulzoni, 2009): 21–38.

26 Gabriele D'Annunzio, *The Flame of Life*, trans. Kassandra Vivaria (Boston: L. C. Page, 1900), 319.

27 René Weis, ed., *Romeo and Juliet*, Arden 3rd series, (London: Bloomsbury, 2012), 79–85.

28 Mercuzio is the Italian form of Mercutio.

29 Gianfranco Bartalotta, *Carmelo Bene e Shakespeare* (Rome: Bulzoni, 2000), 63–86.

30 Ibid., 86.

31 Richard Lassels, *Voyage of Italy, or, a compleat Journey through Italy* (Paris, 1670), 437.

32 George Byron, *Byron's Letters and Journals, Volume V: 'So late into the night', 1816–1817*, ed. Leslie A. Marchand (Cambridge, MA: Harvard University Press, 1976), 126.

33 *Romeo and Juliet* (1936), [Film] Dir. George Cukor. USA: MGM.

34 Maria D'Anniballe, 'Redefining Urban Identity in Fascist Verona through the Lens of Hollywood's Romeo and Juliet', in *New Perspectives in Italian Cultural Studies: The Arts and History*, vol. 2, ed. Graziella Parati (Madison, NJ: Farleigh Dickinson University Press, 2012), 224.

35 Ibid., 234.

36 Ramie Targoff, *Posthumous Love: Eros and the Afterlife in Renaissance England* (Chicago and London: University of Chicago Press, 2014).

37 Anna Villari, *Verona. Casa e Tomba di Giulietta* (Milan: Silvana Editorale, 2011), 3.

38 Paul Fussell, quoted in Luzzi, *Romantic Europe*, 219.

39 Nick Squires, 'Verona commissions replica "Juliet" statue after one too many brushes with tourists', *The Daily Telegraph*, 25 February 2014. Available online: http://www.telegraph.co.uk/news/worldnews/europe/italy/10660642/Verona-commissions-replica-Juliet-statue-after-one-too-many-brushes-with-tourists.html (accessed 25 February 2014).

40 Federico Moccia, *Tre metri sopra il cielo* (Rome: Ventaglio, 1992).

41 Villari, Verona, 3.

42 Club di Giulietta, available online: http://www.julietclub.com/ (accessed 6 June 2015).

43 Lise Friedman and Ceil Friedman, *Letters to Juliet: Celebrating Shakespeare's Greatest Heroine, the Magical City of Verona, and the Power of Love* (New York: Tabori & Chang, 2006).

44 *Letters to Juliet* (2010), [Film]. Dir. Gary Winick (USA: Summit Entertainment and Applehead Pictures).

45 Paul A. Kottman, 'Defying the Stars: Tragic Love as the Struggle for Freedom in *Romeo and Juliet*', *Shakespeare Quarterly* 63, no. 1 (2012): 1–38.

46 Zygmunt Bauman, *Liquid Love: On the Frailty of Human Bonds* (Cambridge: Polity Press, 2003).

47 Umberto Eco, Postscript to *The Name of the Rose*, trans. William Weaver (New York: Harcourt Brace Jovanovich, 1984), 3.

48 Gertrude Stein, 'Sacred Emily', in *Geography and Plays* (Boston, MA: Four Seas, 1922), 178.

Chapter 8

1 See the annotated bibliography for publication details of the works cited.

2 See René Weis, ed., 'Introduction', in *Romeo and Juliet*, Arden 3rd series (London: Bloomsbury, 2012), 94–116, for an in-depth discussion of Q1 and Q2.

3 Brian Gibbons, ed., *Romeo and Juliet*, Arden 2nd series (London: Bloomsbury 1980), 239–80.

4 Weis, *Romeo and Juliet*, Arden 3, 52–94.

5 Dympna Callaghan, ed., *Romeo and Juliet: Texts and Contexts* (Boston, MA: Bedford/St Martin's Press, 2003), 3.

6 *The Bedford Shakespeare* series uses David Bevington's edition of *Romeo and Juliet*.

7 Belsey's text is part of the *Arden Students Skills: Language and Writing* series. Dympna Callaghan is the series editor.

8 Gillian Woods, *Romeo and Juliet: A Reader's Guide to Essential Criticism* (London: Palgrave Macmillan, 2013).

9 Diane Purkiss, *Troublesome Things: A History of Fairies and Fairy Stories* (London: Penguin Books, 2001).

10 Julia Reinhard Lupton, 'Making Room, Affording Hospitality: Environments of Entertainment in *Romeo and Juliet*', *The Journal of Medieval and Early Modern Studies* 43 (2013): 145–72.

11 Alison Findlay, *A Feminist Perspective on Renaissance Drama* (Oxford: Blackwell, 1999), 127–63.

12 Milla Cozart Riggio, ed., *Teaching Shakespeare through Performance* (New York: Modern Language Association of America, 1999).

13 Belsey's essay is also available in *The Yearbook of English Studies*, vol. 23 (1993): 126–42.

14 Kristeva's essay is also available in Julia Kristeva, *Tales of Love*, trans. Leon S. Roudiez (New York: Columbia University Press, 1987), 209–33.

15 See details online: http://www.corestandards.org/ELA-Literacy/ (accessed 7 June 2015).

INDEX